ABORIGINAL, NORTHERN, AND COMMUNITY ECONOMIC DEVELOPMENT
PAPERS AND RETROSPECTIVES

JOHN LOXLEY

ARP BOOKS • WINNIPEG

Copyright ©2010 John Loxley

ARP Books (Arbeiter Ring Publishing)
205-70 Arthur Street
Winnipeg, Manitoba
Treaty 1 Territory and Historic Métis Nation Homeland
Canada R3B1G7
arpbooks.org

Printed in Canada by Imprimerie Gauvin
Design by Relish New Brand Experience
Third printing, September 2017
This book is printed on 100% post consumer paper.

COPYRIGHT NOTICE
This book is fully protected under the copyright laws of Canada and all other countries of the Copyright Union and is subject to royalty.

 Canada Council for the Arts / Conseil des Arts du Canada

ARP Books acknowledges the generous support of the Manitoba Arts Council and the Canada Council for the Arts for our publishing program. We acknowledge the financial support of the Government of Canada through the Canada Book Fund and the Province of Manitoba through the Book Publishing Tax Credit and the Book Publisher Marketing Assistance Program of Manitoba Culture, Heritage, and Tourism.

LIBRARY AND ARCHIVES CANADA CATALOGUING IN PUBLICATION

Loxley, John, 1942-
    Aboriginal, northern, and community economic development / John Loxley.

Includes bibliographical references and index.
ISBN 978-1-894037-46-4

1. Community development--Canada, Northern.
2. Economic development--Canada, Northern.
3. Native peoples--Canada, Northern--Economic conditions. I. Title.

HC79.E44D63 2007   338.9   C2010-907037-2

TABLE OF CONTENTS

Acknowledgements 7
Introduction and Rationale 9
1. The Aboriginal Concept of Stewardship and Enoughness 15
2. Alternative Strategies of Community Economic Development 19
3. Strategies Advocated by Native People 57
4. Casinos as an Economic Development Strategy 73
Retrospective on Chapters 1 to 4 81
5. The "Great Northern Plan" 93
6. Manitoba: The Dynamics of North-South Relations 131
Retrospective on Chapters 5 and 6 141
7. Aboriginal Economic Development in Winnipeg 151
8. Financing Community Economic Development in Winnipeg 189
9. The State of Community Economic Development in Winnipeg 217
Retrospective on Chapters 7 to 9 231
10. Why Native Businesses Fail and How Agencies Contribute 235
11. The Role of Subsidies in CED 245
Retrospective on Chapters 10 and 11 253
12. Challenges and Opportunities 257
Appendix I: Input-Output And Income Flow Analysis 261
Appendix II: John Loxley: Practical Involvement in Aboriginal, Northern, and Community Economic Development 265
Bibliography 271
Index 291

To Phil Fontaine, for his courage and commitment.

ACKNOWLEDGEMENTS

Since the papers in this book cover much of my academic life, the list of people to whom I am indebted is huge. Most are acknowledged in the specific papers. There are, however, people whose influence on my work and thinking over the years on the issues in this book requires additional acknowledgement. In this category there is Phil Fontaine, the late Van Hall, Gerry Helleiner, Moses Okimaw, Jim Silver, Russ Rothney, Louise Champagne, Larry Morrissette, Anna Rothney, Doug Smith (who was accidentally overlooked in my last book), Tom Simms, Harvey Bostrom, Fred Wien, David Newhouse, Wanda Wuttunee, Fred Shore, Cindy Blackstock, Garry Loewen, Lawrie Deane, Nigel Mohamed, Cindy Coker, Brendan Reimer, Parvin Ghorayshi, and Alain Molgat. I've also received enormous personal support from Norah Richards, the Hudson family, Peter Ferris, Colin Kinsella and the rest of cssc, Nicole Ritchot and Jerry Sopko, Don and Karen Hurst, Robert Chernomas, Mark Gabbert, Shauna MacKinnon, Carol Anne O'Brien, Joan Larsen, Betty McGregor Janette Bulkan, and Tara Prakash. I thank my other friends in the Economics Department at the University of Manitoba, at ccpa-Manitoba, and in our cura research project for their ongoing comradeship and intellectual stimulation.

This book was prepared with the generous financial assistance of the Social Science and Humanities Research Council (grant # 538-2002-1003) and the Manitoba Research Alliance on ced in the New Economy, the research consortium headed by the Canadian Centre for Policy Alternatives—Manitoba, which secured and administered the grant. The financial support of the Global Political Economy Research Fund, Faculty of Arts, University of Manitoba, is also gratefully acknowledged.

Thanks to Todd, Esyllt, Rick and John at Arbeiter Ring for their support and patience. The assistance of Daniella Echeverria, Norah Richards, Tibor Brody, Judy Ings and Debby Fiorucci in preparing the manuscript is gratefully acknowledged.

Finally, thanks to Zeeba, Salim, Camille, Aurelie, Raina, and Matthew who, over the years, paid the price for my preoccupation with what is between the covers of this book.

INTRODUCTION AND RATIONALE

The essays in this collection represent reflections on over 30 years of involvement in Aboriginal, northern, and community economic development (CED) and planning, as a practitioner, advisor, teacher and theoretician. An outline of my involvement in this area is to be found at the end of the book. My views have been shaped by my interaction with the Aboriginal community, other CED activists and by many students, at both the undergraduate and graduate level, and I wish to acknowledge the many people involved in that process. The rationale for this book is that there is some interest by practitioners and students in both earlier materials that are difficult to obtain and in more recent pieces. This book brings my papers together and provides an update of my views contained in them based on the evolution of my thinking over the years.

My practical experience dates back to the mid-1970s when I was the Secretary of the Resource and Economic Development Sub-Committee of cabinet in the Schreyer NDP government in Manitoba. I was privileged to work with a committed and gifted group of civil servants and political activists, Aboriginal and non-Aboriginal, on the Northern Plan, which is dealt with in Chapter 5. This planning exercise, unique in Canada, represented a holistic attempt to address problems of poverty and underdevelopment in Northern Manitoba and especially in Aboriginal communities. The article on which this chapter draws was published in *Studies in Political Economy* 6, 1981 and is reproduced here for several reasons. First, it suggests there are no simplistic solutions to the problems facing northern and Aboriginal poverty and underdevelopment. Rather, multi-faceted, across-the-board approaches are called for, which are demanding both conceptually and politically. Second, the plan demonstrated that there are numerous possibilities for economic and social development in the small communities of the North, possibilities which become greater with co-operation among communities and with targeted state involvement and support, including subsidies justified by social considerations. Third, the chapter argues the need for theoretical analysis of social and economic differentiation within the Aboriginal community, this being important to understand the political dynamics and the potential for economic and social transformation within these communities. Fourth, the chapter lays out the theoretical foundations of the Northern Plan, which was C.Y. Thomas's convergence strategy. Finally, it attempts to explain the limited practical impact of the planning exercise in terms of its poor conceptualization, failure to mobilize Aboriginal support, opposition from within the bureaucracy, and lukewarm political commitment to addressing northern poverty. The approach has, however, been well received in the Aboriginal community and has continued to have an influence on community economic development principles and strategies.

For all these reasons, it is felt that this paper is worth reproducing, but especially so in a volume which seeks to situate it within broader theoretical and policy perspectives. Thus convergence is only one of several possible alternative approaches to economic development, each with its own growth potential and class impact. While written after "The Great Northern Plan," Chapters 1 to 4 examine these alternatives, providing a broader context for that planning exercise. Chapter 1 reflects on traditional Aboriginal values and culture and their relationship to land. Chapter 2 was written for the Native Economic Development Program in the mid-1980s and seeks to analyze the many explicit or implicit development strategies observable in Northern Canada, beginning with a pure subsistence strategy and ending with the convergence strategy. It draws to some degree on the author's long experience in Africa and especially in Tanzania, where debates about different development paths were common in the 1960s and 70s. Inspiration was drawn especially from Tamas Szentes, a former colleague at the University of Dar-es-Salaam in Tanzania and his book *The Political Economy of Underdevelopment* (Budapest, 1971). It seeks to blend international development theory with Northern Canadian and Aboriginal realities. Chapter 3 looks at strategies advocated by Aboriginal People themselves. Chapter 4 looks briefly at some factors to consider in the recent development of Aboriginal casinos in Canada and reflects on casinos as a strategy of economic development.

The way the south views northern Canada is, I believe, important in setting the framework within which northern and Aboriginal development possibilities are situated. In particular, earlier views on the desirability and possibility of an integrated northern economy have given way to a near universal emphasis on resource extraction for export to the south and elsewhere. The rejection of the Northern Plan reflected, to a large degree, the preference for an export promotion strategy based on foreign capital, large-scale production, the import of skilled labour and the relative neglect of the needs of the Aboriginal community. Chapter 6 reviews the evolution of thinking on the role of the North and questions the prospects for alternative visions, especially in the light of new technologies and their implications for both scale and location of economic activities.

As more and more Aboriginal people migrate to or are born in Winnipeg, their role in economic development becomes an issue of critical importance. Again, the social and economic diversity of the Aboriginal community is apparent, as is the strikingly high incidence of poverty. Movement to the city has the potential for widening opportunities for the community but all too often it simply reproduces the social and economic problems in rural and remote Aboriginal communities. Migration has, however, led to the formation of many types of Aboriginal organizations concerned with economic development and several competing views of appropriate strategies of development.

Chapter 7, originally written for the Royal Commission on Aboriginal Peoples, to which the author was a policy advisor, demonstrates the complexity of Aboriginal life in Winnipeg and the different approaches to economic development found there. It aims to capture and preserve the historiography of urban Aboriginal approaches to economic development, and to reflect critically on them. It also assesses the record of government intervention in this area, identifying what appears to have worked and where more needs to be done. It examines employment creation, training, employment equity, and community economic development approaches all of which, and more (e.g., education and child welfare reform) are likely to be called upon if poverty is to be eradicated.

There has been a substantial growth in CED activity in the city of Winnipeg in recent years, much of it, though by no means all, revolving around Aboriginal people. Long-term funding of these activities is crucial if they are to survive. Chapter 8 studies the evolution of the structure of CED organizations in Winnipeg and their financing. It examines the efforts that have been made to secure funding, the progress made, and the difficulties which remain. Chapter 9 is a reflection of the state of CED in Winnipeg which probably has relevance for CED activities elsewhere.

Chapter 10 draws on the author's experience in developing Aboriginal business enterprises in order to draw lessons from what it takes for those businesses to succeed and what has contributed in the past to high failure rates. This leads logically to a consideration in Chapter 11 of the circumstances in which it might make sense to subsidize such business ventures, be they private or collective in nature.

The collection ends with a forward-looking chapter on the challenges and possibilities for Aboriginal people in Manitoba given current demographic forecasts. Aboriginal youth could potentially become an important segment of the labour force in the coming years, helping to compensate economically for an aging population generally. Whether or not that becomes a reality and whether or not labour force participation converts into higher Aboriginal employment will depend mainly on how contemporary problems faced by the Aboriginal community are addressed in the immediate future. Successful participation will require that all levels of government and the Aboriginal community itself co-operate to lay the groundwork for dealing with the obstacles to social and economic involvement, which large sections of Aboriginal society currently face. It is hoped that the book as a whole contributes in some small way to suggesting how that might best be achieved.

A note on terminology. Over time termination has changed, but in what follows, the terminology applicable at the time of writing has been maintained to retain the authenticity of the pieces. Thus the term "Indian" is used rarely these days and usually only to relate to legal status. The word "native" persists in the names of university departments but otherwise "Aboriginal" has replaced it. There are some who prefer not to use "Aboriginal," objecting to the term "Metis" encompassed by it, preferring "Metis Nation," but since this is not yet widespread practice it has not been followed in the book.

CHAPTER 1
THE ABORIGINAL CONCEPT OF STEWARDSHIP AND ENOUGHNESS[1]

The Aboriginal community of North America is a possible source of insight into alternative lifestyles and value systems. Traditional Aboriginal values reflect the relationship of the people with land and, in particular, their complete dependence on the land for survival. Land is respected as the giver of life, and together with water, fish, animals, and plants, is considered inseparable from human life itself. The land is the "mother" of human society, the flesh and blood of human existence. It is the basis not only of security, but also the source of Aboriginal Peoples' identity, pride, self-respect, and independence (Berger, 1977: 93–100). No one owns the land, and all can use it but within socially determined patterns of land use distribution.

As custodians, the current generation has responsibility for safeguarding the land and the animal, fish, and plant life for future generations. In practice, this custodial obligation finds reflection in Aboriginal resource management practices that are highly respectful of the need for conservation and replenishment. For instance, the Waswanipi of the Boreal Forest area of Northern Canada practise rotational hunting, moving from one area to another, in order to regulate the production and distribution of animals (Feit, 1987). Aboriginal resource management in Australia seems to have followed similar patterns, the sophistication of which is only now being appreciated by non-Aboriginal society, whose own resource management practices leave so much to be desired (Coombs, 1990: 97–99).

[1] From Chapter 5 of *Interdependence, Disequilibrium & Growth—Reflections of the Political Economy of North-South Relations at the Turn of the Century.* London: Macmillan, New York: St. Martin's and Ottawa: International Development Research Centre. March 1998.

In general in Aboriginal communities, resource management is achieved by consensus based on shared information gathered through harvesting experience, and passed on from generation to generation through oral culture (Usher, 1987). Rules governing trespass, over-hunting or hunting out of season are enforced through social sanctions. Since "production" is for use rather than exchange, consumption is indeed governed by some concept of enoughness and is modest with any surplus being shared with others in need. Sustainability is the result of this modesty and social control over land use.

One should not, however, romanticize the Aboriginal wildlife management experience. "There is fairly clear evidence that early humans in North America were at least partially responsible for extinction of at least 20, possibly as many as 40 species of medium to large mammals" (Pruitt, 1989: 2). The point is that traditional Aboriginal ways of life were and are much more in synchronization with nature than is merchant and industrial capitalism, which has wreaked more destruction in the last 400 years than "that which had taken the earlier human invasions some 10,000 years to achieve" (ibid.).

Together with this highly developed sense of stewardship over land and natural resources, Aboriginal communities maintain a value system which appears to be singularly relevant to the search for a more sustainable form of economic existence. There is a strong attachment to egalitarianism and to sharing (Berger, op. cit.), to "mutual aid ..., family and community life and traditional institutions such as the collective land tenure system" (Ross and Usher, 1986: 150). Central to Aboriginal culture is respect for elders as repositories of knowledge, history, customs, and tradition (Berger, op. cit.). This stands in stark contrast to the values fostered by capitalism, which emphasize individualism, acquisitiveness, and the educational and technological superiority of youth. This type of mentality gives rise to not just lack of respect for the experience, contribution and knowledge of the aged but also a lack of social responsibility for their care seen, in its most heinous form, in the recent phenomenon of "granny dumping" in the U.S.

Though trade and gift giving between regions was often highly developed, Aboriginal economies were very self-sufficient. With the encroachment of merchant and industrial capitalism, and of the state, the Aboriginal way of life has been eroded and constrained, but it still persists and in northern regions remains strong. It is a testimony to the strength of Aboriginal culture that it does persist under such unrelenting pressure, and there is much that can be learned from its values by those seeking a less acquisitive, more community-focused way of life.

CHAPTER 2

ALTERNATIVE STRATEGIES OF COMMUNITY ECONOMIC DEVELOPMENT[1]

This chapter examines the economic dimension of community development as it is treated in the literature. In particular it looks at the alternative recommendations in that literature on the direction and pattern that economic development strategies should take and it evaluates each of these in terms of their strengths and weaknesses.

Since the literature on community development (CD) is voluminous one can only survey a minute portion of it and even then only in very schematic terms. Nevertheless what follows is, hopefully, representative of the major currents of thought in that literature, especially as it pertains to Canada.

1.1 ON DEFINITIONS AND TERMS

i) The Meaning of "Community Development"

The term "community development" is used widely but is rarely defined. When definitions are attempted, they tend to describe a *process* by which people consciously seek to improve their well-being through collective action. Thus, community development "offers a way of involving people more fully in the life of their communities; it generates scope and initiative for participation in economic, social, and cultural life; it provides a basis for more profound understanding and a more effective use of the democratic processes"

---

[1] From Chapter 1 of *The Economics of Community Development*. Report prepared for Native Economic Development Program, DRIE. January 1986.

(Lotz, 1977: 35) "The primary objective of community development ... is to promote, sustain, support, and maintain community action ... (to go) forward towards defined goals, with purposeful activity aimed at real achievement" (Griffiths, 1974: 89). Community development encompasses community *economic* development (CED), frequently entailing "an economic analysis of the community and research and decision making aimed at drawing up a plan of action to create or maintain the kind of community that people have collectively determined to be desirable" (Lotz, 1977: 9). Generally, however, it goes beyond the narrowly economic to encompass social and cultural well-being and presupposes, therefore, an "integrated approach to development" (Wismer and Pell 1981: 3).

In its most general sense the term "community development" suggests a conscious intervention on the part of a group of people to shape their lives in directions they feel to be desirable. The implication is that without this intervention broader forces at work in society, many of them economic, would act to the detriment of the people in question, either by bypassing them or by affecting them adversely. Externally induced crises which, in extreme cases, might threaten the very survival of a community have been cited as an important stimulus to community development efforts (Williams and Scott 1981: 11). Such external threats have undoubtedly been a major factor underlying a number of initiatives taken by Aboriginal Peoples in Canada in recent years. Thus hydro dam and power line construction, oil and gas developments, mining expansion, and the contamination of fisheries by resource extraction industries have all been seen at one time or another in the recent past as threatening to the survival of Native communities (see e.g., Sanders, 1973). They have given rise, therefore, to collective initiatives at the community level. In the process, Native communities have inevitably had to go well beyond the defensive positions designed to preserve an existing way of life and consider adjustments to, and possible improvements in, their way of life in the face of these external pressures.

Yet the threat of externally induced disruptions is not the sole, nor, for many Native communities, even the most important stimulus to community development initiatives. That disruption has long been an historical fact, not an impending threat, and the marginalization of Aboriginal communities that accompanied Canadian economic development in general (Loxley, 1981) provides the rationale for many community initiatives.

Being concerned largely with "process," however, the literature on community development tends to overlook the historical factors that give rise to the need for "conscious intervention" by the community. As a result, it tends also to have relatively little to say about possible economic strategies that communities might adopt to deal with their marginalization. There are exceptions to this, as we shall see below and certainly literature on concrete community experiences tends to be more concerned with history and *strategic* alternatives than is the more general theoretical and policy-oriented CD literature; but as a rule, the bulk of CD literature is relatively silent on crucial aspects of economic strategy that communities must confront if "community development" is to have any lasting beneficial impact.

ii) The Meaning of "Economic Strategy"

Like that of the term "community development," the meaning of "economic strategy" is rarely made clear. In this context we shall interpret it to mean the direction taken by economic policy in a number of key areas. Strategic thrusts will usually be explicit, often the outcome of a planning process in which options are identified and their relative merits assessed, but they can also be implicit in more random decision-taking processes or in situations in which communities have little real input into major decisions affecting them. Some of the key policy areas which comprise economic strategies are as follows:

a) Ownership of capital and natural resources and control over economic decision-taking.

b) The direction of investment and the choice of products and markets.

c) The scale and technology of production and market size.

d) The participation of women in economic activities.

A clearly articulated economic strategy would specify policy in these and related areas, thus setting a clear *direction* in which the community would move in terms of economic development.

Community development literature tends, in general, to focus on only some of these elements. Being preoccupied with "process" it tends to concentrate on *how* decisions are made rather than on the *substance* of those decisions. Thus, the theoretical and policy literature on CD, as well as CD manuals, tend to say relatively little on items (a) to (d) beyond the dimension of process. This is, perhaps, partly because the looseness of the definition of CD means that the range of activities encompassed by CD literature is extremely broad, covering community/social work, urban renewal, adult education and political organizing at the local level (Griffiths 1974: 90–91). One has, therefore, to examine the literature on specific CD experiences (which is not the purpose of this report) or to study the literature in fields closely related to CD in order to throw light on the issue of economic strategy. Regional economics, economic development, international trade, and microeconomic theory are therefore a more fruitful source of insights than is mainstream CD literature. There are encouraging signs, however, that Canadian CD literature is beginning to incorporate lessons from this broader political economy literature, giving it a richer, more rigorous basis than is often encountered in mainstream CD journals and books. Before examining this in detail, however, it seems necessary to look more closely at what is meant by the term "community."

iii) The Meaning of "Community"

The term *community* "is an abstraction which refers to a small geographic and population area having the potential for some form of economic, social, and political cohesion" (Tudiver, 1973: 47). In reality, the potential for cohesion is often not realized because communities are not homogeneous but rather consist of social groups and classes whose interests may not coincide (Conyers, 1982: Chapter 7). Indeed, the relationships between different sections of society at the community level may be antagonistic in some fundamental sense, so that realization of even modest community development goals as outlined in Section 1 (ii) may be possible only with a significant redistribution of economic and political powers. Most CD literature sidesteps this issue altogether, using the term "community" as if it referred to a homogeneous entity.

In addition to failing to address the question of social differentiation and heterogeneity *within* communities, much of the CD literature does not come to terms with the nature of the structures within communities through which *outside* authorities wield economic and political power. Thus, while recognizing that community development may involve the redistribution of power, some writers see this purely in terms of power being shifted towards the community, and away from outside "authorities" (Griffiths, 1974: 93). In reality, however, the authorities tend to exercise their powers through agents residing *within* the community, which raises very complex issues concerning the role of these agents in the community development process. As we shall see, local leaders within Native communities are often in a very ambiguous position, being elected by the community but at the same time being funded by the state and exercising powers delegated by the state. Clearly, any review of CD experience within these communities must address the contradictory pressures and divided loyalties under which Native leadership operates (Loxley, 1981).

In failing to analyze the social and political complexities of power relationships at the community level and their link with authorities outside the community, the literature on CD reveals a distinct ideological bias in favour of maintaining the "status quo." By not acknowledging these relationships and the role they play in the creation or maintenance of the very problems that CD is designed to deal with, much CD literature and advice can at best be peripherally helpful and at worst positively harmful. If the goal of community development really is the transfer of power and resources to the community level, as many suggest it is, this is unlikely to be accomplished unless a careful analysis of the nature of those relationships and their structure *within* the community is first undertaken. Until this happens, the power structures that CD seeks to transform in order to give people more control over their lives will remain unchallenged. An *understanding* of these structures at the community level is therefore crucial to the successful implementation of CD goals as they are usually outlined in the literature (see Dixon, Johnson, Leigh, and Turnbull, 1982).

The recognition that communities comprise a variety of social groups with diverse political interests and viewpoints should serve to caution one against the view that the hallmark of successful community development is social harmony. Yet even those considered enlightened in community development circles tend occasionally to give the opposite impression. Thus, while recognizing the potential for disputes between different groups that CD initiatives might bring, Jim Lotz argues that "(e)ffective community development should enable people to handle these conflicts and tensions in a creative manner ... if people don't hang together they'll hang separately" (Lotz, 1977: 9–10). Yet, if CD is effective in giving some members of the community more control over their lives and over the resources of the community, the chances are that someone else in the community is losing some control or influence. To the extent that this is the case, the process of CD will almost certainly be characterized by disputation and conflict. The irony is that Lotz himself has argued that CD has been used, from time to time, "as a safe ideologically neutral way of keeping people from making legitimate demands for changes in the power structure" (Lotz, 1977: 36).

A similar inconsistency is observable in the works of other, otherwise equally enlightened, CD writers. Thus Wismer and Pell (1981: 141) point out that local businesses and/or social service groups may object to community economic development projects as presenting unfair competition. They suggest that such conflict should be minimized and could be by keeping the community informed and by maintaining good working relationships with "the other groups." The problem with this advice (which of course sounds so plausible and non-intimidating that it has an immediate appeal) is that it underestimates the likely degree of opposition to successful CED projects and mis-specifies the likely nature of some such opposition. Thus, if the advice of Wismer and Pell were followed successfully then, as we shall see later in this report, communities would move in the direction of self-reliance on a "not for profit" basis. This would, of necessity, change the economic relationships between the community and the outside business world and, more than likely also alter the economic circumstances of local agents of that outside world. At the same time, democratically organized, community-based, not-for-profit organizations would, sooner or later, almost certainly pose a threat to privately owned, profit-seeking and outside-market-oriented local business and it is hard to see how good relationships could be maintained in these circumstances. This serves to emphasize again that communities are not homogeneous and community development cannot be a neutral process politically if its objectives are to shift economic and political power. Harmony and avoidance of conflict would be possible only if CD efforts were themselves marginal or insignificant but Wismer and Pell seem to be calling, quite correctly, for more substantial initiatives than that.

1.2 APPROACHES TO ECONOMIC STRATEGY IN COMMUNITY DEVELOPMENT

Having dealt briefly with the meaning of some basic terms, we now move to consider the way in which the literature of CD and that in related fields deal with the *economic* development dimension of community development. Specifically, we shall examine what it says about the main elements of economic strategy outlined in Section 1.1 (ii). To begin with, however, it is necessary to examine what has become a common thread tying together various approaches to economic strategy to be found in the literature; that is, the recognition that development initiatives should, in some way, respond to the *needs* of the community.

i) The Issue of "Need" in Community Economic Development

That economic development should proceed in a way that meets the needs of communities is a proposition, which, superficially at least, appears unobjectionable. It is indeed one that is held widely and by writers of all political persuasions. Yet the rationale for it, the meaning and how it would be put into operation raises complex philosophical and practical problems. For instance, how does one ascertain the needs of a community? What is the relevant concept of needs—those "felt needs" pre-existing a process of ascertaining them and simply articulated or, at most, firmed up by that process, *or* needs which are formed and shaped by that very process and which were not "felt" or were felt differently before the process began? These questions have been the subject of intense debate in the literature on CD because they have enormous implications for the approach of community development workers to their task. Some would argue that quite different types of community development would result from these two alternative approaches to the formation and expression of needs and from subsequent efforts to meet them.

Those arguing in favour of the "felt" needs approach tend to see community development workers as politically neutral "facilitators" whose task it is "to help people think in a more orderly, systematic and logical manner than they would otherwise do" (Batten, 1974: 101). While presenting facts objectively—both pros and cons of each issue—they themselves remain impartial and avoid becoming involved in disputes or arguments. What they must avoid at all costs is adopting, whether knowingly or unintentionally, a *directive* approach which concentrates on persuading communities to accept decisions—and therefore expressions of need—which have been worked out *for* them and not *by* them. Some would go so far as to argue that under a directive approach, community development loses all meaning (Batten 1974: 98).

Opponents of the "felt needs" approach feel that it suffers from severe limitations which would unnecessarily restrict the scope of community development potential—perhaps to the point where CD legitimates rather than seeks to change the "status quo." It is held that the very fact of deprivation and economic backwardness that characterize many communities, which are the target for community development efforts, limits the knowledge of possibilities available to them. People cannot be expected to want what they have no knowledge of. In addition, these circumstances of deprivation serve to constrain the ambitions and aspirations of communities.

For these reasons it has been observed that in many deprived communities "felt needs" often turn out to be relatively few in number, relatively general in nature and very limited by the narrow view of what is possible that characterizes the perspective of a single, not to mention deprived, community. There is, therefore, a case for "an educated and persuaded need" (Batten, 1974: 98) and especially so where a community forms but one element in a broader regional or national economic development planning exercise.

Other community development workers see themselves performing not only an educational role but also one which is best described as a mobilizing role. They see it as not only legitimate but also imperative that they educate and mobilize community groups to form their own organizations to articulate their needs and to press their case politically (Loney, 1982). More often than not, this type of interventionism is informed by a systemic, historical view of the causes of regional inequality and community deprivation. This framework of analysis guides the educational and organizational efforts of the CD worker and inevitably serves to broaden the perspective of the community in the definition of its needs. Furthermore, this approach often suggests, in broad strategic terms, the types of political or economic steps required to deal with economic deprivation, though these suggestions and detailed decisions to implement them are all subject to community discussion and approval (Loxley, 1981). There is, therefore, an activist role envisaged for the CD worker but at the level of education, discussion, debate and organizing; one which would not be considered "directive" by its proponents.

From this more activist standpoint the "neutral" CD worker represents an obstacle to the type of local organizing which is seen as being necessary if communities are to have any impact on resource allocation or power sharing. Once more, therefore, neutralism is seen as reinforcing "the status quo" (Filken and Naish, 1982).

The question of meeting "needs," however defined, raises other important issues in community economic development theory and practice. In Canadian society many needs are met through the marketplace. Needs are, therefore, often equated with "demands" and are met through the exercise of purchasing power. But there are problems in relying upon market forces to meet needs. To begin with, demand is a function of the level and distribution of income. Low incomes imply a low level of effective demand and hence many "basic" material needs will not be met. For a definition of "basic needs" and a discussion of the problems of meeting them, see Streeton, 1979. This is a common situation in deprived communities and one which points, among other things, to the importance of the creation of jobs which pay more than poverty-line wages.

Secondly, there are several basic material needs necessary for the survival and reproduction of the population which in deprived communities are often not "felt" or at least not given the priority they deserve. Available incomes often tend to be spent instead on non-essentials of one kind or another (e.g., in communities where nutrition is a problem significant amounts of money are often spent on soft drinks, chips, and alcohol). Apart from highlighting the shortcomings of relying on "felt needs" as a guide to action, this example also suggests that meeting needs in the sense of "basic needs" may be a very complex and difficult task involving not only education but also, perhaps, the local production of goods thought important for a balanced diet and the discouragement (prohibition?) of certain types of junk food.

To the extent that attempts are made to meet needs, which are not currently met through the marketplace *either* because incomes are deficient *or* because the pattern of demands does not coincide with the pattern of "needs," these attempts may be costly. Rectifying "market" and systemic failures of this type *may* require subsidization of services to communities (e.g., provision of safe drinking water) which cannot be financed at cost recovery pricing, or provision of employment in activities that are not commercially viable. This raises the whole question of subsidization, a topic which is generally avoided in CD literature but one dealt with later in this report. Subsidization may be, as we will argue, a crucial element in successful CD activities designed to meet community needs.

Finally, it must be stressed that not all needs are material in nature, whether basic or otherwise. Non-material or psychic needs are often closely related to production but are generally met by "objects of satisfaction (that) are not produced" (Heller, 1974: 99). Meeting these needs may also imply departure from market criteria, or, and perhaps more significantly, a fundamental realignment of institutions which take decisions affecting the daily life of community residents. Thus, if a need is felt for greater community self-reliance, this may be more costly in material terms than existing market arrangements. If community ownership of and/or control over local business activities is desired, then new institutions will need to be established to give concrete expression to this desire. These institutional innovations *may* also be less efficient in a strict profit and loss sense than other laissez-faire approaches (see the next section). Meeting these types of psychic needs may, therefore, also have implications for funding and subsidization.

ii) The Question of Ownership and Control

Much CD literature expresses no preference for particular forms of ownership and merely outlines the pros and cons of each possible type of ownership vehicle. Priority is placed upon local initiatives stimulating economic development projects rather than upon the specific ownership form that such projects may take. This approach reflects a preoccupation with "process" rather than with the substance of CD and has little to say on the origins of the problems that render CD initiatives necessary or on the likely efficacy of alternative strategic approaches to solving those problems. This "cookbook" approach to CD is very common (Williams and Scott, 1981; Mahmood and Ghosh, 1979, are good examples) and can be of great assistance to communities exploring the mechanics of CD. It is, however, an approach which is quite limited in scope precisely because it lacks an historical and theoretical perspective on *why* communities are deprived and on what might be done to remedy the situation.

There are, however, two alternative approaches that do take strong positions on the appropriate ownership focus for CD. The first of these is common in the literature on urban renewal and on ethnic minority development initiatives in the U.S. It has also characterized the development strategies of colonial governments in different parts of the world, of contemporary foreign aid agencies (including the World Bank) and of many of the federal and provincial funding programs in Canada established to foster community development. This is an approach which emphasizes very strongly the promotion of small private business enterprises as the backbone of community development.

A number of justifications are put forward for this type of ownership strategy. Some people equate different scales of enterprise with different appropriate forms of ownership—the larger the enterprise the greater the justification for social control and therefore, of public ownership. Community enterprises are deemed to be small-scale operations in which the case for public ownership is weakest. In the words of E.F. Schumacher, "in small-scale enterprise, private ownership is natural, fruitful and just" (Schumacher, 1974: 223).

Others see the justification for private ownership in the need to create a "middle class" among disadvantaged groups. This seems to be a particularly important consideration in the ethnic minority literature in the U.S. (see e.g., Hetherington, 1981). It is also a theme dominating development policies of colonial governments, modern aid agencies and public sector funding bodies in Canada. The objective is clear. It is a means of bringing disadvantaged people into the mainstream economy by "building on the best"—by co-opting so-called "progressive" representatives with the lure of private wealth and by providing a model to be followed by those not so fortunate. If successful, this serves to minimize social unrest among the disadvantaged groups and to head off potential opposition from the "progressive" element who often tend to be vocal and politically active. In a sense, therefore, community workers and development agencies pursuing this strategy can be said to be acting as agents of social control since they aim at social integration of potential community leaders into the economic system as a whole (Loxley, 1981).

Within this perspective, cooperative initiatives by members of the community frequently have as their rationale, the promotion of private business activities. Thus, Community Development Corporations in the U.S. have often been seen less as vehicles to directly undertake business activities than as a means of attracting and stimulating private business through the provision of factory space, credit, etc. One observer has gone so far as to suggest that Community Development Corporations "may affect timing, location and amount of investment by private business concerns but the decision as to whether or not to invest remains with the (private) manufacturer" (Gilmore, 1960: 133). The realities of lack of capital *within* deprived communities may be as responsible for this approach as any ideological preference for private enterprise. Shortages of capital may mean "if the economic structure of the ghetto is to undergo dramatic transformation it may be necessary that even the strongest community corporations compromise their desire for complete control by inviting outside firms to participate in community-inspired plans for business development" (Sturdivant, 1972: 46; The Twentieth Century Fund, 1971: 99).

Yet ideological preference is important too and finds expression both in its support for private enterprise and in arguing the inherent weaknesses of collective ownership. "To people who have been denied access to economic opportunity, ownership of a business is a symbol of personal emancipation" (Hetherington, 1972: 14–15). At the same time "the successful operation of communal enterprise requires a strong, cohesive social organization among the members of the group. A disciplined social structure of this sort is inconsistent with the emphasis on individualism and independence which is the dominant theme of the social philosophy of this country" (Hetherington, 1972: 17). In other words, members of disadvantaged communities can be expected to share the values of the larger society, and community ownership and control are not part of those values.

Others argue the case for private enterprise *implicitly* by pointing out the contradiction said to be inherent in the dual goals of community-owned enterprises; namely, the goal of profit on the one hand and that of democracy and community input and control, on the other. This view is one which is held widely among CD theorists. Sturdivant has argued that "it is probably safe to say that the greater the degree of democracy in the enterprise, the less effective its management will be. This weakness is clearly a major flaw in the concept of community based development" (Sturdivant, 1972: 42–43).

The idea of a "trade-off" between efficiency and democracy in community-owned enterprises is to be found in Canadian CD literature too. Thus, Williams and Scott argue that the strength of commercial corporations, the form widely used by private business, lies in their promotion of financial efficiency rather than in generating broader community benefits (Williams and Scott, 1981: 57). They go on to argue, "This is an important reason why the community-development movement has tended to shun this corporation form." They have, however, "noticed a growing sentiment that efficiency is a needed asset in community-based development." The clear implication is that other ownership forms do not promote or are not compatible with "financial efficiency."

It must be emphasized that while, in theory, more collective forms of ownership provide systematically for greater democracy and community input, they do not necessary achieve these goals in practice. In the U.S., Community Development Corporations have a very mixed record in this respect with managers frequently, if unintentionally, gaining disproportionate power through the monopolization of information and technical expertise (The Twentieth Century Fund, 1971: 93; Sturdivant, 1972: 46–50).

At the other extreme from those advocating a private enterprise thrust to CD are writers who feel that the very nature of the problems that CD seeks to address warrants an approach which, explicitly and unambiguously, promotes communally owned enterprises of one form or another. In Canada in recent years, a number of writers have advocated communally owned enterprises as the preferred way of achieving community development (Loxley, 1981; Wismer and Pell, 1981, 1983; Jordan, 1983; Jackson, 1984). Others have advocated strategies which, while promoting local entrepreneurship in general, make specific provision for the "encouragement of all forms of cooperative action" (The Canadian Council on Rural Development, 1976: 9).

The reasons for preferring communal ownership are numerous and vary from author to author. Some have an aversion to the exploitation of one section of society by another that is implied in the capital/labour relationship and would, therefore, oppose private enterprise of any but the owner-run, single proprietor or family type. Some would argue that the deprivation of many communities is the result, in spatial terms, of the pursuit of profit being the main economic motivator in society. They would argue that this motivation leads to uneven geographic development in which some communities, and even whole peoples, become "functionally irrelevant" (Watkins, ed., 1977). On this perspective, CD represents an attempt to reverse these historical forces by, to some extent at least, changing the rules of the game. Community ownership of capital and resources is seen as essential if spatial patterns of economic activity more congenial to existing locations of communities are to become a reality and to remain so over any extended period of time. Local ownership and control are considered essential if patterns of investment are to change to promote community development and if surpluses are to be reinvested locally to guarantee long-term development.

Communal ownership is also thought to be the only type compatible with the strong democratic and participatory philosophy underlying some approaches to community development. There is, as we have seen, no guarantee that this philosophy will always find practical expression in communally owned enterprises; much more than the question of legal forms of property is involved in securing community input and control over decision-taking. There is, nonetheless, recognition that communal ownership is at least a *necessary* condition for such democracy, even if it is not a *sufficient* one.

It follows, therefore, that much more is expected of CD projects than mere profit-making (difficult enough though that in itself might be!). The desire to meet broader community goals would undoubtedly lead communally owned projects to behave in numerous ways differently from the manner in which private businesses might operate. The desire to avoid dependence on the state would also rule out the Crown corporation option as a substitute for private business. Thus, communally owned vehicles of one type or another are considered by some to be a "third sector" (Wismer and Pell, 1981), "neither public nor private but making use of the resources of both public and private sectors" (Wismer and Pell, 1983).

It is because of these broader dissatisfactions with private enterprise that some would argue that the option of attracting private business by the offer of state- or community-financed subsidies is not a desirable one. Also, many believe that public funds should not be used for the purpose of enriching a few individuals but should rather be employed in the interests of the broader community.

The principal forms of communal ownership are client- or worker-owned cooperatives, community development corporations and non-profit incorporated entities, but communal ownership can also be exercised through partnerships and through enterprises incorporated for profit. The advantages and disadvantages of each of these are well covered in the literature (Wismer and Pell, 1981; Williams and Scott, 1981; Jordan, 1983; MacLeod, 1979; Jackson, 1984). Three observations might, however, supplement the information in these sources. To begin with, choice of vehicle is less important than the commitment of the community to the collective ideal. Even companies incorporated as profit-making entities can be operated in a manner that permits community input and control if the desire is there. They can operate with broader community goals in mind than mere profit maximization and they can be subsidized if meeting those goals entails losses. At the same time, other forms, which are less obviously profit and loss oriented, can survive over time only if deficits are either avoided or financed in some way. Secondly, the cooperative or CDC forms have an advantage over other forms because there are national organizations which can be drawn on for technical support and advice, although some Native communities avoid these forms because they fear the possible interference of these national bodies (Development Education Centre, 1983: 201). Thirdly, some provinces have legal provision for community-based Crown corporations. In some situations, these can be operated as if they were community-owned and -controlled and hence this type of vehicle should not be ruled out of consideration as a matter of principle, but should rather be examined from the point of view of the degree of dependence it is likely to entail in any concrete situation.

Since community ownership is the form assumed in the strategy of convergence proposed in this report, it is important to deal with a view, commonly encountered in Canada, that community ownership does not work. The best possible response to this is to refer such cynics to the wealth of material which demonstrates that community ventures are prospering throughout Canada and that many of them are owned and operated by Native People (Wismer and Pell, 1981; Williams and Scott, 1981; Jackson, 1984; Development Education Centre, 1983; Thalassa Research Associates, 1983). One might therefore appropriately describe this view as "the myth of community enterprise failure."

It cannot be assumed, of course, that communities will necessarily have a commitment to community ownership or, even if the commitment is there, that the ability and expertise required to initiate and operate a successful community-owned venture will be. Communities may opt for privately owned businesses for either practical or ideological reasons. The point that must be made, however, is that funding agencies can play an important role in vehicle choice and that their preferences need not always coincide with those of community.

iii) The Direction of Investment and the Choice of Products and Markets

Once communities have decided that they wish to actively promote their own economic development and have decided on the types of vehicle they feel are appropriate, the central question that needs to be addressed is what kinds of economic projects should they consider initiating. Though this is obviously a vital question, it is ironically one about which most CD literature says little. Generally, and again this is a reflection of a preoccupation with process, the emphasis is on *how* decisions will be arrived at and not on the possible nature of those decisions. Sifting through the literature, though, it is possible to identify several different strategies of development that are being advocated or implemented. These are as follows:

a) Subsistence strategies

b) Welfare and/or migration strategies

c) A government services strategy

d) Export promotion strategies

e) Import substitution strategies

f) Dual economy strategy

g) Convergence or self-reliance strategies.

We shall discuss each of these in turn in the context of an income and production framework to be found in Appendix 1. This framework analyzes the structure of an economy in terms of product inputs and outputs and in terms of the sectoral origins and disposal of income. It enables one to ascertain how strong are the *linkages* within an economy, in terms of sectors or firms buying from and selling to each other, how dependent is the economy on outside markets for sales or sources of supply, and how open or inward looking is the economy in terms of retaining income generated locally.

a) Subsistence Strategies

The essence of this type of strategy is production for direct use by the producer. Subsistence production does not involve market exchange or monetary transactions and, therefore, neither the export nor, in extreme cases, even the import of goods. Production can be used for direct consumption but it can also provide intermediate inputs into other products (e.g., skins for clothing) or even investment goods (e.g., bones of animals for tools, wood for housing or transport, etc.). The essence of subsistence production is the direct link between use of the resource base and the meeting of basic human needs.

This convergence of resources with needs is characteristic of pre-capitalist economies but survives in a limited form in modern society. Subsistence production is also characterized by social relationships different from the dominant ones in societies in which production for exchange is the order of the day. Cooperative ties based on kinship or tribal relationships contrast with the competitive, individualistic and wage relationships of modern capitalist systems.

Some argue that subsistence transactions are much more important in contemporary society than is generally realized. The Vanier Institute of the Family is well known for advocating this position and for arguing that the "informal economy," as they call it (Nicholls and Dyson, 1983) should be greatly expanded in preference to and at the expense of the money economy. They do not advocate the complete replacement of the "formal" economy and hence their approach is not a true subsistence one but one which is better located in the "self-reliance" group of strategies discussed below. Nevertheless, the subsistence element is a major one in their economic strategy proposals. Their reminder that cooperative relationships frequently characterize the informal economy, even in the midst of contemporary capitalism, is an important one and one which provides support for those who believe in the cooperative philosophy which underlies much CD literature. They believe that expansion of the informal economy in a cooperative manner would also reduce sex-role stereotyping and the exploitation of women in the home (Nicholls and Dyson, 1983: 48).

Subsistence strategies have great appeal where resources are abundant (including land and wildlife) and where market intrusions are still relatively limited. They are rarely advocated as a total strategy as the money-exchange economy has numerous attractions in terms of the products and services it makes available and these attractions are only realizable if would-be purchasers have commodities they can sell in return. Nevertheless, subsistence production is important in many communities and is likely to remain a key element in whatever overall strategy is adopted by such communities. It should be noted, though, that other strategies might undermine the role of the subsistence economy by depleting the resource base or by siphoning off labour to wage employment.

b) Welfare and/or Migration Strategies

These strategies are rarely if ever the outcome of deliberate community development initiatives. Usually they are the product of a community being unattractive as a location for private or state investment. If members of the community are immobile they will tend to continue residing in the community even if job prospects are dim or non-existent; a welfare community then persists. Such immobility is regarded by mainstream economic theory as a market imperfection and there is a school of thought (supply side economics) which would argue that the appropriate state response should be to reduce welfare payments and subsidies to these communities to induce labour to move to locations where job prospects are better.

Welfare-dependent communities are characterized by relatively low levels of economic activity. Where communities are small and isolated, consumption of goods locally tends to exceed the value of goods produced locally, the balance being provided by imports, from outside the community. As a result imports tend to constitute a very high proportion of total spending and, often, are in excess of the value of incomes generated by economic activity within the community.

Migration away from such communities may take place over time simply as a reflection of deteriorating social conditions—this is common in welfare communities—and may, therefore, be the result of a lack of community development initiatives. On the other hand, certain types of positive community initiatives may have the unintended effect of stimulating a greater rate of out-migration. Community-sponsored education and training programs not accompanied by the creation of equivalent employment opportunities may serve, therefore, to drain communities of the educated and the skilled, through migration. Such education and training programs are often state-initiated and, where this is so, their impact on migration may or may not be intended.

By and large, the objective of most formal development strategies is to give communities an alternative to "de facto" welfare and/or migration strategies and a complement to whatever remains of the subsistence sector. Policies of deliberately encouraging migration reflect a belief that alternative community development strategies are not feasible due to a poor resource base or a small and/or isolated economy.

c) A Government Services Strategy

The assumptions underlying this strategy are that economic opportunities in the communities in question are quite limited but at the same time many basic needs of the community are not being met. The state, therefore, intervenes to provide certain infrastructural investments in housing, water supply, garbage disposal, fire equipment, recreational facilities, health, education, and transportation. Funds for these initiatives will usually come from capital and operating budgets, and from outside the community if the community tax base is small or non-existent. Sometimes, short-term job creation projects will be used for these purposes.

The advantage of this strategy is that important basic needs of the community are met which might otherwise not be met. In the process, some employment and additions to local income are generated.

The first disadvantage is that the community often has little input into the decision about *what* is delivered and *when*, especially if it is dependent on outside funding. Also, many of the jobs so created are short-term—often on make-work schemes—covering the construction phase of projects; thereafter, a high proportion of the small numbers of permanent employees in such jobs as health, education, police, etc. are often recruited from outside the community, especially if it is a poor, remote one. The permanent effects on local incomes are, therefore, not likely to be significant. During the construction phase most materials are also likely to be imported into the community and hence linkages to any local economy that might exist are minimal or non-existent. Finally, this strategy clearly offers no permanent, viable solution to long-term community economic growth although it may be an important prerequisite for it.

d) Export Promotion Strategies

Where production within the community is geared to satisfying market demand outside the community, the strategy being pursued is that of export promotion. This is a very common strategy in Canada and usually involves the export of a raw material or a staple. The staple theory of growth is in fact a Canadian theory designed to explain the economic development of Canada as a nation in terms of the impact that different export staples had on the domestic economy and on the social and political structure of the country (Watkins, 1963, 1977).

Export promotion strategies are advocated because export markets offer communities a much larger market for their products than do local community markets. This enables communities to earn larger incomes and to use larger, supposedly more efficient production methods. Competing with others for outside markets is also held to promote efficient resource allocation. Earnings from exports then permit communities to buy the consumption and investment goods they need from large-scale producers outside the community (i.e., imports), thereby obtaining goods more cheaply than they could produce them themselves. This strategy is also held to conform to the theory of comparative advantage, which would suggest that in a resource-rich country production should focus on resource-intensive exports.

The staple theory examines the type of growth resulting from the particular staple in question, measuring its forward, backward, and final demand linkages as well as its impact on the structure of income distribution. This approach to growth is mirrored in a technique which is used widely in regional and urban (community) economic development literature—the economic base technique. This technique makes the assumption that export markets are "the prime mover of the local economy" (Tiebout, 1962: 13). It then goes on to measure that contribution by calculating the relationship between income (or employment) generated in the export or "basic" sector and total income (or employment) in the form of income (or employment) multipliers.

These multipliers are then used to calculate what would happen to total local income and employment in the event of export income or employment rising or falling, so that

k.d.X = dY or k.d.EX = dET, where X = Export earning, Y = Income,
ET = Total employment, EX = Employment in the export sector,
k = the multiplier.

Thus, the economic base technique is supposed to represent a planning aid to communities or regions. It is a very crude technique often using average or minimal requirements data obtained from elsewhere to allocate activities between basic and non-basic sectors. Its weakness is that it assumes all other activities to be a function of export activities, which is rarely the case, especially where the state is an active employer or where production for direct use (subsistence) is important. It also has numerous shortcomings as a forecasting or planning device due to the crudeness of its assumptions. (For a discussion of the approach and its weaknesses see Tiebout, 1962; Kenny, 1981; North, 1975; Bendavid, 1972; Nourse, 1968; Lane, 1966). For these reasons others have suggested the use of input-output analysis to measure more precisely the direct and indirect contribution of exports to local economies, either complete input-output tables (which are difficult to compile in practice) or more limited intersectoral or partial flow tables. (See Kenny, 1981; Hansen and Tiebout, 1963; Lee, Lewis and Moore, 1971; Clapp, 1977).

The assumption of the staple theory is that economic development would involve economic diversification around the export base. Over time, therefore, "autonomous" or internal factors would gradually reduce the importance of exports in their role as "prime mover" in the economy. Critics of export strategies argue that, historically, this is frequently not the case. To begin with, profits and rents on land need not be retained nationally, leave alone regionally or within the particular communities where resource extraction is taking place (Watkins, 1977; Loxley, 1981). The result is that diversification does not take place and production areas remain excessively dependent on one or more staple exports. The control of the use of profits and rents is, therefore, crucial in strategies informed by the staple approach. Secondly, and related to this point, linkages are rarely established at the point of production of the staple. The result is that the local economy has very few linkages—usually of a service or utility type—and most inputs of intermediate or capital goods are imported. The product is exported with little if any further processing from its raw state and therefore few forward linkages exist beyond a few services. At the same time, because production is geared to export, the consumption requirements of the population are also met by imports of goods. In some cases, even the labour is brought into the area from outside thereby reducing even further the benefits to the local community of staple production. The result is that staple economies are often very open, divergent economies in which what is consumed is not produced locally (Thomas, 1974).

Other criticisms of export strategies, particularly those involving staples, are that demand and prices are highly volatile so that local production and/or local incomes are highly unstable. It is perhaps useful to break down possible export promotion strategies by the type of export product involved. Staples can be of two general types, the traditional staples of furs, fish, wild rice, etc. and the modern mineral, forestry, hydro, and oil and gas staples. While sharing many of the positive and negative characteristics described above in terms of large external markets on the one hand, of volatility, lack of linkages, surplus drain, etc. on the other, there are important differences between the two types. Traditional staple activities have provided a way of life for Native People for two to three hundred years and are much more closely woven into the cultural and social fabric of Native life than are modern staples. Traditional staple activities tend to rely more on traditional skills, and to be relatively labour intensive and small scale. They also seem to require less rigid management and organizational systems than modern staples or other types of factory production. Moreover, traditional staple exports are generally consumed, in part, directly by the producers. There is, therefore, a subsistence element which can provide a significant proportion of certain types of basic need (e.g., protein). Finally, while the marketing side of traditional staple industries has tended to be controlled by non-Native people, this has generally not undermined Aboriginal rights in land since land ownership "per se" was not crucial to merchant capitalists in their pursuit of profit.

At the same time, traditional staple industries have not been untouched by cost-reducing technical and organizational innovations. The profit-induced search for greater efficiency has often led to downward pressure on labour requirements, to the centralization of processing facilities and to larger and more capital-intensive harvesting operations (e.g., fish, wild rice). For some staples, these tendencies have also accompanied market stagnation or at best only modest market expansion, raising serious questions about the scope such products are likely to offer for future community economic development.

Modern staples tend to employ highly capital- and skill-intensive techniques of production. They offer, therefore, few job prospects for local residents although the wages paid are the highest in Canada. Many such staples are non-renewable resources and therefore projects have a finite life. While markets vary from product to product, and many are currently depressed, most have experienced very high growth rates in the past 25 years and are thought to have sound long-term prospects. Such staple products have no positive links back to subsistence or to traditional staple production. They do, however, tend to have two negative links. First of all, their production requires a clear title to land and, therefore, a resolution of Native claims to land ownership. In effect this tends to take the form of the extinguishment of remaining Aboriginal titles to land ownership. Secondly, the expansion of modern staples has often adversely affected subsistence or traditional staple production by frightening off wildlife or depleting their food base, by flooding lands used for hunting or trapping, by raising water levels and thereby altering fish stock patterns, and by polluting land, water, and air. Pursuit of a strategy of modern staple exports may therefore be quite incompatible with a strategy of promoting traditional staple exports. We shall, however, consider below proposals for a strategy of a dual economy involving both but in which the traditional, or in this case, renewable resource sector, suitably modernized, will regulate the expansion of the non-renewable sector.

It should be noted that small manufacturing or even service industries (tourism, guiding, etc.) could be export-oriented and may avoid some of the above shortcomings of staple production. The evidence from Native communities seems to suggest, however, that in terms of linkages and community value added, they often tend to function in a similar fashion to staple exports so that this potential is seldom realized. These types of exports must, however, be given serious consideration in reviewing strategic options for Native communities.

e) Import Substitution Strategies

This strategy takes as its starting point the criticisms of export-oriented strategies concerning lack of linkages. It seeks to expand the local economy by establishing projects which produce goods previously imported or provide services previously purchased outside the community. In the literature of economic development certain stages of import substitution are usually proposed, with simple consumer goods such as textiles coming first, more complex consumer goods thereafter, followed at some interval by the local production of intermediate inputs and finally by production of capital goods previously imported (Balassa, 1982). The argument for this progression over time is based on available market size.

The main advantage of import substitution is that a ready-made market exists for the product. The market is known and quantifiable, and this forms a firm basis for project planning. Import substitution can provide communities with higher incomes, more employment, and enhanced labour force skills. In certain situations it may also improve the local tax base. Furthermore, it may create final demand linkages which help to further strengthen the economy.

The main critiques of this strategy are:
   i) The level and pattern of production it leads to are geared to the existing level of *demand* which in turn is based on the existing level of income and the prevailing pattern of income distribution. These may have little relevance to the real *needs* of a community and especially so if the community is a very poor one.

ii) Strategies of import substitution have often led to high cost, inefficient, small-scale production necessitating tariff protection, increased finished product prices, or heavy subsidization.
iii) Often import substitution simply reorders the *pattern* of imports without reducing the total leakages by very much. Thus, finished product imports may merely be replaced by imports of capital goods and intermediate inputs. Often the import substitution process does not go beyond the manufacture of simple consumer goods due to market size consideration and to the business strategies employed by the large corporations (often Transnational Corporations) which control the production of these more sophisticated products.
iv) Local incomes generated by import substitution are often "leaked" out of the production region by virtue of the non-local ownership of capital (including bank loans) and reliance on outside management and skilled labour. Often royalties need to be paid for the use of machinery or processes and these, too, leave the area.
v) Where import substitution industry is grafted on to a staple economy, demand for the substitute will still be almost as volatile as demand for the staple. Thus import substitution industrialization need not be much more stable than export promotion. Nonetheless, it is clear that in an economy in which demand dictates what is produced, import substitution possibilities will always be looked at carefully.

Furthermore, the import substitution approach can be extended to the government services strategies above to maximize the local spin-off effects of that particular strategy. Housing is one sector which offers enormous local benefits if planned properly and has been singled out in CD literature as a sector of particular potential importance to community economic development (Garrity, 1972). Import substitution could also be extended to encompass skilled labour positions held by non-residents of the community. This thrust is considered an essential component of convergence or self-reliance strategies discussed below.

f) Dual Economy Strategy

This proposed strategy encompasses elements of the subsistence and the export promotion strategy. It has been advocated by Watkins (1977) and Usher (1978) for the Dene Nation of the Northwest Territories as a means of preserving Dene self-determination. The essence of the strategy is that the Dene would build a modern renewable resource sector for both subsistence and export, and finance it by rents charged to non-Dene corporations exporting non-renewable resources on Dene lands. In this way the Dene would retain ownership and control of the land and strengthen that sector of the economy to which they are attached historically. They would regulate the non-renewable resource sector to prevent it from adversely affecting the renewable sector and indeed would "tax" it to actually consolidate and expand the latter sector.

This strategy will be discussed later in Chapter 3. At this point it will suffice to note that it presupposes that the Dene possess clear legal title to the land they occupy; that non-renewable resource projects could be regulated in the way proposed; that a modern renewable resource base could be created that would be large enough to support the Dene Nation economically; and, finally, that the Dene do not desire to participate in the non-renewable sector other than through regulating and taxing it (i.e., other options such as equity participation, wage labour participation, or participation as input suppliers, which could be exercised in addition to the one proposed, are not deemed desirable by the Dene). Whatever the situation in the Northwest Territories, these types of assumptions are considered too restrictive for the strategy to be applicable to other parts of Canada (Loxley, 1981: 179).

g) Convergence or Self-Reliance Strategies

This strategy seeks to converge local demands with local resource use and, ultimately, local needs with local resource use—to reverse, therefore, the main structural weakness of dependent economies (i.e., their divergent production structure). In a nutshell, the goal of this strategy is for communities to produce what they consume and to consume what they produce. On the income side, the objective is to reverse the outflows of profits, rents, and other incomes which also characterize dependent economies, in which local property and skilled jobs are often held by outsiders.

This strategy focuses on the production of a range of "basic goods." In this context the term "basic goods" means goods which are used extensively in the production of other goods—other intermediate, consumption, or investment goods. It has, therefore, almost the exact opposite meaning of the terms "base" or "basic" as used in Section 1.2 (iii), d) where it refers to *export* products. Indeed, the convergence strategy can be looked upon as being at the polar extreme from export promotion strategies. Instead, the objective is to build up the local economy, maximize the retention of spending power, and develop as many local backward, forward, and final demand linkages as possible. Basic goods are, therefore, those which have extensive linkages and which exhibit high growth elasticities (Thomas, 1974; Loxley, 1981). A whole range of products fall into this category and a whole constellation of industries therefore suggest themselves as being worthy of examination for planning purposes, among them food, machine tools, and construction.

The convergence strategy presupposes a systematic approach to development since production and demand/need linkages are planned in advance. It is also quite explicitly demanding in terms of participation (Loxley and Rothney, 1983). It assumes community-owned or -controlled enterprises because these are felt to be necessary (though again, by no means sufficient) to reverse surplus flows, to reduce income inequalities and to ensure that production proceeds along the lines desired by the community residents. It requires, therefore, that democratically based community structures be in place to regulate and direct all phases of the planning cycle: from the articulation of community needs to the determination of planning priorities; the establishment and monitoring of projects; and the periodic review of goal achievements and realignment, if necessary, of those goals and objectives. In this context, therefore, community "participation" means community control.

Though this strategy may appear to have much in common with an import substitution strategy, there are major differences between the two. To begin with, import substitution strategies tend to be based on and limited to meeting the existing pattern of *demand*. Convergence strategies depart from this in two ways. First of all, they recognize that the existing pattern of income distribution on which current demand is based may be the product of an inherited structure of class and economic dependence that might not be acceptable to residents. Generally, it presupposes a more equitable income distribution and retention of income leakages. This might, therefore, give rise to a different level and pattern of demand than that assumed by import substitution strategies. Secondly, the convergence strategy recognizes that inherited demand patterns often do not reflect the real *needs* of the community. It advocates, therefore, the gearing up of the local production structure to meet needs for housing, public health, recreation, nutrition, education, etc. that might not be adequately, if at all, reflected in the marketplace (i.e., in demand patterns).

Convergence departs from an import substitution strategy in its view, both of the degree of substitution that is possible and the phasing of that substitution. It rejects the stages of substitution approach outlined above and determines substitution strictly in accordance with the basic goods approach. The choice of product will depend entirely on the nature of the resource base and the structure of needs. As we shall see in the next section, it also makes assumptions about the desirable scale of economic activity that are very different from those usually made in import substitution literature.

A convergence approach would not be incompatible with a subsistence strategy—indeed the very essence of subsistence is the convergence of local resources with need. But a convergence strategy goes well beyond a subsistence strategy to encompass production for monetary exchange and to suggest how this might be organized. It can be based on, but will most surely extend beyond, traditional subsistence pursuits.

A convergence strategy could also encompass, as one element within the much broader overall strategy, the government services strategy. It would, however, have a lot to say about *how* that element should be approached. It would see the state *responding* to community priorities in the service area, planning collegially with the community to determine the timing and manner of implementation of service projects, using or building up the local capacity to construct, operate, and manage projects and, hopefully, setting the groundwork for such projects to be self-financing in the long term. Thus the principles of convergence would be applied to government services, and as far as possible, the material and personnel requirements for such services would be found locally. This might often mean that training programs might need to be established in *anticipation* of service provision or that local production enterprises need to be set up as the first stage of service provision.

Although designed specifically to deal with the shortcomings of export strategies, convergence does not rule out altogether the possibility of exporting products. What it prescribes, however, is that exports should be residual to local needs if efficient scale warrants production of basic goods in excess of the quantity that can be absorbed locally. In modified versions of the convergence strategy, it is also assumed that certain modern staple industries will continue to be a fact of life independently of community desires and that communities might wish, therefore, to "converge" those export industries as much as possible by attempting to maximize local spin-off benefits from them (Loxley, 1981).

The strategy of convergence is not commonly encountered by that name in the literature on community development. Very similar strategies are, however, proposed under different names. Thus, the community-based economic development approach described by Wismer and Pell which advocates community self-reliance, community control, and integrated not-for-profit initiatives has much in common with a convergence strategy (Wismer and Pell, 1981, 1983). So, apparently, does the call for the reinforcement and extension of self-reliance for communities by Lotz (1977: 128) and by Nicholls and Dyson (1983, 1973). A comprehensive development strategy for the Mid-North of Canada by the Canadian Council on Rural Development looks remarkably like a convergence strategy and seems to have borrowed heavily on a convergence planning exercise that was underway in Manitoba at that time (Canadian Council on Rural Development 1976). The C.C.R.D. advocated a "locally based" development strategy and a shift in government policy to accommodate this that would have entailed radical departures from the "status quo."

Some similarities with the convergence approach are to be found in literature on black ghettos in the U.S. Thus, Kotler has argued that the primary economic problem of such communities is that of preventing income and expenditure leakages; this can only be done "if the neighbourhood can create an internal economy and political control to attract and keep its expendable income for commodities and public services" (Kotler, 1972: 11). Jacobs has identified convergent-type growth as the driving force behind the expansion of cities (1970).

Stein has argued that the problems of economically depressed communities require "attention to local production for local needs, rather than for export" (emphasis in the original, Stein 1974: 86). He goes on to argue that exports "will, in any case, automatically follow if efficient production is demonstrable in the home market ... (therefore) it appears logical to move toward the replacement of imports rather than the generation of exports" (ibid.).

There is, therefore, a range of CD literature that explicitly or implicitly advocates a strategy of community economic development along lines very similar to those of the convergence strategy. The advantage of the convergence strategy is that it is one that generally has an obvious intuitive appeal to people. Producing to meet needs directly and basing that production on local resources are concepts communities generally find attractive. The idea of planning community activities for some years ahead and of communities owning and controlling businesses and resources, likewise, is often an attractive one.

There are, however, some major difficulties with the strategy. To begin with, the political assumptions on which the pure strategy is based are very demanding. It is assumed that one is dealing with a political entity that can regulate or prohibit trade flows, impose taxes, take property into public sector hands, redistribute income, and plan production. These assumptions are obviously not met in Canada and certainly not at the regional or community level. Yet, a number of proxies can be utilized to approximate the political requirements of the pure strategy. The importance of state funding to many communities and the openness to community-owned economic development vehicles provide rough proxies to some of these assumptions but obviously, the broader economic system continues to be dominated by private enterprise (or by Crown corporations which operate on similar lines) and by the market system. Where land is Crown owned, however, or where ownership can be negotiated through land settlements, communities can obtain exclusive use of local resources and there are precedents for this (Loxley, 1981). In much of Canada, however, land is privately owned and mineral and other rights are not in the hands of the Crown or of local communities. Inevitably, therefore, the Canadian reality is such that only approximations can be made of pure convergence with the principles providing guidelines that are followed to the extent that local conditions permit.

The second major potential drawback of the strategy is its assumption that production can be organized on a small scale at the community level and survive economically in the face of competition from larger operations located elsewhere. This question is so crucial and so central to many proposals for approaches to community economic development that it requires examination in a separate section.

iv) The Scale and Technology of Production and Market Size

Common to all who advocate strategies of convergence, self-reliance, or community-based development is a belief that small-scale production is both desirable, in and of itself and, at the same time, economically sensible. Small-scale production is desirable because it permits a more spatially balanced economy, a less impersonal work environment, the possibility of community participation and control, and the chance to gear technology to local skill and employment levels. The issue of scale is, therefore, of central importance to this approach to community development (Schumacher, 1974; McRobie, 1981; Thomas, 1974; Stein, 1974; Loxley, 1981; Wismer and Pell, 1981; CCRD, 1976).

In addition, small-scale production is held to be generally more efficient than commonly perceived. While there is a positive association between scale and technical efficiency, the loss in efficiency from operating below the "optimal" is not great in most industries.

Moreover, dis-economies of scale are common in large *firms* (though not plants); large firms frequently operate inefficiently, but this is hidden by their sheer market and financial power. It is not known what the minimal efficient scale of production is for any product—but it is suggested that for a number of industries "a firm employing on the order of a hundred persons may well be competitive" (Stein, 1974: 25). This paragraph summarizes some of Stein's conclusions from a comprehensive review of the literature on scale. The apparent strength of firms much larger than the minimal may often be the result of receiving favourable treatment from government in the form of finance, etc.

Thomas (1974) believes that the economies accruing to large-scale production are frequently exaggerated in the literature on economic development due to faulty or dubious measurement yardsticks. In any given situation, the local prices of products or factors, or high transportation costs, might in themselves justify a smaller-scale operation than the so-called optimal. Most importantly, one can capture most scale economies at relatively small levels of production since at output levels beyond these, the rate of fall of unit costs is often relatively small. Thus, he recommends producing at scale levels at which the rate of fall of unit costs is greatest; this *critical minimum level* will usually be well below the optimal or least cost scale level.

In the convergence strategy, therefore, the aim is to produce basic goods at a critical minimum level of scale. The assumption is that the additional costs of producing goods locally relative to the price of imports will be offset by savings in transport costs and by long-run gains to community income from this economic activity which would not, otherwise, take place.

Where communities are attempting convergence in the midst of a market economy, the need for subsidization of local community development projects may arise from two sources. Firstly, if the average cost of locally produced goods is greater than the price of imported goods, including transport costs, then local residents may not buy the local product unless it is subsidized, whatever may be the long-term benefits of local production. Secondly, if the local market is smaller than the critical minimum scale of activity and if prices outside the community are lower than community prices plus average transport costs, then the export surplus may also need to be subsidized. These situations assume that local products are of comparable quality to non-local ones; if they are inferior, the level of subsidization may need to rise.

Given the extremely small size of many Native communities (see Section 2), even plants employing 100 persons are relatively large-scale. It follows from this that if convergence type strategies are to be followed then:

i) Cooperation between a number of communities is likely to be essential if the critical minimum scale is ever to be reached. This will require the development of some coordinating mechanism. Jordan has recognized this point and called for a federated system of cooperative ventures to deal with the "external environment" (Jordan, 1983). Others have recommended that provincial or other levels of government or Crown corporations perform this regional planning role (CCRD, 1976; Loxley, 1981). It is conceivable (and, perhaps preferable) that Native organizations perform this role, which could extend beyond the question of scale as it applies to markets, and encompass related issues of planning and managerial capacity, regional transport systems, and shared social service systems.

ii) Reliance on sheltered markets may be necessary as a substitute for overt subsidization. Thus, a community store may refuse to purchase from outside the community products which are produced within the community, or else the local council may use local labour and materials to build houses, offices, etc. that could be purchased more cheaply outside the community. Wherever possible, the purchasing power of government or large Crown corporations should be used to shelter local projects from destructive market competition. The degree of shelter would, of course, need to be negotiated so as to limit the exposure of purchasers to unduly high prices caused by inefficiency. These limits could be calculated in a number of ways, relative to estimates of the following:

a) additional costs due to the training or learning experience of communities;
b) the net social benefits accruing to the community(ies) on account of local enterprises; or
c) the net improvement in the government budget, when capital costs and other expenses are compared with reduced welfare outlays and expanded tax revenues (all expressed in present value terms) that local projects imply. The upper limit on such shelter outlays could be expressed as a percentage of the cost or price of close substitutes.

Clearly, the idea of sheltered markets and of subsidization does not sit well with those concerned about community dependence on the state. This perhaps explains why scant attention is paid to them in the two mostly widely used CD manuals in Canada (Williams and Scott, Wismer and Pell). But, equally clearly, if the export option is given low priority in very small communities then the prospects for any kind of development, leave alone integrated, self-reliant development, look somewhat bleak. This is insufficiently appreciated in Wismer and Pell's *Community Profit* in which (p. 107) a table lists the number of inhabitants required to support various kinds of stores. This table refers to U.S. national averages and is printed without commentary. The suggestion is that bicycle shops require the support of an average of 100,000 people, dry goods stores, 34,000 people. This table is a curiosity in a book so committed to small-scale enterprises and, if followed to its logical extreme, would mean that most Native communities could support only a grocery store and an eating place. The possibility of multi-purpose stores, of stores opening only a few hours a week, of direct-order stores, of cooperative buying clubs, of using volunteer labour, or of simply very small-scale stores seems ruled out altogether in this table. These and a whole range of small-scale production enterprises are, as Wismer and Pell would most certainly agree, real possibilities. The potential scope is widened considerably if allowance is made for the possibility of drawing on the purchasing power of government to support local initiatives, though undoubtedly at the cost of new forms of dependency.

The key to successful community-scale development may also lie partially in the adaptation of technology (Schumacher, 1974; McRobie, 1981). The development of appropriate technology can enable efficient use of available resources and foster the spirit of self-reliance. In this context "appropriate" technology is defined as "a set of production methods that are simple, cheap and easily lent to decentralization; but capable of producing goods at prices competitive with other technology" (Schumacher, 1965).

In and of itself it has limited possibilities but within a comprehensive community development strategy appropriate technology can play an important supporting role. "Its usefulness lies in the fact that it *may* be applied in such a way that it releases the economic potential of a rural population, as sophisticated technology has not" (Brox, 1968). For this to be a reality, communities must, however, have access to information concerning alternatives and/or resources to develop their own forms of technology.

Where small community size is accompanied by extreme remoteness there will be only limited possibilities for pursuing convergence strategies, even with the adoption of intermediate technology. There will still be some possibilities of which advantage should be taken but, realistically, a convergence strategy may not provide adequate income and employment possibilities. In such communities, of course, subsistence strategies may still be important and should be encouraged as a form of non-monetary convergence. Thereafter, the community would need to dispassionately assess all its alternatives and pursue those which offered the best prospects. It is felt however, that in larger communities and in smaller ones where possibilities do exist for regional cooperation, there are often excellent prospects for the pursuit of convergence-type strategies.

v) The Participation of Women in Economic Activities

The role of women in CD has begun to receive specific attention only in recent years, as a byproduct of the women's movement becoming more powerful and more radical. As recently as twelve years ago it was possible to publish an important work on community economic development without addressing women's issues at all

(Weistart, 1972). Moreover, that work contains articles which, while championing the cause of ethnic communities and minorities, are distinctly and crudely discriminatory in their treatment of women. Thus, in answering the question of whether or not the black community possesses entrepreneurial abilities Sturdivant (1972: 41) states "One need only observe the charismatic leadership of articulate and dynamic *men* within the community to be convinced that the potential seems to exist" (emphasis added). Others speak consistently of business *men* with no reference being made at all to business *women* (e.g., Faux 1971).

This negative portrayal of women is, however, less of a problem than the failure of CD literature to deal formally with the role women have played in CD in the past and with the problems that women face, *as women*, in their current and possible future contributions. Lotz (1977) is silent on these issues in his assessment of CD in Canada, as are Mahmood and Ghosh (1979) in their handbook aimed at the U.S. market. By way of self-criticism, a major planning effort in which the author was involved ten years ago also left much to be desired in this respect (Loxley, 1981).

On a more positive note, Wismer and Pell (1981) explicitly recognize the needs of women in CD. Their manual gives an example of a women's manufacturing project and shows photographs in which women are actively participating in CD meetings. Their most recently published piece (1983) goes further in emphasizing the importance of CD providing opportunities for women which would not otherwise be available. Williams and Scott (1981) also consistently portray women in positive, non-traditional roles in their manual. These represent a vast improvement over the CD literature referred to earlier but they stop short of integrating fully, in their prescriptions for the CD process, the specific needs of women and the problems women might face participating in community decision-taking. These were addressed, explicitly, by the CCRD in its strategy for the Canadian Mid-North (1976: 87–88). This specifies some of the unique problems facing women in general, and Native women in particular, when they attempt to work outside the home. It places special emphasis on the exclusion of women from decision-taking roles. It also points out the need for a whole host of support services to assist women as wives, mothers, and homemakers. Further, it stresses that women may choose not to perform traditional roles, and that community programs should recognize and facilitate this.

One should not underestimate, however, the problems women are likely to encounter when they attempt to organize to deal with their problems. Low-income women have to contend not only with sexism but also with bureaucratic and professional arrogance and elitism, and with political opportunism of many varieties. These problems are graphically, and depressingly, portrayed in a recent article by Dorothy O'Connell (1983) which should be made compulsory reading for all staff of agencies dealing with women in community development (one suspects that what is described there might apply in large degree to low-income *men* too). It is not, therefore, simply a question of writing "women's issues" into the CD agenda, essential though this is, but rather of going beyond this to subject the whole process of CD efforts, and the relationship between communities and state employees, to a thorough feminist critique (see Dixon, Johnson, Leigh, and Turnbull, 1981 for a similar argument).

In practical terms this would mean analyzing the extent to which CED confronts problems faced by women in the community in question, the nature and degree of participation by women in problem specification and decision-taking, the involvement of women in building and operating new community institutions, and the sharing of women in the direct and indirect benefits flowing from CED initiatives. It would also mean analyzing how state institutions influence women's initiatives and aspirations at the community level.

It has been noted that CED might give rise to friction in communities by recasting power relationships based on wealth and traditional influence. Where, as in most North American communities, patriarchy is part and parcel of traditional influence, it can be expected that CED will be far from a harmonious process if it is to be the vehicle for improving the well-being of all members of the community, women as well as men.

CHAPTER 3
STRATEGIES ADVOCATED BY NATIVE PEOPLE[1]

The approaches of Native People to economic development, like those of government, have evolved over time and vary from one part of the country to another. Moreover, given the considerable differentiation *among* Native People which has emerged over the past twenty years, there is not surprisingly a diversity of views *within* the Native community of any given part of the country as to what constitutes an appropriate approach to development strategy. Nevertheless, this section will identify some common themes in the positions taken by Native People and will attempt also to capture some of the diversity of viewpoints and the reasons for it.

SOME COMMON THEMES

A review of Native economic development literature reveals a reasonable degree of consensus on the following issues:

a) Sustained economic development will only be possible if accompanied by a greater degree of Native self-government than hitherto.

b) The preferred approach is one of broadly based community economic development leading to greater community self-reliance.

c) Points a) and b) presuppose much greater local control over the local resource base than hitherto.

d) The settlement of outstanding land claims is a vital element in Native strategies of economic development.

[1] From Chapter 3.3 of *The Economics of Community Development*. Report prepared for Native Economic Development Program, DRIE. January 1986.

e) New Native-owned and -controlled institutions will be required for successful development efforts.

f) As far as possible economic development should be compatible with and strengthen Native culture and tradition rather than undermine it.

g) Native economic development presupposes, in general, a planned comprehensive approach.

h) A planned comprehensive approach in turn requires that government activities and the use of government resources are planned and coordinated.

i) In turn h) requires that government efforts to assist Native development be sustained, reliable, and predictable.

j) Government assistance should be supportive and calculated to enhance greater Native self-reliance rather than to perpetuate dependence.

k) A major theme in Native literature is that of the need to replace government welfare and remedial expenditures with economic development and preventive expenditures.

l) Funding for Native economic development should be long term, reliable and flexible. It should also subsidize activities which are socially and economically viable even if commercially non-viable.

Turning to an elaboration of these points, Indian People have long argued that the right of *self-government* is an Aboriginal right which must be acknowledged by Canadians. While the precise *form* of self-government has never been agreed upon, there is a general agreement that an important link exists between greater self-government and economic development aspirations. Recognition of this was central to the Indian response to the 1969 White Paper. The "Red Paper" rejected the proposed repeal of the Indian Act and the abolition of the Department of Indian Affairs, but at the same time called for the Act to be rewritten to provide for local self-government at the tribal level. It emphasized that this was necessary because present arrangements "often (frustrate) Indians in their individual efforts to earn a living" and "the entire tribe in its attempts toward ... better stewardship of the assets of the tribe" (Indian Chiefs of Alberta, 1970: 12).

The Indian Chiefs of Manitoba pressed for an extension of local government powers in *Wahbung-Our Tomorrows* (1971: 150–156). While recognizing that "band councils and local government is the hub around which localized economic and social progress can be generated, "they also advocated a series of regional-level commissions and boards through which Indian People would share decision taking at that level with the Department of Indian Affairs" (ibid.: 159). One such body would be an Economic Development Board. This would help to formulate policy and would also evaluate departmental programs and community development projects.

The link between self-government and economic development was specified even more clearly by the Socio-Economic Development Strategy Work Force in 1976 (NIB/Department of Indian Affairs). This saw the Indian Band as the focal point for Indian self-government. This view surfaced with even greater clarity three years later in the Beaver Report (National Indian Socio-Economic Development Committee, 1979) which spoke explicitly of "Indian (band) self-government" as the basis for community economic development. It was on the strength of documents such as these that the Liberal government introduced its draft legislation to extend band government in 1983–84. By that time, however, while still subscribing to the notion that self-government is essential to sustained efforts at community economic development, many Indian organizations in Canada were of the view that the precise form of self-government should be left for Indian People to decide upon. Certainly, among Manitoba Chiefs there was a feeling that the precise form of self-government should not be prejudged, but should be for decision by Indians. There might be an important role to be played by Indian governmental institutions at levels other than the band, e.g., at the tribal, regional, provincial, or national levels (Assembly of Manitoba Chiefs January, 1983). The necessity for open-mindedness and flexibility received a sympathetic hearing in the Penner Report (pp. 56–57).

The Métis National Council has also advocated self-government within Confederation. It envisages local autonomous councils and similar organizations at the regional and national levels. Organizations at each level would include economic development among their functions (Métis National Council 1984).

It should be noted that it is particularly unclear what self-government might mean for Native People resident in urban areas.

While the Department of Indian Affairs has only quite recently come to espouse a policy position favouring *community* economic development, Indian organizations have argued this for many years. The Red Paper had a clear community development focus (17), as did *Wahbung* (141). In the early 1970s the National Indian Brotherhood was advocating community self-reliance (NIB, 1973), while in 1976, it joined with the Department of Indian Affairs in calling for community self-sufficiency (NIB/Department of Indian Affairs, 1976: 21). The Beaver Report also explicitly viewed economic development as being community-based (80ff) and it was Indian representations along these lines (together with an analysis of case studies) that led the Penner Committee to conclude that "economic development succeeds best when carried out at the community level" (House of Commons, 1983: 75).

Recent documents of the Métis National Council do not refer specifically to community-based economic development as such (Métis National Council 1983) but their emphasis on a land and resource base does suggest such an approach. The Manitoba Métis Federation, by comparison, tends to put a much greater emphasis on community economic development and incorporates this into its training programs. Moreover, the whole thrust of recent MMF economic development initiatives has been very much community-oriented (Constitution and Land Claims Secretariat, MMF, 1983).

It has long been recognized by both Status Indians and other Native Peoples that *control over the local resource base* is vital for sustained economic development at the community level. This was put quite clearly by the Indian Chiefs of Manitoba in 1971 when they argued "particular consideration must be given to the extension of the right-of-first-priority to those closest to resources to ensure an equitable distribution of economic opportunity and benefit" (op. cit. 141). In addition, however, the restricted nature of that resource base for many communities led to them concluding, "it becomes essential ... that the natural resource base adjacent to reserve communities become a part of the economic base of the community" (ibid.). It was this kind of thinking that prompted the NDP government of Manitoba to allow northern communities to have first call over forestry resources within a twenty-five-mile radius of their boundaries (Loxley, 1981: 169).

The Socio-Economic Development Strategy Work Force reiterated these demands, stating that "preference should be given in allocation and utilization of natural resources on reserves, around them and around Indian non-reserve communities, to maximize benefits to Indian People" (NIB/DIA, 1976: 15). The Beaver report went further, arguing the tripartite process should be used to allow have-not communities to expand their resource base on provincially controlled Crown lands (op. cit.: 83). Similar demands for expanded access to local resources are central to Métis strategies as well (Métis National Council, 1984: No.3). Some Métis envisage the establishment of "alternative resource communities," set up by and staffed by Native People so that they reap the full benefits of northern mineral resources (Fulham 1981: 102–103).

Of course the need to demand special access is quite secondary to and additional to a more fundamental political demand for *the settlement of outstanding land claims*. The importance of such claims to economic development strategies varies from one part of the country to another depending on the nature and size of land claims outstanding. The most important claims by size pertain to areas of the country where Native People argue that their title to land has not been extinguished by treaty or superseded by law. The basis of these claims is that Native People have traditionally used or occupied the lands in question. Such claims are outstanding In British Columbia, the Yukon and the Northwest Territories, and the land area involved is truly massive, 450,000 square miles in the N.W.T. alone. Because the federal government envisages settling these claims by a mixture of land grants, cash settlements, the provision of a variety of services, and the recognition of certain usufructory rights, it labels these claims "comprehensive."

A much larger number of smaller claims have their origin in grievances over the way in which land provisions of the Indian Act and/or Treaties were administered. There are between 900 and 1,300 such "specific" land claims awaiting settlement (DIAND Discussion Paper, 1980).

In addition to these claims by Status Indians, the Métis in various parts of Canada also have land claims based on the failure of governments to adhere to legislative commitments in the allotment of Métis lands and the distribution of scrip. In Manitoba, for instance, the Métis Federation has developed a claim for over one million acres of prime land along the Red River Valley, some of it within Winnipeg itself, and is attempting to secure compensation through the courts for the loss of this land.

The scale of these land claims is huge which is why settlements are seen by Native People in several parts of the country to be central to their strategies of economic development. It must be emphasized, however, that the manner in which settlements are made will have a profound influence on the nature of economic development strategies to be pursued by Native groups. Two extreme examples should clarify this point.

The federal government sees the James Bay Agreement as a blueprint for future settlements. Under this agreement the Cree and Inuit of the region of Northern Quebec affected by the James Bay Hydro Project agreed to the extinguishment of their title to their traditional lands in exchange for (1) relatively small parcels of land in and around their reserves, (2) exclusive hunting rights over an area equal to 20% of the lands actually used traditionally, (3) more limited rights over the remaining area, (4) total compensation of $250 million, (5) an income security program for hunters and trappers, and (6) economic development funds of $15 million to be invested through a James Bay Native Development Corporation.

Under this agreement Native People retain no rights to minerals on any of the lands in question. A whole series of institutions were created to administer the agreement, the most important of which have representation from the federal and provincial governments. Powers of municipal government have devolved to the Cree while in most areas of government the Cree now find themselves dealing with the province rather than the federal government.

By comparison, the Dene of the N.W.T. have developed a negotiating position around land claims which goes to the other extremes.

The Dene hope the claims process will *confirm* rather than extinguish their title to ownership of land. They hope then to retain ownership and to generate funds for economic and social development by leasing lands for development to those enterprises willing to pay economic rents for the use of Dene land. Some of the rent proceeds would be used to strengthen the traditional economy which would, it is hoped, continue to thrive alongside a carefully regulated "modern" economy (Watkins 1977).

Continued ownership of traditional lands is considered vital if the Dene are to assert their nationhood within Confederation, if they are to be able to manage the delicate task of regulating modern staple development to the benefit rather than the detriment of more traditional sectors of the economy. A land settlement confirming rather than extinguishing their rights would reduce Dene dependence on government handouts and would enable the Dene, in contrast to the Cree and Inuit of James Bay, to develop their own concepts and institutions of self-government free from outside intervention.

The critiques of the James Bay approach are several. To begin with, since the decision to build the dam had already been taken, the settlement could only be an exercise in extinguishing title. Indeed, other parallels with earlier treaties are obvious. The Cree and Inuit were negotiating with a gun to their heads, did not fully understand the implications of the agreement and have subsequently met resistance from government in implementing the agreement (Thalassa Research Associates, 1983: 61–76). The bureaucratic demands of the institutional structures created under the settlement have drawn leadership talent out of the communities and locked the Native People into an unequal partnership with the federal and provincial governments. Under pressure from these quarters the major economic development institutions have invested extensively outside the region and have tended to be biased against community projects and convergence-type projects, preferring small-scale, privately owned service sector investments (ibid.). While preserving the traditional way of life to some degree, the income security program has introduced yet more bureaucracy into the lives of hunters and trappers, rendering well-intentioned income supplements little different from welfare payments, and requiring recipients to artificially adjust their hunting and trapping timetables simply to retain eligibility for payment (LaRusic, 1978).

It must be recognized, however, that the concrete situation facing Native People will itself shape their bargaining ability. Native organizations with specific claims will be limited in what they can negotiate; likewise, where lands have been irretrievably lost, claimants may have no option but to settle for cash compensation. In all cases, however, the object should be to maintain the broadest possible range of options available.

Sometimes, Native People facing one concrete reality tend to project that reality onto other groups facing quite different circumstances and in the process tend to be unsympathetic to the tactics of aspirations of the latter. Thus Stan Fulham, writing as an urban Métis, seems to show a singular lack of empathy towards the Dene or Nishga reality when he writes "A few Native leaders whose responsibilities are limited to the extreme north are demanding a halt to all development until the land claims issue is settled. Other Native leaders, whose political responsibility extends to the thousands of Native People in urban centres, understand very well that they cannot afford to use the continued economic and social deprivation of their people as a weapon in the land claims issue" (Fulham, 1981: 107–108). He then goes on to argue that resource development should proceed in parallel with land claims settlements.

What this position overlooks is that urban Native People are in no position to halt development or to use the threat of doing so as a lever to achieve land claim settlements. Most urban Native People are not involved in land claims anyway. Fulham's argument also overlooks the fact that unregulated resource development in the North has often contributed to the very economic and social deprivation which he wishes to avoid. In order to retain a full range of economic development options, those Native organizations involved in comprehensive claims are entirely justified in opposing developments until their claims are settled. The federal government has estimated that if comprehensive claims were settled on the same (and highly questionable) basis as the James Bay Agreement, they would cost $275 million per year, in 1980 dollars, from 1985 to the year 2000, in cash compensation alone. A similar amount would be involved in the non-cash elements of compensation—harvesting rights, land, social and economic programs, etc. Thus, in the next fifteen years the total cost would amount to some $8.25 billion in 1980 dollar terms or $11.8 billion in 1985 dollar terms over the same period (DIAND, 1980). No estimate has been made of the likely value of any Métis or Non-Status claims (e.g., the Manitoba Métis claim). These figures give some indication of the importance of the land claims issue though they represent only a minute fraction of the overall value of the land involved.

Most Native groups acknowledge that sustained economic development will probably require them creating entirely *new Native-owned and -controlled institutions*. Historically, Native institutions have consisted of community-based organizations (e.g., band councils or Métis locals) which were designed to perform functions other than the promotion of economic development, and provincial and national political organizations which have in part acted as pressure groups for development but which have had, at best, only peripheral roles in terms of development policy, programming, or implementation.

In recent years, a number of institutions have evolved with specific orientation towards the promotion of economic development. These have taken the form of development corporations operating at the community, regional, tribal council, or provincial level, of training programs, planning initiatives, marketing organizations, and even national trust companies. These are as yet still embryonic and few in numbers due largely to the lack of capital and expertise required.

This has been long recognized by Native groups who have argued for far-reaching institutional development to provide necessary inputs into projects, to facilitate community development, and to support individual entrepreneurs and partnerships (see e.g., NIB/DIA, 1976: 17–18).

In general it is recognized that effective community development will require institutional expression at the community level and support from new institutions at higher levels. The balance between institutional development at these two levels will, of necessity, be a delicate one. A proliferation of institutions at levels other than the community will almost certainly deprive communities of scarce planning, administrative, and implementational talent. On the other hand, there are clear limits to what can be accomplished in communities if broader-based support systems are not in place. Potential problems of imbalance can be avoided if communities themselves retain control over the nature and pace of institutional developments at other levels.

A recurring theme in Native literature is that economic development must be consistent with and help strengthen *Native Culture and Tradition*. On the surface this is a problematical proposition. Culture does not evolve in a vacuum but is, instead, a reflection of the material base of society. Significant changes in that base can be expected to put pressure on inherited culture and traditions and possibly, eventually to foster the rise of new ones. What sense can we make then of the Native desire to promote economic development in a way which preserves and reinforces tradition and culture? Is this simply an unfulfillable romantic dream?

First of all, there is the fundamental question of what remains of Native culture and tradition at this point in time. It is, of course, apparent that Native culture was deliberately suppressed by the Church and the State in the years following the fur trade and until quite recent times. Furthermore, the encroachment on traditional Native economy of merchant and industrial capital has been accompanied by a parallel encroachment on traditional Native culture and values, one which has become more pronounced with increasing Native migration to urban centres. For many Native groups, therefore, it is now as much, if not more, a question of "revival" of culture as it is of "survival" (*Wahbung*, 1971: 34–36). Such a revival has been taking place for years and involves recapturing Native art, poetry, music, oral history, and religion. While this is of the utmost importance in terms of restoring Native self-respect, rebuilding Native history and purging that history of its racist devaluation and rejection of Native culture and tradition, for many Native People the material context which created that culture and tradition in the first place no longer exists. At best, therefore, the revived culture can play only a minor role in the lives of these people, it cannot shape their lives the way it did before. Only where there had been some continuity in the traditional Native *economic* way of life, as there has been in the North and in more remote parts of Canada, have traditional culture and values survived to play a significant role in the contemporary affairs of Native People.

The compatibility or otherwise of culture and tradition with economic development would seem to be dictated to some degree by the type of development strategy being pursued and, to a lesser extent, by the pace of development. Native culture is inextricably tied to the land and to land-based economy. Those strategies that emphasize strengthening the "traditional" economy—hunting, fishing, trapping, and gathering—need not necessarily threaten Native culture or tradition and might even reinforce them.

Similarly, outfitting, guiding, and forestry work, while not being "traditional," do draw on traditional skills and underscore Native attachment to land. But in all these and similar areas, the impact on culture and tradition will go beyond the "land" element. Social relations are also crucial and Native culture and tradition are based on a clearly identifiable set of relationships in production and decision-taking. By and large production and distribution are organized on communal lines, kinship is important and decision-taking is quite collegial with an emphasis being placed on the views of "elders" who are seen as the repositories of accumulated communal wisdom. It is apparent that contemporary non-Native production relations and values are quite antithetical to these, emphasizing private ownership and accumulation, hierarchical and bureaucratic labour processes, and focusing on economic power and status, on the individual and on technocratic skills. The preservation of tradition and culture may not be possible even in land-based or land-related ventures if the building of contemporary non-Native social relations is an integral part of the development initiatives.

This point seems often not to be appreciated by those sections of the Native community which argue, simultaneously, for *both* expansion of private enterprise in Native communities *and* retention of traditional values and culture. The Red Paper is, perhaps, the best example of this, arguing that "it is, therefore, imperative that we enlist the energies, resources and talents of private enterprise" (15), and at the same time that "giving up on Indian identity is not necessary for economic development" (15), although "private sector development must be in tune with the life and spirit of the community" (17). It simply assumes that compatibility and coexistence is possible, yet this is not self-evident and there are strong grounds for believing otherwise. It is in this respect that convergence-type community economic development with its emphasis on communal ownership and collegiality might act as a link both to the best aspects of the past and to a future which transcends certain negative aspects of current power relationships, values, and organizational systems.

It is highly unlikely, however, that pure traditional values and culture could survive intact even the successful pursuit of convergent-type CED. To begin with, certain traditional values are no longer acceptable to society at large and a considerable proportion of Native People. The role of women is a clear case in point. Native women are by and large no longer prepared to accept narrow economic roles or the type of second-class status implied in the Indian Act.

Native society is, however, not free from sexism and Native women will have to struggle for many years to come against their traditional, and what many Native men would see as their "rightful" status.

Modern economic development initiatives will also inevitably imply that those with certain technical skills will, regardless of age, be called upon to assume decision-taking responsibilities. Furthermore, many Native People are not prepared to accept the dictates of Chief and council where these deprive them of basic rights available elsewhere to both Native and non-Native people. An example of this would be the recent case of a Chief and council attempting to deprive workers on reserves of the right to unionize. Preservation of culture and tradition, therefore, may not always be desirable or possible.

Where it *is* desirable, we conclude that the extent to which they can be preserved will depend upon the choice of development strategy both with respect to sectoral development and to the nature of ownership and decision-taking models. To the extent that a convergence strategy would lead to the development of modern staple industries and of secondary industrial development, it is highly questionable that one could preserve much of traditional culture and values. Even so, the adoption of communal ownership strategies and collegiality in decision-taking, would still seem to be more in tune in Native tradition than is private ownership and hierarchical, authoritarian decision-taking. In this respect a convergence strategy would still appear to be preferable whatever the sectoral configuration of activities to which it gives rise.

Native literature on *ownership* of community-based enterprises gives no unambiguous preference for one type over another. As already mentioned, the Red Paper strongly favours expanding private enterprise. It maintains, "It is probable that the lack of private enterprise participation is one of the main causes of failure to solve the problems of the poor and underdeveloped" (16). Stan Fulham has a similar perspective and his strategy presupposes extensive private enterprise in Native communities, while the Manitoba Chiefs also envisaged cooperation with the private sector (*Wahbung*, 1971: 145). Each of these would see the government playing a role which would support and strengthen private sector initiatives. The Red Paper, for instance, called for the government to offer a range of development incentives in the form of tax concessions, training grants, and labour guarantees (17). As recently as 1986, the Assembly of First Nations was making similar requests, in the form of investment tax incentives and tax-free zones (Assembly of First Nations, 1984: 5).

This emphasis on promoting private enterprise stands in sharp contrast to the position taken by the National Indian Brotherhood (1973) when it argued "most Indian Communities, allowed to freely choose, will develop structures and institutions that will avoid concentration of wealth into the hands of a few members. The communities do not want a mere transfer of exploitation from the present outside interests to a few individual members of the community" (15).

Yet government policy has deliberately aimed at creating economic differentiation in the Native community by promoting private enterprise. There now exists in that community a small but influential number of small business owners, mostly state-financed, who represent a vocal lobby for "community" development based on private ownership. A number of these are leaders or ex-leaders of Native political organizations who have used their influence to secure state assistance to accumulate private wealth through business (Loxley, 1981: 163). This point of view is echoed in recent declarations on economic development by the Dene (Dene Advisory Committee, 1982) which focuses their efforts instead mainly on community ownership. This will vary from community to community depending on cohesiveness and the strength of the desire to minimize economic differentiation. Given the relative scarcity (in any community, Native or non-Native) of leadership talent, it can be a major blow to communal initiatives if leaders seek their own self-enrichment through business.

Whether business is privately or community-owned, the reliance on state finance and assistance is likely to be great given the shortage of capital and supportive resources in Native communities. Yet, almost all Native organizations are agreed that this type of dependence is preferable to welfare dependence. Indeed, one can trace back over the years the consistent call for converting "maintenance" or "remedial" government spending into *economic development spending* (e.g., *Wahbung*, 1971; Beaver, 1979; Penner Report, 1983). It is now recognized, or course, that self-sustaining Native self-government will require a commitment of state resources to economic development greatly in excess of amounts currently paid for welfare and the annual costs involved of administering poverty. But this can be conceptualized as "capitalizing" these costs which, it is hoped, would no longer be incurred if development efforts were successful.

Native People argue that sustained development will require that government activities and expenditures be *planned* and *coordinated*. This will be necessary if the most is to be made of integrating economic development initiatives with these activities and expenditures. Providing products of labour to meet government requirements will only happen if demands can be projected into the future in a planned way encompassing all facets of government spending. It will only succeed if supported by all areas of government working in concert. Thus capital expenditure plans of government agencies should be coordinated in such a way that community enterprises and community labour can contribute fully towards them. This, in turn will have implications for funding agencies and training programs operated or assisted by the government.

The provision of state resources should be guaranteed over a *considerable period of time*. Conventional programs of the government focus too much on "early returns and early viability" (*Wahbung*, 1971: 142) whereas what is needed is a "sustained joint effort by the Indian People and the government for not less than ten years and by mutual agreement for twenty years, to achieve the objectives that will be identified by communities within the broad goals" (NIB/DIA, 1976: 12). This may require *long-term subsidization* of economic projects, and perhaps even of labour, given the general lack of competitiveness of Native projects in which, however, net social benefits may exceed the commercial ones. State funding would be required for equity and loan finance, loan guarantees, and the creation of Native development organizations, training programs, and employment subsidies. In order to enable Native institutions and enterprises to take root, this funding must be long-term and must be guaranteed, subject to certain clear prerequisites being met. Ideally, funding should be made available in forms which allow discretionary use by Native People. In the long term, therefore, some form of equalization grant is envisaged to self-governing Native organizations (NIB/DIA, 1976: 15; Penner Report, 1983: 97). In the immediate future, Native People are requesting greater use of consolidated contribution agreements which allow discretion as opposed to other types of contribution agreements which do not (All Chiefs' Budget Committee, 1982: 11).

It is the desire of Native People to lessen their dependence on the state but there is recognition that this can only be achieved through successful community economic development and that this will take time. In the interim, it is vital that state funding be made available in sufficient amounts and with predictability and dependability so that the goal of community economic development is, in fact, ultimately realized.

CHAPTER 4

CASINOS AS AN ECONOMIC DEVELOPMENT STRATEGY[1]

Legalized gambling is becoming an important new source of revenue for First Nations in Canada. This paper outlines some of the economic characteristics and attractions of casinos. It does not address issues of addiction or racism, both of which figure prominently in the Manitoba debate, but these are dealt with in the article from which this chapter is drawn.

WHAT PROPORTION OF JOBS CREATED GO TO ABORIGINAL PEOPLE?

This varies widely from place to place but in the U.S., it is estimated that Indian gaming of all types had created about 290,000 jobs by 1995, 85% of which were held by non-Indians (Hill, 2001). This would still mean that some 43,500 jobs were held by Indian people. Two studies of casinos in Minnesota in 1992 reported that 13 casinos employed about 5,700 people of whom 1,350, or 24%, were Native Americans (DesBrisay, 1994). It appears that quite high rates of Aboriginal employment can be achieved, witness the Lummi Tribe securing two-thirds of the 400 jobs in its casino for its own members in the first year of operation (ibid.). In some cases, tribes are simply too small for their membership to occupy a high proportion of jobs; in other cases, location is probably a factor while in yet others it may be simply decisions by outside managers and weak ownership control which limits Aboriginal employment. In

[1] From "Gambling on Casinos," with Wanda A. Wuttunee and Alison Dubois. 2002. *Journal of Aboriginal Economic Development*, 2, 2.

Saskatchewan, the four First Nations casinos employ 1,100 people, 70% of whom are Aboriginal (SIGA web site, 2001). In their Yorkton casino, 79% of the 210 employees are Aboriginal (Helen Falding, May 2000). One of the prime objectives of First Nations casinos in Manitoba is job creation (Manitoba First Nations Casino Project Selection Committee, 2000: 3).

ARE CASINO JOBS UNIONIZED?

This depends on the casino. Unionization is important, not just to ensure reasonable wages, which in Yorkton start at $7.75 an hour plus tips (compared with over $13 in Windsor) (Hutchinson, 1999), but to address issues of working conditions. Casinos present workers with some unique conditions of noise, stress, violence, and harassment which owners need to address but seemingly do not without pressure from workers through their unions. Union representation is important, therefore, for both non-Aboriginal and Aboriginal workers.

In Saskatchewan, the Canadian Auto Workers union (CAW) is representing workers at the Prince Albert casino. CAW represents workers at the largest casino in Canada, at Windsor, and so has experience in the area. The Saskatchewan Indian Gaming Authority (SIGA), which leases casinos from First Nations, has been extremely resistant to unionization, arguing that there is no room for a provincially regulated union on First Nations land that is under federal jurisdiction. On these grounds, SIGA has launched a series of legal challenges and appeals against CAW representing its workers, losing the argument at every level so far. Currently they are waiting for permission to appeal to the Supreme Court of Canada. SIGA seems not to have much of a case, since its gambling operations are regulated entirely by the province, but is prepared to spend huge amounts of money on the issue. What really seems to be motivating SIGA is opposition to the union movement generally. After two years of trying, CAW has still not been able to negotiate a collective agreement with SIGA, the main stumbling blocks being grievance procedures, seniority, and collection of union dues, before issues of salary and working conditions have even been aired properly. SIGA has recently applied to have the union decertified (interview with Doug Olshewski, CAW Winnipeg, CBC Information Radio, March 12, 2001).

There is a tradition of similar hostility towards unions among some First Nations leaders in Manitoba, with claims that they are not Indian organizations and that they challenge First Nations sovereignty. These are spurious arguments having more to do with First Nations leaders not wishing to have the authority of Chief and Council challenged. Aboriginal workers have been at the bargaining table with SIGA and have been appalled at its intransigence. In particular, SIGA's expressed wish to have elders deal with grievances does not sit well with First Nations workers, let alone with other Aboriginal and non-Aboriginal workers in the casinos. Neither does the attempt to place Indian status at the forefront of seniority considerations, ahead of qualifications and length of service. It is reported that Manitoba casino proponents also share SIGA's view about the inappropriateness of provincially regulated unions operating on First Nations territory (CBC op. cit.). Again, this makes little sense if the authority of provincial agencies to regulate First Nations gaming in Manitoba is accepted and one wonders how First Nations leaders would react if federally registered unions were to appear on the scene. The report that Aboriginal casino proponents in Manitoba are, however, prepared to accept more informal employee associations, is even more puzzling and suggests that formally organized unions pose an unacceptable threat to their leadership and authority.

WHAT PROPORTION OF GAMBLING INCOME ACCRUES TO FIRST NATIONS, DIRECTLY AS OWNERS OR INDIRECTLY?

In 1995, 106 U.S. tribes received $1.6 billion in net income from Class III gaming activities (casinos, slot machines, horse and dog racing, jai alai), representing 38% of revenue from gambling after payouts. This compares quite favourably with figures of 20–25% for similar facilities in Nevada and Atlantic City.

In Saskatchewan, the 73 First Nations reportedly shared $13 million from casinos in 1999. This includes a 37.5% share of the profits of the four First Nations casinos and 25% of the profit of Casino Regina, which is operated by the province. The four First Nations casinos also pay 37.5% of their profits to the province and 25% goes to community development corporations which fund both Aboriginal and non-Aboriginal charities (Falding op. cit.).

The revenue sharing formula arrived at in Manitoba provides for as much as 70% of all net revenue to be paid to the host First Nation and the owners, with only 27.5% accruing to all First Nations and 2.5% reserved for addressing problems of addiction. The main differences from the Saskatchewan situation are that the province receives no share and the owners clearly receive the lion's share. There are, however, no public estimates of what dollar amounts might be involved.

DO ALL FIRST NATIONS INVOLVED IN THE GAMING INDUSTRY MAKE MONEY?

There is great unevenness in the size and profitability of Indian gambling facilities in the U.S. About 40% of all gaming revenue was generated by just eight out of 112 facilities operated by the 106 tribes mentioned earlier (House of Representatives, Ways and Means Committee, May 1997). Ten tribes received at least $50 million each, accounting for overhalf of the $1.6 billion transferred. Twenty tribes showed no transfers from their gaming operations.

A survey of 24 Indian gaming facilities in California in 1991 found that ten were profitable, at least four have closed down, four were marginal and the rest marred at some point by controversy including fraud, mismanagement, and allegations of gambling-related murders and the involvement of organized crime (DesBrisay, 1994).

Of the four Saskatchewan First Nations casinos, the $4 million casino and resort at the more isolated White Bear Reserve was said to be struggling (Falding, op. cit.). In the U.S., managers brought in from the outside to assist First Nations have not always acted appropriately. Thus, the White Earth Band of Chippewa, at Mahnomen in Minnesota, took control over its Shooting Star Casino after the managers, Gaming World International, had reportedly breached its contract by taking a larger share of profits than agreed and by not repaying loans made by the band ("Gaming World International/

White Earth Contract Breached." At <yvwiiusdinvnohii.net/upnews/ojibgame.htm>). Casinos and the like are not, therefore, guaranteed cash cows. Even profitable operations may not be sustainable in the long run. Some observers see U.S. tribes having no more than ten years to use gambling revenues to diversify their economies before profits are eroded through competition (Frantz, 1999: 298).

WHAT EXPLAINS SUCCESS OR FAILURE OF FIRST NATIONS CASINOS?

Factors held responsible for the success of casinos are population density and accessibility, quality of management, and political stability of the First Nation organization (DesBrisay op. cit.), but competition for business must also be important. In the Manitoba context, all four successful casino bids will operate close to or in urban centres and the Manitoba Lotteries Commission will closely regulate and monitor all management operations. The MLC is also in a position to regulate competition. There are, however, limits to its ability to do this. At least one of the proposed First Nations casinos, at Brokenhead, is quite close to Winnipeg and its ability to compete with existing casinos there is an open question. Also, competition from Internet gambling and from casinos in neighbouring provinces and adjacent states of the U.S. are potential threats over which the MLC has little control. Neither can the MLC be expected to do much about political instability should this become a factor.

The planned casino on the Opaskwayak Cree First Nation, a joint venture of six First Nations in the North, may also not be guaranteed success because of a small population base, a fragile economy and possible saturation of the market for gambling. Opaskwayak has a population of 3,500 and is adjacent to The Pas, a town of only 6,000 people. Both are quite remote although there is some tourist traffic in summer. Recently, the main employer in the town, Tolko Industries, a sawmill and lumber operation, shut down, putting some 600 people out of work. While the closure may be only temporary it will, according to the Chief of the First Nations community, have a significant impact on the local economy (*Winnipeg Free Press*, March 10, 2001). The other problem with this particular choice of location is that gambling revenues there are already significant (they were as high as $5.8 million gross as early as 1991!) (see DesBrisay, 1994: 22), presumably from bingo and VLTs. Perhaps the saving grace of this proposal is its relatively modest capital cost of $4.6 million, compared with over $30 million for the Brokenhead proposal.

IS ACCOUNTABILITY AN ISSUE IN FIRST NATIONS GAMBLING ACTIVITIES?

Most definitely. The amounts of money involved are, relatively speaking, huge. In Saskatchewan, the office of the Provincial Auditor has found that the Saskatchewan Indian Gaming Authority has been guilty of improper and questionable use of public money, involving some $1.7 million. It found that the CEO of SIGA improperly used debit and credit cards, board and management expenses were unsupported, unauthorized salary advances were made, contracts were let in excess of market value, and board members were sometimes in conflict of interest situations. Both the SIGA Chair/CEO and the whole board have been replaced (Saskatchewan Liquor and Gaming Authority, November 15, 2000). Since there was an intention that SIGA would assist First Nations casinos in Manitoba, this development must not only have been a disappointing one for First Nations, it must also have been an alarming one for the Manitoba Lotteries Commission (MLC).

There are important lessons for the MLC in what happened in Saskatchewan. The Provincial Auditor there has taken the position that the Saskatchewan Liquor and Gaming Authority (SLGA) could have prevented some of the improper use of public money if it had done a better job managing the public money under SIGA's control (Saskatchewan, Provincial Auditor, 2000). The First Nations of Saskatchewan were let down, therefore, not just by SIGA, but also by the SLGA. This is bound to make the MLC more cautious in its regulation of First Nations casinos. Indeed, successful casino applicants have already begun to complain that the MLC is not only being unduly restrictive in negotiating management agreements but is also expecting Aboriginal casinos to pay for an expensive regulatory infrastructure (Falding, March 14, 2001).

The other aspect of accountability is the use of gambling proceeds in the communities themselves. While the issues involved here may appear to be no different from those arising with the use of other sources of revenue, U.S. experience suggests that if inflows are large, gambling revenues can be particularly contentious. Questions arise about whether monies should be paid out on a per capita basis or pooled for collective use. Off-reserve residents have also claimed a share in such revenues when these have been large (DesBrisay, 1994: 44).

WHAT ARE THE ECONOMIC IMPACTS OF GAMBLING?

No systematic studies of the economic impact of First Nation gambling facilities appear to have been carried out. In gross terms, U.S. tribes derived about $300 million or 7% of their gross revenue in 1995 from food, beverages, hotel rooms, and interest as sidelines to gambling. But the economic development impact goes beyond these direct linkages in more successful operations. Thus, the Sault Ste. Marie Tribe of Chippewa Indians in Michigan used proceeds from its casino to create many spin-off businesses including two convenience stores, a janitorial service, a cleaning supplies outlet, a dry cleaner, an air charter service, a tribal newspaper, and other successful businesses.

Of the five proposals for First Nations casinos accepted in Manitoba, all but one (the one on Opaskwayak First Nation) are accompanied by a hotel, offering additional potential spin-offs and employment.

RETROSPECTIVE ON CHAPTERS 1 TO 4

I am reasonably comfortable with Chapter 2 on the Aboriginal concept of stewardship and enoughness, although my friends and colleagues Fred Shore and Wanda Wuttunee expressed unhappiness about the association of Aboriginal Peoples with past animal extinctions. They claim, correctly, that Pruitt (1989) provides no evidence of this. The broader literature does, however, assign some responsibility to Aboriginal People, even when other factors might also have been involved in extinctions, although this is hotly debated. Shepard Krech (1999) offers a sceptical view of the Ecological Indian. Pruitt's main point is, however, still valid. Aboriginal societies were much more in sync with the environment than merchant capitalist and capitalist societies.

There has been a huge improvement in the literature on women and CED since 1986 so many of the reservations cited in Chapter 3 need updating and qualifying. The work of Melanie Conn in Canada (1989 and n.d., for example) has been extremely important. More recently, Callahan (1997) and Amyot (2007) have continued to ask searching feminist questions about approaches to CED in Canada, while McCracken et al. (2007) have focused specifically on the contribution that CED might make to alleviating problems of poverty among young women. The participation of Aboriginal women in CED has been addressed directly by Findlay and Wuttunee (1997), both in principle and in practice. They draw on three case studies of women's involvement in CED to outline problems and potentials, two of which, Neechi Foods of Winnipeg (see Chapter 8) and ET Developments of Grand Rapids, are in Manitoba.

There have been some interesting recent developments in the literature on strategies advocated by Aboriginal and especially Canadian

Aboriginal authors. These add to and in some ways, are directly in contradiction with, the strategies I outlined in my earlier papers. What follows should be essential reading for those interested in development alternatives.

Calvin Helin (2006) has argued that Aboriginal communities are dominated by "Shaman economics," or the economics of the welfare trap, in which communities have been economically isolated and made dependent on federal transfers for "typically 100% of the wealth" (131) flowing into them. The lack of private sector activity is at the heart of the problems of dependency and the lack of development and is what principally distinguishes Aboriginal economies from the mainstream economy.[1] Aboriginal employment is unduly concentrated in public administration, which inhibits business development (134–135). The emphasis on communal ownership in Aboriginal communities leads to neglect of property and lack of incentive to generate high returns to capital (136). Aboriginal elites control their communities, and are often corrupt, incompetent, nepotistic, undemocratic, and unaccountable financially.

Rectifying these problems and building self-reliant local economies will mean creating an environment that "encourages and nurtures" individual Aboriginal entrepreneurs. This will only happen when communities recognize the need to change their reality and take responsibility for their own future. This will entail changing their mindset and their approach to governance, taking charge of their fiscal resources and creating accountable governance institutions which can provide a long-term stable political and economic environment in which entrepreneurship can blossom. Helin draws heavily on the recommendations of the Harvard Project on American Indian Economic Development (Cornell and Kalt, 2005) which stress the importance of stable governance and the separation of the political from the economic in decision-taking and in institutional structure (199–201). There should also be dispute mechanisms

---

[1] There is inconsistency in Helin's view of the role of government in mainstream society. At one point he claims that the U.S. economy is 90% private (p. 128) while at another he quotes it at a more realistic 40% (p. 139). His approach to economic development is premised on the first figure and might have been more hedged had it been premised on the second!

which are fair and transparent and a cultural "match" between values in the community and the way in which institutions work. Within this framework, development strategies should be drawn up accompanied by decisions and actions to implement them.

He cites examples of successful Aboriginal economic development in North America and New Zealand which have drawn on this approach. In Canada he cites the Northeastern Alberta Aboriginal Association, Memberton First Nation, Osayoos Indian Band and the partnership of Aboriginal groups with the Alberta-based ATCO Group. An interesting feature of the Memberton experience is the conscious effort to attract trained and qualified members of the band back to the reserve from urban areas.

Helin sees the 1999 First Nations Land Management Act, which allows First Nations to develop land codes, as offering more local control over land use by bands (201–202). Such codes replace the land provisions of the Indian Act and are enforceable in law. They cover issues such as land allocation and registration, occupancy rights, transfers, use of natural resources, pledging of land as security, provisions for expropriations for band use, protection of rights, and dispute resolution mechanisms. Since 1999, 23 bands have developed and operationalized such codes while as many as 90 have opted into the process (Flanagan et al. 2010: 109). While codes differ greatly over such matters as band rights, proponents claim that they encourage and speed up development of private investment on reserve.

Helin also believes that the First Nations Fiscal and Statistical Management Act of 2004 offers "a whole new fiscal framework for doing business on reserves" (202). It enables First Nations to borrow for infrastructure projects, to levy taxes, set financial standards, and improve access to data, thereby reducing reliance on Ottawa and putting reserves on a similar footing to other levels of government.

Improving educational achievement is seen as being crucial in Helin's view as "the only path out of poverty" for most Aboriginal People (205). He calls for a national Aboriginal education strategy and approaches to education which emphasize and demand quality rather than "segregation of the Aboriginal students with a lot of vague...touchy-feely support" (213). Aboriginal parents must take ownership of the educational system.

Helin argues that more needs to be done to assist Aboriginal People wishing to live in urban areas. Efforts should be taken to 1) help retain connections of migrants with their home communities, including political connections, 2) better prepare reserve residents for life off-reserve, 3) examine how best to support people making the transition, and 4) find ways of diverting some federal monies destined for rural bands to support the transition. His proposals under point 3 echo precisely what the Indian and Métis Friendship Societies do at this time, though he makes no mention of them. He does not propose a specific urban Aboriginal development strategy or make any reference to the several Aboriginal proposals for urban economic development made by the Aboriginal community itself. Instead, he stresses the importance of good housing, education, and political empowerment but the last only with regard to continuing involvement in on-reserve issues (244–252).

There is much in Helin to recommend it: The need for Aboriginal People to make greater efforts to take over their own destiny, the desirability of greater transparency and accountability in the Aboriginal political and government processes, the need to get out from under the tutelage and control of the colonial Indian Affairs department and to escape the welfare trap, and the stress on the importance of education and the desirability of reconnecting migrants who have acquired skills and experience with their home communities. The weakness in Helin is his ideological fixation with the private sector and his underappreciation of the role and importance of the public sector. This leads him to see a concentration of Aboriginal employment in the public sector as a weakness of the Aboriginal economy. From an historical point of view, however, the growth in Aboriginal employment in this sector represents real progress. It demonstrates how the provision of services by bands has increased over time as the influence of outside actors, such as the Indian Agent and non-Aboriginal education, health, and social service providers, has declined. This is a form of import substitution and service extension that has been relatively successful.

Some of the success stories that Helin identifies are in fact examples of successful community initiatives, with state support. The best example of this is the Alaska model based on generous treaty settlements and Aboriginal-owned entities, working with private companies. Other successful examples have close proximity to cities or large resource projects. To what extent are these examples relevant to the more typically remote Aboriginal community? Good leadership seems to be a common element, but how is this reproducible elsewhere?

There is also an over-arching question about the compatibility of private enterprise and capitalist values with those of Aboriginal culture, about which Helin is surprisingly silent. Other Aboriginal scholars have, however, taken up this issue.

David Newhouse (2000), of Trent University, has developed the notion of Capitalism with a Red Face. He argues that Aboriginal People have long adapted to capitalism, being actively involved in merchant capitalism and more recently in modern trade, and have "accepted the fundamental premises of capitalism" (57). Moreover, he believes that there is a desire in the Aboriginal community "to adapt this particular political-economic system and to make it work in accordance with Aboriginal belief systems" (56). These systems comprise seven traditional values: kindness, honesty, sharing, strength, bravery, wisdom and humility, all within "the collectivist orientation of Aboriginal society" (58). Adapting these to capitalism will entail going beyond economic development to encompass all four dimensions of the Medicine Wheel, which embraces economic, mental, emotional, and spiritual (59). Development will be viewed as a process or journey, the quality of which will be important, perhaps favouring long-term as opposed to short-term projects. The journey will be a collaborative and respectful one, in which individual entrepreneurs will work closely with the collective and will also be mindful of our insignificance in the world in which we live and wish to change. It will emphasize investment in human capital and the quality of life generally, rather than personal acquisition of wealth. The whole development process, including planning, may be subject to review by elders, drawing on their wisdom. Sharing of wealth by successful business people may be implicit in this model. Development institutions will be capitalist in nature, but their operations will be adapted to the local environment. Decision-making about development will be arrived at in a consensual manner and accountability will be driven by notions of honesty and respect.

Newhouse believes that much of this is already happening and the challenge is not to preserve Aboriginal worldviews and values, but to "find ways to assist in the creative interpretation of these worldviews and values in the contemporary reality, a process which is already underway" (61). Newhouse himself admits that "(t)here is and will continue to be considerable debate about whether traditional values are indeed compatible with capitalism" (58), and his is certainly a more sanguine view of the compatibility of development with Aboriginal culture than the position I took in Chapter 4. I am now more inclined to accept his arguments, based on case studies. Some of these are presented by Wanda Wuttunee (2004), who takes a theoretical approach similar to that of Newhouse. She recommends the use of Salway Black's Elements of Development Model which is, itself, based on the Medicine Wheel. This emphasizes balance in community development and respect for traditional culture, language, values and the land. Her case studies from across Canada underscore Newhouse's argument that "modernization" has proceeded apace in the Aboriginal community and Aboriginal culture and values have had a perceptible impact on approaches to development. Her examples are drawn from urban to remote communities, from straight capitalist initiatives with community-owned capital, to direct community-owned investment projects, from those with a land settlement and capital, to those with very little land or funds. She addresses both the positive and the problems and uses a combination of data and personal interviews; the result is a plausible and often subtle analysis of the complexities of "red capitalism." Once more, leadership seems crucial.

Dean Howard Smith (2000) is a Mohawk born in Canada but working in the U.S. His contribution to the literature is to argue that, while Aboriginal culture and values have been under assault since first contact with Europeans, they have survived and are meaningful. Poverty and deprivation make it difficult, however, for them to thrive and evolve. If people are struggling to survive, they may have no time, energy, or resources to participate in cultural activities. In particular, many cultural activities cost money. Economic development is, therefore, a prerequisite for cultural fulfilment, provided it is consistent with underlying values.

Drawing inspiration from the work of Jane Jacobs, Smith outlines a four-stage cycle of economic development for reservation economies. This starts with an initial export-import economy. Imports are financed by the income from extractive industries (exports), gaming (often "export" in nature), government activities, transfer payments, and trust income. The second phase consists of import replacing industries, primarily retail and service activities. The third phase is an extension of import replacement in which new products and technologies are introduced, the example he gives (which doesn't really fit) being the use of new techniques for dyeing and spinning wool used by Navajo artists. The fourth stage draws on these new techniques to expand exports, thereby raising imports and new import substitution possibilities. These phases are not necessarily sequential and may overlap; export possibilities might, indeed, be independent of prior import activities. The phases are designed for "narrative simplicity" (49).

The measure of successful development will be the extent to which the community will be self-supporting and free of dependence on the federal government. Movement in this direction will require a positive environment for growth in which tribal government becomes stable and self-supporting—echoes of the Harvard Project again, with which Smith is associated. The tribe must court outside private investors and give support to local would-be entrepreneurs by, among other things, making procedures less bureaucratic. The tribe needs also to develop a "comprehensive plan of action" (68). The planning process for this phased development starts with a census of the resource base, including human resources. The planning horizon must be long-term and allow, for instance, for the development of required human capacity. The whole process will be guided by "Native ideals and cultural norms" (ibid.). While aimed primarily at tribes in the U.S., Smith believes his approach will be relevant for Aboriginal Peoples elsewhere, and especially for those in Canada whose historical experiences have much in common.

On casinos as an Aboriginal economic development strategy, a comprehensive look at Canadian experience by Belanger (2006) has concluded that it was too early to say whether or not the costs of gambling outweighed the benefits in Saskatchewan or Manitoba (122). That remains the case at the end of the first decade of the new century.

To late 2010 only two of the planned five Manitoba First Nations casinos have been established, the one in The Pas and the one in Brokenhead. The latter has proven to be quite successful to date, proximity to Winnipeg not being a handicap as I thought it might be, but a boon. As it happens, proximity to a large urban area appears to be a feature of success of Indian casinos in the U.S. (Royal Society of Canada, Panel on Aboriginal Casinos 2007). The South Beach Casino and Resort Hotel situated on the Brokenhead Ojibway Nation now employs 250 people, of whom 57% are Aboriginal. The First Nation has received a dividend of $600,000 over the first two years of operation. In total, the casino generates about $7 million a year in profits. The First Nation recently built a gas station and convenience store across from the hotel and also provides supplies to the complex (Owen, 2008).

A third casino has also been approved recently in SouthWest Manitoba. After two proposals were rejected by the citizens of Brandon, the Spirit Sands casino will be built by the Swan Lake First Nation. Profits of the casino will be shared with the 63 First Nations in Manitoba, each of which is expected to receive $60,000 per year. Between 200 and 300 jobs will be created for Aboriginal People (Owen 2010). If this proceeds as planned, it is likely to be the last for the foreseeable future, as the consensus appears to be that the market is now saturated and that the original plan for five casinos was over-optimistic. In 2008, however, the province did support a $20 million First Peoples Economic Growth Fund, financed by Manitoba Lotteries Corporation to provide interest-free funding for First Nation businesses (Cash, 2008).

Perhaps the most significant development since these papers were written was the Report of the Royal Commission on Aboriginal Peoples (RCAP)(1996). This report took five years to complete and was based on extensive grassroots meetings with Aboriginal and other people. It made far-reaching recommendations on economic development but also on governance and other crucial preconditions for economic development. Its main recommendations were that the approximately 60 Aboriginal Nations should have self-government separate from other levels of government, and that such governments receive long-term block grant funding so that they could pursue their own vision of economic development (Wien, 1999: 111). Community development would function, therefore, under the broader ambit and larger scale of national governments. Appropriate institutions of government would be established to help foster economic development. These would ensure a capacity to undertake economic planning and development on a day-to-day basis at arm's length from political leaders, and would establish dispute resolution mechanisms and controls over abuse of political power.

RCAP recommended that the Department of Indian Affairs and Northern Development be eliminated and replaced by a Minister for Aboriginal Relations, and a new Department of Aboriginal Relations to negotiate and manage new agreements and arrangements. A Minister of Indian and Inuit Services, and a new Indian and Inuit Services department would deliver the gradually diminishing services coming from the federal level until self-government was fully established.

The land basis of Aboriginal People would be expanded significantly. South of the 60th parallel, Canadian Aboriginal lands are much smaller than those of Aboriginal People in the U.S. outside of Alaska, a 0.5% versus 3%. The Commission recommended that Aboriginal People be given sufficient land to pursue traditional interests and build a financial base for self-government, through land claims and other processes. Existing treaties should be strengthened and adhered to.

The Report made various recommendations to strengthen Aboriginal business development, including measures to increase capital availability (including a national Aboriginal development bank), entrepreneurial support and improved access to markets, through set-asides and trade promotion (Wien, 1999: 115). Traditional pursuits would be strengthened not only by extending the landmass but also by provision of support for trappers and hunters, in the form of cash and equipment.

Increasing Aboriginal employment was seen as a critical need. Training people for the institutions of self-government would be a key requirement for Aboriginal job growth, as would the development of organized employment services geared to Aboriginal People so that information would be readily available to both those seeking work and those seeking workers. Greater contact would also be required between Aboriginal organizations and large employers to overcome barriers that job seekers face when they are Aboriginal and have little direct contact with those seeking workers. Finally, improved and culturally appropriate childcare was seen as essential to increase Aboriginal and especially female Aboriginal employment (Wien, 1999: 18)

The Report also recommended that social assistance funds be topped up and made available for community economic development projects that provided people with jobs or, as in the case of the James Bay Cree, continued and used to subsidize access to traditional pursuits. This might mean shifting from individual entitlement to community entitlement to these funds (Wien 1999: 18).

The costs of doing nothing were measured by the Commission at $2.9 billion a year for Aboriginal People in forgone net earned income and at $4.6 billion a year for governments in terms of direct expenditures and revenues forgone on lost incomes. The RCAP strategy would entail an increase in government funding in the initial years by between $1.5 and $2.0 billion per annum (McCallum, 1999: 125). But over time these costs, especially of land claims, would decline and eventually, would be more than offset by increases in government revenues. McCallum (1999: 125–126) concluded that the additional spending recommended by RCAP to eradicate what he called "Canada's shame," would be affordable to the nation through anticipated growth in government budget surpluses. Grand Chief Phil Fontaine proclaimed that RCAP's "recommendations to pump investment into First Nations' communities is a forward-looking one. The time to move our people away from dependency towards self-sufficiency is now" (Fontaine, 1999:141)

Unfortunately, progress in addressing RCAP's recommendations has been very disappointing. The AFN (2006) argued that ten years after the RCAP report, very little had changed. In reviewing 65 recommendations of the Commission, the AFN concluded that there was a complete failure to deliver on 37 of these; in the case of 24 others, the government was awarded a C or less for performance, and only four were given between a C+ and an A. In short, the AFN concluded that the restructuring of the relationship between First Nations and the government recommended by RCAP had not taken place, "and the status quo continues today. The federal response has been limited to providing some funding to targeted areas such as early childhood development, diabetes, housing, sewage infrastructure, some aspects of education reform, water management, and social assistance." They argue that the reality for First Nations is ongoing poverty, an increasing income gap with the rest of society and a failure to invest "in meeting the needs of First Nations communities, or in addressing key determinants of health/well being." Regrettably, that remains the situation today.

CHAPTER 5
THE "GREAT NORTHERN PLAN"[1]

Manitoba's brief social democratic interlude provided the context for launching a series of reforms designed to promote equity and participatory democracy. This paper examines one of these, the "Northern Manitoba Development Strategy," in which the author, as senior policy advisor, was intimately involved. The object of the Strategy was to map out a comprehensive economic and social development project for the northern part of the province aimed at transforming the living conditions of one of the poorest sections of Canadian society. The exercise was unique in that it attempted to apply a modified version of a development strategy designed to meet the needs of a small underdeveloped economy in transition to socialism, to a region within the province. The strategy was never implemented, in part a victim of the fiscal crisis reverberating throughout the Canadian state by the mid-70s. However, its failure cannot be attributed to this alone. The composition of the budget, even in periods of scarcity, registers the political strength of various forces. The main failure, then, was that of the planners who failed to build the political support required to implement the Plan.

This paper seeks to describe the conditions of underdevelopment in Northern Manitoba that necessitate far-reaching and urgent political action. It outlines the theoretical basis of the strategy and the modifications made in order to implement it in one region of a larger nation-state. The examination of the reasons underlying its failure provided the basis for an assessment of the conditions

[1] From "The Great Northern Plan," in *Studies in Political Economy*, Number 6, 1981

necessary for its successful implementation in similar regions of Canada.[2]

THE SYMPTOMS OF UNDERDEVELOPMENT

In 1973 the total population of Northern Manitoba was about 79,700, two-thirds of whom were residing in ten urban centres based on mining, forestry, hydro construction or government administration activities. The majority of these were white and many were recent migrants from Southern Manitoba and elsewhere, but in all these centres were residents of Native ancestry. The remaining 26,360 were living in 46 generally much smaller communities. Almost all of these were either Indian (19,000) or Métis (7,000).

In that year total employment was estimated to be 25,630 and over 80% of these jobs were located in the ten urban centres. The participation rate in these centres was above the Canadian average and unemployment appeared to be below average.[3]

For the remainder of the North the natural rate of population growth was in excess of 3% per annum and about 48% of the population was under 15 years of age, both well above provincial averages (Hickling-Johnston, 1975: Appendix 1, 2). The labour force participation rate was only 29% and the unemployment rate was thought to be well over 20% in 1973, which would be consistent with the well-publicized crude unemployment rates (those not working as a percentage of those in the age group 15–64) of over 75% (Evans, 1976).[4] On Indian reserves in Manitoba 43% of the people over 15 years old had never been formally employed (Elias, 1975).

Northern employment patterns found inevitable reflection in income figures. The average personal income in the ten urban centres

2 I would like to thank RED staff members and especially George Davies and Fred Gudmundson for their parts in the exercise and for helping shape my views on it. I also acknowledge the very helpful comments on an earlier draft received from Michael Lebowitz, Colin Leys, Mel Watkins, Henry Veltmeyer, and Russ Rothney.
3 Population and employment date derived from Manitoba Planning Secretariat of Cabinet, *Macro-Data Working Group Report,* Mimeo (July 1975).
4 This figure was quoted by J. Evans of the Department of Indian affairs at a conference on Northern Development organized by the Communities Economic Development Fund, Manitoba, March 10–12, 1976.

was at $ 4,019, which was 11.8% higher than that for Manitoba and 4.7% higher than that of Canada, while the average income of those living in the other 46 communities was only $793, a mere 22% of the Manitoba average and less than 21% of the Canadian. Of this $793, fully 34.4% was accounted for by transfers from government including welfare, family allowances, etc. and 5% from income in kind (fishing, hunting, firewood, etc.).[5] To help put this average income figure into perspective it would yield a family income 24% below the 1970 Economic Council of Canada poverty line figure for a family of five.[6] Indeed the per capita figures were very close to those for Mexico and Chile (Meier, 1976: 22).

The picture was even more depressing when income inequalities within communities were considered. The average per person quintile range was from about $200 to $1,600 in the non-urban centres and between $1,300 to $6,500 in the urban centres. Meanwhile prices in the non-urban centres were 20–50% higher than in Winnipeg, implying much lower real incomes than cash incomes indicates (Hickling-Johnston, 1975).

Health statistics reinforced the above picture of poverty in the smaller non-urban centres. Infant mortality rates were two and a half times those for Manitoba as a whole, and the incidence of a number of diseases such as pneumonia, TB, intestinal infections, skin diseases, and eye infections were several times higher than for Manitoba as a whole. Other serious health problems included a high rate of dental decay and nutritional deficiency (Elias, 1976: 2–13). Accidents, suicide and violence were leading causes of death among young Native adults with suicide and homicide rates being, respectively, three times and 11 times those for the province as a whole. The rates of hospital discharges for accidents and poisoning were over twice the rate for the rest of Manitoba. The serious health care problems of

5 Northern income figures are taken from the Macro-Data Working Group Report and from the Northern Transportation Study. Urban centre incomes are based on tax returns and welfare data. Non-urban centre incomes are based on income tax returns, welfare data, and data from Indian Affairs governing earned income and transfer payments.

6 For information on how the ECC Poverty Line is calculated and why it is too low, see I. Adams et al., *The Real Poverty Report* (Edmonton, 1971), 1–24.

the North were compounded by levels of health care service that were well below standards elsewhere in the province.

Many of the health problems in the North can be traced directly to grossly inadequate incomes and diet but also to poor housing and infrastructure. In 1974 it was estimated that almost a half of all the Indian houses in Manitoba required immediate repair or replacement and most were overcrowded. Only 5.2% of Indian houses had a water system to the house and no less than 86% of Indian houses had no internal sewage facilities. In addition such basics as fire protection, sports, recreation and cultural and educational facilities were either deficient or non-existent in most of these communities (Department of Indian and Northern Affairs, 1976).

Data for 1973 show that 19% of all Native northern people had never attended school, while the proportion of Native children receiving secondary level education was between a third and a half of that for Manitoba. Teacher turnover rates and student drop out rates were high throughout the North but especially so in the non-urban centres (Planning Secretariat of Cabinet, 1976: 7–8).

The evidence is overwhelming. There were serious problems of poverty and inequality in the North both within communities and between communities. These problems were not confined to non-urban centres, nor simply to Native People, but this was the section of northern society most acutely affected and to a degree that was simply scandalous. What is more, the problems were such that poverty, if left unchecked, would become more serious over time since inadequate diet, health, education, social, and cultural facilities serve to reinforce the inter-generational transfer of deprivation.

It was felt that these problems indicated a situation which might properly be termed "underdevelopment"—one in which there was "a blockage of potential, sustained economic and social development geared to local human needs." (Rothney and Watson, 1975: iii). The aim of the northern strategy was to help realize this development potential by tackling the process of underdevelopment at its roots.

EXPLAINING UNDERDEVELOPMENT

The northern strategy exercise sought to provide an alternative explanation of the causes of underdevelopment in Northern Manitoba to the conventional wisdom, espoused by both the federal and provincial governments, which attempted to explain it in terms of orthodox theories of dualism, vicious circles and the "subtraction approach." These crudely divide the North into a white, industrial, modern north and a Native, backward, traditional North. They then list a number of deficiencies in the "Native North" which are supposed to explain its backwardness. The absence of skills, failure to adjust to job opportunities, excessive population growth rates, lack of leadership, and remoteness itself, are offered as explanations.[7] In particular it is felt that "their traditional values systems may be in conflict with modernization ideals," inhibiting progress, discouraging individual initiative, hard work, and leadership, and encouraging rapid population growth (Hickling-Johnson, 1975: Executive Summary, 11). These factors reproduce themselves in a vicious circle, thus perpetuating the problems of poverty.

The northern strategy exercise rejected this "blame the victim" dualist explanation as being at worst racist and at best oversimplified, static, and ahistorical. It is racist to the extent that it equates white northerners with industrialization and progress and Native People with backwardness. By making such generalizations it is at a loss to explain the existence in the North of Native workers or Native business people. Neither can it accommodate a community such as Matheson Island—a Native community in Northern Manitoba that is largely self-reliant with a high standard of living and little unemployment or welfare. By making superficial generalizations it also fails to see in white society many of the problems it identifies as being specifically Native (e.g., problems of labour turnover and alcoholism).

It is static and ahistorical in that it treats the problem of the poverty of Native People as being an original state (i.e., as a problem of undevelopment) as if Native People had no history and are living now more or less as they have done since earliest times.

---

7 See, for example, Canada Department of Regional Economic Expansion, *Manitoba's Changing Northland* (Ottawa, n.d.).

Presenting the problems of Native People in the framework of vicious circles simply adds to the confusion for it fails to isolate the historical origins of those problems or to trace their development and changes in relative importance over time.

The listing of deficiencies of traditional society relative to the attributes of advanced industrial society is described by Szentes as the "subtraction" approach (Szentes, 1971: 26). The methodology involves analysing a society that has been transformed by industrial capitalism, listing its characteristics and comparing them with those to be found in pre-industrial societies. Characteristics not found in the latter are then said to be the cause of the failure to industrialize. Baran criticizes this approach for confusing cause with effect, i.e., for revealing nothing more than the fact that pre-industrial societies have not been industrialized by capitalism, a fact which the subtraction approach, bound by its narrow empiricism, is not able to explain (Baran 1957: 235).

Having rejected dualism, vicious circles, and the subtraction approach, the northern strategy sought to explain underdevelopment in Northern Manitoba within a Marxist framework of analysis. There is, of course, no single Marxian theory of underdevelopment, but rather a Marxian paradigm replete with controversy and competing theories. The perspective adopted recognized this and can be regarded as a left-wing variant of dependency theory, one which acknowledges the vital importance of world exchange relationships in the shaping of the economies of underdeveloped regions but which, at the same time, subordinates these to the social relationship of production which underlie them.[8]

There has been little analysis of Northern Manitoba from this perspective and what little there has been can be regarded only as an important first step. Thus Elias divides the external penetration of the North into three distinct phases. The first, from the seventeenth century, he describes as that of the rise and fall of "balanced reciprocity" in which Native People initially traded commodities of about equal value with merchant capitalists. In the second phase,

---

8 This perspective is similar to that developed by James Petras. See J. Petras, *Critical Perspectives on Imperialism and Social Class in the Third World*, (New York, 1978).

from the early nineteenth century to the signing of the treaties, the monopoly of the Hudson's Bay Company was complete, exchange was unequal and "true colonial relations between the Whites and Natives were established." In the third period, since that time, Native People have been separated from their means of production and incorporated into Canada's class system "as a class of permanently unemployed persons" (Elias, 1975b: Ch. 1).

Rothney's work points to a number of weaknesses in Elias's analysis.[9] The profit record of the Hudson's Bay Company indicates that balanced reciprocity was, at best, a very short-lived phenomenon which had disappeared well before the end of the seventeenth century. Indian dependence on European trade goods was also widespread by that time. Secondly, class relationships were clearly developed in this period. Indian petty commodity producers, owning their own means of production, confronted the local agents (Company officers) of an exploiting merchant capital class resident outside of the area. Within the merchant companies class relationships were essentially feudal, "mercantile capital assum(ing) the overhead cost of labour in various ways as well as signing it to contractual bondage."[10] Hierarchy was also based on ethnic background and Native People were excluded from employment.

This period was, therefore, one in which a primitive communal mode of production was penetrated by foreign merchant capital, gradually giving rise to a society in which a class of predominantly petty commodity producers was exploited through the mechanism of unequal exchange by a merchant capital class. Until the late eighteenth century Cree and Assiniboine Indians acted as middlemen between the companies and the direct producers but lost this position with the inland expansion of trading posts. Taking their

9 R. Rothney, "*Mercantile Capital and the Livelihood of Residents of the Hudson Bay Basin*" MA, Department of Economics, University of Manitoba, 1975. The author's analysis owes much to this work and to that by Rothney and Watson, *A Brief Economic History*.

10 The analysis of the class basis of the fur trading companies is drawn from the exciting but as yet unpublished research of Ron Bourgeault which, as an untitled mimeo paper of his states, has the "specific intent ... to show that the history of the native struggle is indeed the history of class struggle with the secondary struggle being that of national rights, or the national question."

margins in the form of consumer trade goods, they did not accumulate capital and were not able to build an economic base independently of the companies.

The second period is more problematic. There is no doubt that with the merger of the Bay and the North West Company Indian dependence increased significantly. Yet Elias' term "colonial" hardly captures the complications that marked emerging social relationships during that time. Within the company feudal relationships eroded, giving way to an officer class now sharing directly in profits and to a proletariat receiving wages. Outside the company the Red River Settlement became increasingly class-stratified with a petty bourgeois class of farmers and merchants, a proletariat, and a reserve army of the unemployed, the size of which fluctuated with the fortunes of the fur trade. Since land grants varied according to one's place in the hierarchy of the company, the racial basis of class was carried over into the settlement.

Most importantly of all, after 1821 relationships between Indian primary producers and the company underwent profound changes. With monopolization of the industry, the depletion of the resource base, and the development of economic alternatives outside of the industry, the company began to regulate the organization of production and to exercise control over the work process in an unprecedented fashion. This took the form of conservation measures, of restricting the mobility of trappers, and directing trappers to specific trading posts.[11] At the same time debt was used to tie producers to the company. All these measures combined to restrict severely the independence of producers, so much so that one can legitimately question the extent to which their property was real or merely sham (Marx 1973: 510).[12] In other words, notwithstanding the fact that labour power was not exchanged for wages in the commonly accepted form, there is a legitimate question of the extent to which Indian producers were proletarianized during this time.

11 See Rothney (1975) and Bourgeault, Untitled.
12 I am indebted to Mike Lebowitz for bringing this point to my attention. Marx raises the issue of sham property with regard to the status of weavers and spinners in their dealings with merchants in the early days of manufacturing.

However one answers this question, it is apparent that by the time of treaties and the penetration of industrial and finance capital into the area, society was already highly stratified. As primary producers and members of the reserve army Indians occupied the lowest strata. Mixed bloods dominated the proletariat proper and were well represented in the reserve army. With the collapse of the fur trade the ranks of the reserve army were swollen by Native People. Mixed bloods also comprised a portion of the intelligentsia and petty bourgeoisie and it is these who led the Red River Rebellions. The remainder of the petty bourgeoisie and the large farmers were non-Native as was the officer class that, while accumulating some capital in its own right, was essentially a comprador class acting on behalf of a capitalist class resident outside the region.

These social relations of production had important implication for the structure of the northern economy. Production was almost entirely for export and, within mercantile restrictions of the day, exports were in unprocessed form to be manufactured in Europe. Aside from the early years of the trade the means of production, and hence technology, were virtually all imported from more industrialized centres outside the region, as were many important means of consumption. Surplus value was remitted outside the region since for the most part the capitalist class was non-resident and had little interest in diversifying its mercantile pursuits within the region. Surplus value generated by the fur trade was, with the exception of the years of intense competition (1763–1821), enormous relative to the capital employed. Finally, Native People were excluded from the class appropriating surplus value and indeed from almost all positions of authority in the trade or in the government region.

Following the decline of the fur trade, Native People participated in a wide range of occupations in mining, forestry, cottage industry, farming, fishing, transportation, surveying, and prospecting. From as early as the turn of the century, however, racial discrimination restricted Native employment, especially in the more highly paid, highly skilled jobs and particularly when labour was abundant (Rothney and Watson 1975: 29). They were, therefore, forced back into trapping and fishing for their livelihood, becoming heavily indebted to merchant capitalists who controlled these industries. In recent years, declining yields and low cash returns have drastically reduced the number of Native People engaged in petty commodity production and few can survive on the cash income from this source alone.

Since the Second World War the rate of growth of output and employment in the North has been impressive as a result of the expansion of modern staple industries, mining, forestry, and hydroelectricity. Yet, structurally, the economy has much in common with that of the fur trade era. It is still very much a "divergent" economy, like most underdeveloped national economies of the world, in that it lacks internal linkages: what is produced locally is not consumed locally and what is consumed locally is not produced locally. A measure of this divergence between domestic resources use and domestic demand is Thomas's import-domestic expenditure coefficient (Thomas, 1974: 139). This indicates the extent to which an economy is dependent on external demand and on external sources of use values, and ranges from zero to one for national economies. For Northern Manitoba as a whole it must be quite close to unity, with little change from the early days of the fur trade. For the non-urban centres of the North, in which the majority of Native People reside, this coefficient is probably in excess of one, imports being larger than gross product. This is a possibility which Thomas, dealing with national economies, ruled out of consideration but it can be explained by the high dependence of Native People on state transfer payments from outside the region. This in turn reflects the peculiar way in which the dominance of the capitalist mode of production was established in Northern Manitoba.

Modern staple industries required that the process of primitive accumulation begun in the fur trade era, that of divorcing Native People from the land, be completed and legalized formally. This was necessary in order to provide industrial capital with clear rights to the use of land; rights that, as Watkins has pointed out, are vital for modern resource extraction industries (Watkins, 1977: 88). The treaties extinguishing Indian title robbed Native People not only of their rights to land but also of their right to that share of surplus in industrial capital ventures corresponding to land rents.

At the same time the expansion of these industries has frequently had negative effects on direct production for domestic need and on petty commodity production around Native communities by impinging on hunting, trapping, and fishing grounds. Mercury pollution in Lake Winnipeg, the flooding of northern communities by Manitoba Hydro, the destruction of timber berths by the forestry operations, and the spread of sport fishing by white workers and tourist operators, are cases in point.

While industrial capital has brought modern housing, infrastructure, social services, and jobs to the north, it has not brought them to Native communities. Even where a choice was possible, profit maximization has dictated that these facilities be located close to the resource base, so that while Native communities have suffered the negative effects of industrialization, they have not received the benefits. This, of course, partly reflects the fact that industrial capitalism sees few profitable opportunities in the North except in resources extraction. Other types of industry which might more directly meet the needs of Native People and which could conceivably be located in native communities are more profitably located in "advanced" centres elsewhere in Canada or the U.S.

Even when Native People have been prepared to migrate they have been all but excluded from permanent jobs in these resource industries and in the state apparatus. In 1975 they occupied fewer than 900 jobs, less than 5% of the total number of jobs in the North. In a paper prepared for the Planning Secretariat of the Manitoba Cabinet, Elias explained this by the poor health, diet, and education of Native People, by nepotism among white northerners, and by institutionalized racism. The jobs that are open to Native People are unskilled, often temporary, dead-end, and low paying. This in itself discourages Native employment. Yet government training programs tend to prepare Native People for these very jobs, thus offering "northern natives who are unemployed, underemployed and impoverished, the opportunity to be unemployed, underemployed, and impoverished" (Elias, 1975).

Cultural barriers to the employment of Native People in industry are real but not of the form of significance usually ascribed by orthodox dualists. The most significant is the importance of one residing in one's home community to preserve or extend one's personal and kinship influence in social, economic, and political affairs. This places a real constraint on movement out of one's community to seek industrial employment. Obviously it is a constraint that many Native People have chosen to overcome, but perhaps at considerable cost in terms of disruption of community structure and process. A recent study of Indian migration to Regina revealed that 40% of Indian males left the reserves to seek work and 13% to get more education. As many as 70% of all migrants said they would return to the reserves if the conditions and opportunities there were improved.[13]

Such stereotypical "Indian problems" as "slowness to adjust or adapt to change" or "difficulty of keeping time" have no basis in historical fact, argues Elias, and do not represent cultural barriers but simply another form of blaming the victim.

The problem is not that surplus value generated in the North is too small to sustain a rate of accumulation adequate to provide for the basic material requirements of Native People. Surplus has in fact been huge. Thus between 1968 and 1970 the mining companies recorded book profits of no less than $192 million, while over the same period Manitoba Hydro paid interest and retained earnings of around $70 million, most of which was attributed to the North. Between 1970 and 1978 Hydro surpluses so defined amounted to $450 million.[14] The problem is that Hydro surpluses accrue to bondholders resident elsewhere and to those consumers of electricity, like the mines and U.S. corporations, who pay well below cost for the product. The surpluses of the state-owned Manitoba Forest Industries paper plant (Manfor) were capitalised and lost to foreign capitalists long ago in the fraud surrounding its creation, while the surpluses of mining companies and of Abitibi, the other major paper plant, accrue to capital outside the region.[15]

The role of the state in the North also needs clarification. In general, all states perform three basic functions, which find expression

13 Cited in the *Winnipeg Tribune*, January 28, 1978. The study was conducted by the Federation of Saskatchewan Indians.
14 Data taken E. Kierans, *Report on Natural Resource Policy in Manitoba*, Government of Manitoba (February 1973), for mining companies and from *Annual Reports of Manitoba Hydro Electric Authority* for hydro.
15 For a thorough analysis of the scandal surrounding the building of Manfor, or Churchill Forest Industries as it was originally called, see P. Mathias, *Forced Growth* (Toronto 1971), Chapter 6.

in their budgets: assisting the accumulation of capital, providing for certain reproduction cost and maintenance expenses of labour, and repressing opposition to the status quo (Panitch, 1977: 8). In the history of Northern Manitoba the accumulation function has tended to dominate government activity with the second function gaining in relative importance only in the last 20 or so years in response to demands from the working class generally throughout Canada. Thus the major role of the state has been that of subsidizing merchant and industrial capital activities. The Rupertsland monopoly of the Hudson's Bay Company, the vesting of state powers in that company, and the subsequent handsome compensation of the company for the loss of its powers were but early examples of state-assisted accumulation. In more recent years the Indian treaties and subsequent amendments, the building of railways, roads, hydro dams, town sites, schools and the use of police to break strikes, are all examples of state action designed primarily to foster the accumulation of capital by the owners of resource extraction industries.

It is in the last 20 or so years that the state has been forced to play what O'Connor would call a significant legitimizing role in Northern Manitoba, the impetus for this coming largely from the growing political consciousness and organizations of Native People and from the general struggles of workers for an increase in the social wage (O'Connor, 1973: Chapter 1).[16] Before that time Native People were simply administrated. In recent years they have been not only administrated but also have won from the state the concessions of welfare and some access to health and education facilities, training programs, and make-work projects.

It should be noted that some of the very measures taken by the state to facilitate accumulation served, themselves, to undermine political pressures for increasing legitimization expenditures and to prevent Native People from participating fully in the development process. This is particularly true of the Indian Act and the treaties

---

16 The problem with O'Connor's approach is that he denies the real social struggles underlying gains in legitimation expenditures, reducing them to a form of cooption by the state to facilitate, indirectly, capital accumulation. On this point see J. Loxley "Fiscal Sociology and the Fiscal Crisis of the State," Journal of Contemporary Crises, (6), 1982.

which, apart from enabling the North to be opened up to industrial capitalist expansion, also effectively tied Status Indians to the reserve system and restricted their basic freedoms to engage in any economic activities at all and especially those involving non-reserve residents or communities (Rothney and Watson, 1975: 24). In this way, therefore, Native People were restricted not only in the degree to which they were proletarianized but also in the extent to which they could join the petty bourgeoisie class. This legislation also split the Native People into a number of distinct groups—Status Indians, non-Status Indians and Métis—creating artificial divisions among them and denying basic democratic rights to the first group. Once sanctioned by law, these divisions began to take on real political significance weakening the strength of Native People as a whole in the classic "divide and rule" manner of colonial state strategy.

Indeed, as Watkins and others have argued in recent years, the Native People of the North are colonized and their economy bears all the characteristic traits of a colonial economy (Watkins, 1977). Yet there are unique features of the colonization of Native People in Canada. The Native economy depends for up to a third of its income on state transfers. This level of dependence on "aid" has no parallel in the history of colonialism in Africa, Asia, or Latin America and is possible only because Native People represent a colonized minority within one of the wealthiest countries of the world and because a sizable state bureaucracy and a number of capitalist and petty bourgeois enterprises thrive on Native dependence on these transfers. It is necessary because the long history of exploitation of Native People by external capital has created a situation in which such payments are required for the very physical survival of the community.

CLASS STRUCTURE

The poverty of Native People is a reflection of the marginalized positions they occupy in the class structure of Northern Manitoba. It is not correct to say that Native People as a whole constitute "a class of permanently unemployed persons." Rather it appears that the majority (perhaps 55% with dependents) are members of the proletariat albeit frequently occupying positions in what Marx called the stagnant form of relative surplus population. This would be consistent with the figures given earlier which show that the majority of Native People over 15 years of age have had experience in the formal work force but that most of these are unemployed. Their employment tends to be largely impermanent, frequently seasonal or very short term, hence their incomes are low.

Beneath these is a much smaller but nevertheless large and growing group of Native People (maybe 25%) who really are permanently unemployed as far as the formal labour market is concerned. They depend totally upon state transfers for their cash income but in other respects are roughly equivalent to what Marx called paupers or "the lowest sediment of relative surplus population" (Marx, 1972: 711). This group is distinguished from the reserve army by having no impact on wage rates but it is still highly functional within the capitalist system, as Elias stresses, in that it assists the process of realization of surplus value through its dependence on state transfers and through the administration of its affairs by large numbers of bureaucrats (Elias, 1975b: 117).

As Marx argued, the creation of this group of paupers "is an inevitable outcome of the production or relative surplus population—the two together form indispensable conditions of the existence of capitalist production and the development of wealth" (Marx, 1972: 712). That this group is disproportionately represented among Native People is therefore a reflection of this disproportionate size of the reserve army among Native People.

A very small proportion (maybe 4%) of Native People are pure petty commodity producers in the more traditional pursuits of hunting, fishing, and trapping. A somewhat larger group (maybe 12%) occupies what Wright has termed a contradictory class location combining petty commodity production with wage employment, their earnings from the former often enabling super-exploitation in the latter—the payment of wages below the reproduction costs of labour.[17]

Each of the classes is engaged, to varying degrees, in direct production for subsistence (which also permits super-exploitation of

---

17 For discussion of the term "contradictory class location" see E.O. Wright, *Class, Crisis and the State*, (London, 1979), 61–97.

those engaged in wage labour), and hence each has an attachment to land and to certain traditional communal production and consumption practices. These, in turn, are solidly rooted in northern community life, being stronger the more remote the communities and, therefore, act as a deterrent for Native People to migrate to more developed centres. As petty commodity production and direct production continue to decline in importance, class delineations can be expected to become clearer.

Apart from these classes there is a very small petty bourgeois class (maybe 1%) owning stores, garages, trucks, etc. which is the product of the post Second World War state policy of trying to build an Indian middle class. The businesses of this class are almost entirely state-financed with a very high failure rate due to competition from established white businesses, undercapitalization, and poor management support system.[18]

Finally there is a group of Native People occupying a further contradictory class location. These are the state and band employees, band-elected officials and elected officials of the Native organizations, the Manitoba Indian Brotherhood (MIB) and the Manitoba Métis Federation (MMF). They own no means of production and are not policy-makers. Yet they hold positions of authority within the ideological apparatus and exercise powers of hiring, funding, and sometimes of coercion. They are subject to contradictory pressures from the state on one hand, from whom they receive their finances, and from the Native communities on the other, whose interests they supposedly serve. At the community level the latter pressures often outweigh the former giving rise to quite radical leaders, but the complete dependence of even elected officials (such as Chiefs) on state finance places severe limitations on the independence of their actions. In the MIB and MMF the contradictory pressures are there but the influence of the state is more direct since these bodies operate at one remove from communities.

18 These observations are based on the author's personal experiences as Chairman of a Provincial Crown Corporation Loan fund established to lend to residents of remote communities in Manitoba and on personal experiences with Federal lending and granting agencies such as Special ARDA, and the Indian Economic Development Loan Fund.

In some respects this section of Native society (no more than 2–3%) acts as an agent of colonialism or, since the state is increasingly implementing policies and programs through Native organizations, more accurately, of neo-colonialism. A number of members of this group use their influence to secure state financial assistance for themselves or their families and hence move into the petty bourgeois class.[19] At the same time they are unanswerable directly or indirectly to communities and therefore must demonstrate at least minimal commitment to dealing with community problems. In this situation they cannot be ruled out as potentially progressive agents and they frequently act to protect or further the interests of Native People generally.

The poverty of Native People is therefore the outcome of the historical process of capitalist penetration of Northern Manitoba in the structural manner described which positioned Native People in marginalized class locations. The burden of poverty is, however, not borne by the class responsible for its generation. It is borne, not by capital but, as Marx emphasized, by "the working class and the lower middle class" (Marx, 1972: 712).

In Northern Manitoba these classes are predominantly white, relatively better off than their counterparts elsewhere in Manitoba, and frequently racist. The white proletariat does not generally recognize the common roots of its own explanation and of Native poverty, tending instead to see Native People as a burden upon them through taxation. This, it will be shown, has important implications for the forging of political alliances between these different segments of northern society.

THE THOMAS STRATEGY

Having thus theorized on the causes of underdevelopment in Northern Manitoba the next step was to select a development strategy consistent with this analysis. The one adopted was a modified version of the strategy advocated by C.Y. Thomas.[20]

19 See for instance, J. Burke, *Paper Tomahawks—From Red Tape to Red Power* (Winnipeg, 1976) for an account of the role of the Manitoban Indian Brotherhood and of certain prominent Indian leaders active in it in the early 1970s.
20 See Thomas, *Dependence and Transformation,* part 2 for this and all references to the strategy of this section.

This sees the divergent nature of dependent economies as their major structural weakness, a weakness to be rectified by a two-stage strategy of convergence. The first stage is that of the convergence of domestic resources use and domestic demand, while the second is that of the convergence of domestic demand and domestic need. Since the structural aspects of dependent economies are themselves the product of the social relationship of production generated by the capitalist penetration of pre-capitalist economies, it follows that strategies of convergence presuppose an end to the class forces underlying divergence and reproducing dependence. Thus the basic assumption of the Thomas strategy is that society is in transition to socialism. From this follows both the willingness and the ability of a sovereign state to reverse the consequences of the uneven development of world capitalism within its own borders, by socializing the means of production, halting the outflow of surplus, and building up a structure of production which caters to the requirements of its population.

The convergence of local use and demand will be achieved, according to Thomas, through the creation of a series of industries producing "basic goods"—goods which feature prominently in the production of a wide range of consumption and investment goods. They are characterized by extensive forward and backward linkages and by high growth elasticities (increase in per capita value added in a given sector relative to changes in per capita income). It is the dominance of these goods in the production structure of developed capitalist and socialist economies which distinguishes their economies, structurally, from those of dependent underdeveloped economies. The precise constellation of industries and their phasing will be dictated, of course, by the nature of the resource base and the pattern of demand. The essence of the approach is that production is planned, and planned first and foremost to meet local demands and only secondarily if at all, as an extension of the domestic market, to meet foreign demands.

Thomas's strategy was conceived with small economies in mind—specifically the West Indies and the balkanized nations of black Africa. In consequence he devotes much attention to the issue of scale and to the decentralization of activities. Conventional wisdom has tended to discount the possibilities of rapid integrated development in these economies on account of the limited size of the domestic market and has, accordingly, prescribed specialized production for export as the main strategy. Thomas questions the validity of this notion of prohibitively restricted market size and argues that the importance attached to economies of scale in development literature is frequently exaggerated. Empirical measurement of optimal scale is complicated by price distortions resulting from the existence of monopoly, external economies, and the use of exchange rates in making international comparisons. In any given situation departures from what might be regarded as technically optimal size may be justified by the prices of local resources or factors or by attempts to minimize transportation costs. But the evidence is unambiguous, says Thomas, in showing that the *rate of fall* in average cost as scale increases is far from being uniform, and is often at its greatest at scale sizes which are well below the optimum; at sizes which may even be relatively small by the prevailing standards of Europe and North America. Thus the scale guideline to be followed in the Thomas strategy is not that of the optimum, or least cost, but rather that of the critical minimum where the rate of fall in average cost is greatest. Countries would produce goods the planned market for which would be sufficient to enable this critical minimum scale to be adopted. The benefits to be derived from integrated domestic production at these levels are assumed to outweigh the social costs involved in producing at less than optimal level, those costs being the savings forgone by not waiting until the market size is large enough to warrant optimal scale of production.

Thomas places much less weight on the choice of technique than is customary, arguing that in practice this choice will be dictated, more or less, by the choice of product configuration determined by the strategy. In his view the possibility of substitution of different raw materials in the production of a given commodity is likely to be a more significant policy consideration than the possibility of substitution between the labour and capital. He does, however, provide for technological choice after selection of the product configuration and argues that a domestic capital goods sector is a prerequisite for the development of a dynamic, indigenous technology appropriate to local conditions. Even in this long-run sense, therefore, Thomas sees the choice of commodity as the critical decision with choice of technique being subordinated to it. This is to be contrasted with the widely held view that effective technology choice is, or can be made, available to underdeveloped countries independently of the production structures of these countries.

In the Thomas model the machine tool sector plays a key role in the development of basic goods production and Thomas points out that, contrary to popular belief (a belief strengthened by the application to this sector of such emotive descriptions as "heavy industry"), the machine tool sector is typified by small-scale, labour-intensive custom production which makes it ideal for small labour-surplus economies.

The construction industry is also crucial since it plays a prominent role in satisfying many of the basic needs of society. In addition, it provides unparalleled opportunities for the convergence of domestic needs with domestic resources, the nature of the industry being such that it can exhibit rapid rates of growth at very low levels of per capita income and has an unusual flexibility in terms of the choice of input mix, technology, scale, and location.

Thomas is not advocating autarky. There is a clear role in his model for foreign aid and foreign trade provided they service the convergence strategy.

In the early stages of transformation the domestic market will itself be determined by demand. The longer-run aim of the strategy, however, will be in the convergence of domestic *need* with *demand*. This will be achieved in part by a progressive equalization of incomes and in part by the raising of material living standards. The market will continue to function but will be restricted to the extent that convergent production requires a scale too small to permit the range and variety of output that completely free choice might dictate. Also, many needs will be met through the provision of public goods especially in the areas of housing, public health, recreation, nutrition, and education, the quantity, form, and timing of which will be determined through democratic process. This provision of public goods will also progressively reduce the influence of the market.

This strategy is clearly premised on two critical political assumptions: first, that the economy in question is a sovereign nation and second, that society is in transition to socialism. Neither of these was valid in the context in which the strategy was applied and this raises the issues of the appropriateness of the choice of this particular strategy and of the wisdom of the exercise as a whole.

It can be argued that the latter assumption is more crucial than the former for if society were in transition to socialism, convergence principles could be applied at all levels of planning, regional as well as national. The problem of the non-applicability of assumption 1 starts when assumption 2 does not hold. What possible relevance could such a strategy have when society is not in transition to socialism? How can one plan a region in a capitalist economy with its openness at this level in terms of the flows of surplus, trade, investment, and labour? Likewise, why should a capitalist state wish to reverse the process of underdevelopment given what has been said above about the contribution of the state in this process? Why then was the exercise attempted in the first place?

First of all it was hoped that the specification of the various production possibilities in the North consistent with such a strategy would help dispel the prevailing mythology that the resource base of the North is inadequate to support current and anticipated population levels. This myth was subscribed to by many senior provincial politicians (including the premier) and bureaucrats and led to the view that the only future for most Native People lay in their migrating to towns. Since the vast majority of Native People in towns fail to find employment this is not much of a future. The formation of an urban lumpen-proletarian stratum of the Indian pauper class described above, now visibly in process in western cities, can hardly be considered an answer to the problems Native People face on reserves. Thus the very technical specifications of such a strategy might, it was hoped, challenge this orthodoxy of hopelessness.

Secondly, it was felt that participation by Native People in strategy formulation, itself a prerequisite for fulfilment of the strategy, might contribute to the development of political consciousness among Native People as to the causes of underdevelopment in the North and to the conditions required for its eradication. The aim, therefore, was to help mobilize Native People to struggle politically for alternative strategies of development in the North that put people and their needs, material, social, and cultural, at the centre of the development process. As victims of colonialism and as a minority group in their own homeland it is not surprising that Native People themselves frequently accept both the orthodox paradigm of development theory and the limited prospect for improvement in their lot—short of migration, assimilation, and a complete abandonment of their culture and communities—that the paradigm posits as being possible.

Thirdly, the pure Thomas model was never attempted. A major modification was made to it by not challenging the private ownership of existing northern mining or forestry ventures nor the current outflow of surplus from these enterprises. At the same time the state was heavily involved in the northern economy. The province owns Hydro in its entirety, owns one of the two pulp mills and was considering building another, and had legislative power giving it the option of participating up to 50% in all new mineral exploration projects and in the development of new mineral ventures. Almost all the land in Northern Manitoba is Crown land and the province has full constitutional power over natural resources. Finally, it regulates not only mineral and forestry production with the power to tax both profits and rents, but it also regulates the fishing and trapping industries. In the circumstances it was felt that these powers would act as a useful proxy to social ownership of the means of production should the province express a desire to formulate a Thomas-like strategy. It was also felt that the financial implications of a convergent transformation of the North could be met by diverting huge state expenditures already flowing into the North, i.e., without attempting the hopeless task of restricting private surplus flow from existing resource industries.

Finally, the exercise was attempted because, implicitly, there was an assumption on the part of the planners that under the NDP government the nature of the state as a whole had changed in Manitoba and that some reversal of past patterns of development might be possible. Direct state intervention in the economy, support of community cooperatively owned enterprises, the use of state purchasing power to meet broader social goals, the adoption of a "stay option" policy under which no one should be forced to leave the province or any region of the province because of lack of economic opportunity, and the oft-repeated calls for public participation in development decisions, all seemed to be consistent with a Thomas-type strategy and, indeed, the strategy was legitimized by reference to these positions.[21] The NDP controlled the five provincial seats in the North, its reformist platform attracting the support of much of the white proletariat and of the Native proletariat and underclass. It was assumed that with this class base of support for the NDP government and with increased political pressure from Native People, the state as a whole might well be pushed into implementing a modified Thomas strategy. We shall return to this assumption when analyzing why the exercise failed.

METHODOLOGY AND RESULTS

The occasion of the strategy exercise was the expiry of the Northlands agreement between the province and the federal Department of Regional Economic Expansion (DREE). Until that time three agreements constituted virtually the essence of what passed for planning in the North but they contained no explicit strategy, being rather a shopping list of barely related social infrastructure projects aimed at only a small section of the population in the provincially administered non-urban centres, i.e., excluding the large towns and the Indian reserves. Responsibility for negotiating and administrating the DREE agreement lay with the Resource and Economic Development (RED) Secretariat, a wing of the Planning Secretariat of Cabinet which advised the RED sub-committee of cabinet on all matters related to economic policy and on new or problematic expenditure requests. The proposal for the northern strategy exercise was conceived by the RED Secretariat, of which the author was Secretary or Deputy Minister.

The idea was that the exercise would provide a framework into which a longer-term Northlands agreement would fit by aiming at

21 For a review of these and related policy statements see Province of Manitoba, *Guidelines for the Seventies* (March 1973), Vols. 1, 2, and 3.

a general strategy, a five-year broad outline plan and a detailed first-year plan for the whole of the non-urban north, including Indian reserves. This framework would be generated by line departments and Crown agencies under the direction of the RED Secretariat and the Department of Northern Affairs (DNA), which had a mandate to coordinate provincial state activities in the non-urban, non-reserve communities. Once the general principles of the approach—convergence, reversal of surplus flow, and participation by northerners in both planning and controlling northern development initiatives—had been approved by Cabinet, eleven working groups were established reporting to a synthesizing group composed of RED and DNA staff. These groups covered the following areas: 1) macro data and historical review, 2) physical resources, 3) financial resources, 4) health, education, and social policy, 5) manpower, 6) community participation, 7) industrial development, 8) transportation and communications, 9) agriculture, 10) services to Treaty Indians, and 11) community services and local government. The synthesizing group was responsible for overseeing and coordinating the work of these groups although two Plan Coordinators, a senior DNA Planner and the DREE coordinator in RED Secretariat, had day-to-day contact with the groups. Overall bureaucratic responsibility for the exercise lay with the Deputy Minister's Liaison Committee composed of the RED Secretary and the Deputy Minister of the DNA whose task it was to ensure cooperation from departments and state agencies and to report to Cabinet through the RED sub-committee.

Participation by Native People was to be achieved by inviting the MIB and MMF to send representatives as members of the working groups, although the task of the Participation Working Group was to develop a model to ensure ongoing community input into the planning process. In addition, this group was to advise on the best vehicles for achieving community ownership and control of both resources and enterprises.

The exercise commenced in May 1975 and by March 1976 the first attempt at concrete proposals was submitted to cabinet. At this brief span of time the Macro Data group had produced statistical profiles of the North and of individual communities covering such items as income and employment. The Physical Resources Group had collated available information on the resource base of the North, both renewable and non-renewable by major commodity, and its potential. This data was mapped in relation to individual communities.

The Community Participation Working Group analysed transcripts of three sets of public hearing in the North and various submissions by the MIB and MMF to the government in order to derive first estimates of needs. Listed by community and by type these needs were then circulated to each working group. Collectively they constitute a strident demand for improved living conditions, for jobs and for dignity.[22]

The reports of the other groups laid down the major sectoral policies to be followed in line with the convergence strategy and made detailed proposals, sector by sector, for both investment and employment possibilities. A summary of the recommendations of a few of these groups should suffice to illustrate the nature of the planning exercise.[23] Thus convergence in the forestry sector would take the form of creating/reviving fifteen local sawmills to produce lumber for local construction, the mines, etc. These would be fed by 32 community harvesting operations which would also help replace by attrition a portion of the 70% of the labour force in the two large forestry operations which was drawn from outside Northern Manitoba. All forestry resources within 25 miles of communities would be reserved for community use. There would be more direct employment of Native People in Manfor and Abitibi, achieved by a levy/grant system which would penalize employers not employing Native People and subsidize those that did. A small particle board plant would assist the viability of community operations, as would a small thermochemical process pulp and paper mill, by purchasing 65% of wood wasted in harvesting and sawmilling, and would provide forward linkages to furniture and house building.

By projecting forward demand/need in the housing and related sectors it was ascertained that the construction industry could

---

22 Working Group on Community Participation *Representation by Northern Communities* Province of Manitoba, mimeo (July 1975).

23 The recommendations themselves were summarized in a submission to Cabinet entitled *Representation by Northern Communities* Province of Manitoba, mimeo (July 1975)

support at least a dozen new enterprises producing trusses, windows, doors, stairs, furniture, etc. with linkages back to forestry and other industries. Northern building specifications would, however, have to be rewritten to permit the use of local resources.

A very comprehensive program of agriculture development was drawn up aiming at self-sufficiency in basic foodstuffs in the North by 1985. This covered the production of vegetables, berries, eggs, hogs, broilers, beef, honey, wild rice, and feed grains and the creation of depots for reconstituting powdered milk. Apart from convergence and job creation a major aim of this program would be to help solve nutritional problems. It would require two demonstration farms, extension workers, community storage facilities, an abattoir, a feedmill and a subsidization scheme to cover fertilizers, feed grains (until northern production commenced), storage, and loan interest.

Similarly detailed reports were prepared for all other sectors including not only production sectors but also transportation, health, education, etc. In each report questions of scale, appropriate technology, and the recruitment and training of local Native People were addressed where relevant. The end result was, therefore, a comprehensive set of coherent and internally consistent proposals dealing with the economic, social, and cultural development of the North with their physical, human, and financial implications spelled out as clearly as possible.

Community projects identified would generate 2,300 jobs directly while the proposed 20% minimum Native employment targets for existing industries would create 3,000 jobs for Native People by 1981. The overall capital costs of the strategy would be between $245 and $370 million over five years, while additional recurrent spending, including subsidies, would amount to about $20 million. These figures were thought to be reasonable given the outflow of surplus from the North, which is much larger, over a five-year period and given provincial government expenditures of $206 million in the North in 1975–6 alone. Hydro capital development expenditures ranged between $200 and $600 million per annum in the early 1970s while federal expenditures are unknown but were as high as $20 million as long ago as 1970. It was felt that with the judicious reallocation of existing expenditures, especially away from Hydro development, and with modest additions to annual expenditures, financing of the strategy was feasible.

It was recognized that these were merely preliminary and somewhat crude proposals which needed to be assessed and developed by communities, so part of the package provided money for each community to hire its own planner and for each to send representatives to regular regional meetings to ensure regional coordination and the development of the strategy over time. All working papers and reports on the strategy were to be made available to communities and a team of three Native liaison workers would travel to each community explaining and discussing the strategy in detail.

These proposals were greeted by certain of the RED committee members with a mixture of humour ("there are three ways to spend money—on women, gambling, or, most recklessly of all, by listening to the advice of a professional economist") and incredulity at their total cost. Above all there was a complete failure on the part of the committee as a whole to appreciate the internal coherence of what was being proposed, reflected in statements to the effect that "we should proceed cautiously, perhaps adding a couple of cutting operations in the next year" or "we should shake the tree and see which proposals fall out." There was a categorical reluctance to "turn money over to communities."

In any event, after much pressure from the northern MLAs the package was accepted in principle. The Secretariat was requested to obtain departmental reactions to the details and to put together proposals for inclusion in the budget for the coming year. From this point on there was a steady erosion of what little support there had been for the exercise and within twelve months it was clear that, with the exception of the odd small item here and there, the recommendations would not be implemented. Certainly, there would be no concerted effort to implement the strategy on a full-scale basis. Also, until very recently the exercise had little impact on the struggles of Native People in the North to improve their lot and in fact at one point was attacked by them. We now turn to attempt to explain why this was the case.

WHY THE EXERCISE FAILED

In retrospect it appears that the most important reason for the failure on the Northern Strategy exercise was the neglect of the planners to analyze the class nature of the state in Manitoba under the NDP government. As a result there was facile equation of the class basis of the party in power with the class nature, or at least potential class nature, of the state as a whole. The unspoken premise behind the exercise was that with a little pressure from Native People inspired by the exercise itself, the state machinery in the North could be transformed; that somehow the victory for a mildly social democratic party would make it possible to reverse the historical role for the state in the North from that of assisting capitalist accumulation to that of facilitating the convergent development of Native communities.

This premise was completely misguided, indicating that the planners failed to comprehend the political coherence of capitalist development, and the extent to which their proposed strategy challenged both the ideology of capitalist accumulation and the political institutions which serve it. The role of the state in Northern Manitoba after 1969 changed marginally with only minor concessions being made to the workers and underclass of that region who had helped make the NDP victory possible. Essentially the state continued to support the accumulation of capital by a non-resident class of property owners. Hydro development dominated state policy and state expenditures in the North on an unprecedented scale, even though a significant part of the NDP's electoral support had come from Native People and others who opposed this type of development. The building of Leaf Rapids townsite, a reformist move to the extent that the miners benefited from unusually comfortable living conditions, represented in essence a subsidization of multinational mining capital. Policy shifts making it possible for the state to participate with the private sector in mineral exploration and development in no way threatened rates of profits in this sector and changes in mineral taxation did so only to a negligible degree. Each of these measures reinforced the traditional role of the North as a resource extraction enclave. All of this was known by 1975, and indeed the strategy exercise recognized this implicitly by not proposing the socialization of the existing means of production, and by proposing that convergence principles be applied as far as possible to existing mining, forestry, and hydro enterprises.

Given that the strategy was modified so as to leave the existing private appropriation of surplus intact, financing of proposals was to depend entirely on state funding. This subjected them to the acute fiscal constraints faced by the state at all levels in 1976–77 and, in effect, prevented even the highly selective implementation of individual strategy proposals that the politicians envisaged. First of all the federal government announced that the annual average sum of DREE Northlands money available over the ensuing five years would not exceed the average received by Manitoba in 1975 (i.e., not only would there be no increase but there would also be no provision for inflation). In effect the province would receive only about half of what it required.

Secondly, the provincial government also tightened its belt with the inevitable result that legitimization expenditures, and especially those to politically weak groups, were cut back. Since most of the Northern Affairs budget fits this category, it is not surprising that there was a decline in real dollar terms in its budget for 1977–78. The northern budgets of other departments also came under strong attack with proposals to cut or abolish a number of progressive programs providing educational services to Native People.

Not only was the Northern Strategy not implemented but the existing level of state non-accumulation expenses in the North was severely cut back even by the NDP government. With the election of the Conservatives, the Department of Northern Affairs was systematically dismantled. Indeed, the very election of the Conservative government with its emphasis on reduced state spending and on taking the state out of business can be explained in large part by the fiscal crisis itself, reflecting the underlying crisis of capitalism in Manitoba and Canada generally. Since 1977, northern policy has been geared much less unambiguously to the requirements of individual capital operating there, as evidenced by the closure of community projects, the laying off of Native staff, the cutbacks in social services, the reduction of taxes on mining companies and the emphasis on expenditures on infrastructure in or to the urban centres.

Even before the 1977 election, however, there were clear signs that the state was prepared to sacrifice the interests of northern Native People in order to boost the provincial economy, including that of the urban centres of the North. Thus the state actively cooperated in the preliminary investigative work of Polar Gas Pipelines Co. Ltd., which was seeking to build a $7+ billion pipeline through the northern part of the Province. Neither the NDP governments nor its successor has paid much attention to the concerns of Native People who fear the dislocating effect of the project. The state has made no offer to fund Native People in their efforts to educate themselves about the proposed line and its possible impact and to make representations on it to the appropriate authorities. The whole project is proceeding quietly and systematically in spite of the protests of Native People. What is more, the pipeline is seen by the City of Churchill, suffering badly from state spending cuts, and by City of Thompson, suffering from mining layoffs, as a panacea for their problems and has the support, therefore, of the state, of the northern Chambers of Commerce and of northern unions. This project, above all others, is indicative of the class nature of the state in Manitoba and of the fact that state-assisted developments in the North continues to strengthen the process of underdevelopment in Native communities.

The failure of the planners to articulate the class nature of the state led to other errors. It was a grave mistake to believe that the state apparatus could be used as a vehicle through which to root the strategy exercise in the concrete class struggles of Native People, or of any other section of society for that matter. It soon became apparent that not only was much of the central bureaucracy hostile to the strategy, but field staff who worked in communities felt particularly threatened by it.

A serious split developed in the Participation working group over the nature and purpose of "community participation." Traditional extension staff members allied themselves with the extension staff of Northern Affairs working in the communities to promote a notion of participation which consisted of series of confessional-type meetings where residents unburdened themselves of their problems to field staff. A more progressive wing of the Participation group argued that this unstructured approach was simply a means of reinforcing the status quo, since no attempt was made to encourage northerners to put their problems into a broader theoretical and historical perspective of underdevelopment. The traditionalists opposed this view on the grounds that since northern people live there, they should know best what their problems are and what they want. The progressives countered that without an understanding of how their problems originated, northerners would never really appreciate their precise nature and how best they might be tackled.

The extension staff also had quite different views of how the process of participation would evolve once implementation of the strategy began. Those who initiated the strategy saw participation as eventually becoming synonymous with ownership of and control over the means of production. Most extension staff on the other hand were opposed to the collective ownership of the means of production, either in principle or because they believed that communities were not ready for it, and saw participation as being roughly the equivalent of consultation or limited local government powers.

The result of this conflict was that field staff became a barrier to the exercise, helping to shield communities from contact with it rather than helping to promote their involvement, and opposing any kind of planning from the centre even though this is clearly vital for the success of most community projects. A commonly heard comment from field staff, and one which echoed the paternalism of some politicians and Winnipeg-based bureaucrats, was "We don't want to give them (i.e., Native People) unrealistic expectations." A literal interpretation of this would be that "We don't want Native People *demanding* an improvement in their way of life."

There were also serious deficiencies in the conceptualization of the way in which Native involvement in the early stages of strategy formulation would be achieved (i.e., by the representation of the Native organizations in the various working groups). Copies of all background documents were in fact forwarded to the organizations and each was promised funding for a planner to work on the strategy. This funding never materialized and, even if it had, it is doubtful that this would have permitted more than merely token involvement by these organizations.

More seriously, this approach presupposed that the interests of the leaders of the organizations and those of the working and underclasses in the communities were the same and, as argued above, this cannot always be assumed to be the case. Thus the organizations tended to be somewhat sceptical of community ownership because this threatened the petty bourgeois aspirations of their leaders. The talk of extending community power also challenged the role that the leadership envisaged their organizations playing, that of taking over administrative responsibilities from state organs. Thus the class interests of the leadership conflicted sharply with some of the basic tenets of the strategy, and especially so since there was no pressure on them from the communities to support the strategy.

From their point of view, therefore, the leaders of the organizations saw a planning exercise being carried out from Winnipeg by a handful of bureaucrats, without their involvement; an exercise which, if successful, would seriously undermine their own class aspirations. For these reasons they opposed it. In November 1975 the MMF and the MIB complained publicly about lack of consultation in the exercise, claiming, quite inaccurately, that they had only just learned of the existence of what they called, pejoratively, "The Great North Plan." The MMF organised a 200-strong march on the Legislative Building and attempted to organize a boycott of classes by children throughout the North. The boycott did not materialize, indicating a failure on the part of the MMF to mobilize support for their position at community level.

From that time on, though, the provincial politicians avoided the organizations and instructed that the strategy be taken directly to community meetings. While the ideas behind the strategy were warmly received at this level, once the hurdle of existension staff had been bypassed, no funds were provided to ensure even a minimal involvement by communities in the exercise. It seems that the objective of holding a limited number of meetings directly with communities was one of diffusing any negative political impact the MMF actions might have had at that level rather than of securing community involvement in planning.

The upshot of all this was that when the strategy proposals were shelved there was no outcry from Native People because they had not identified with the exercise or actively participated in it from the start. Thus while the planners could claim to have demonstrated the enormous range of technical possibilities of convergence in the Northern economy, which had never been done before, they could lay no claim to having made the slightest positive impact on Native struggles in Manitoba. They had failed miserably to mobilize Native People behind the strategy exercise. As one commentator on an earlier draft of this paper wryly observed, "the only people in motion are the planners."

Neither did the planners seek to gain support for the exercise from the urban working class in the North or in the province generally. This was partly because they recognized that the NDP government had made it a point to distance itself from labour in order to reassure capital that its reformism did not threaten property interests in Manitoba. It would, therefore, have been unacceptable for policy advisors to attempt to mobilize support by approaching workers' organizations. It was also partly because the planners never really thought through why workers might be persuaded to support the exercise. After all, the immediate interests of the white proletariat seem so often to be at odds with those of Native People.[24]

As beneficiaries of employment in resource industries, as taxpayers, and as a group with landuse claims that compete to some extent with those of Native People (especially in the area of leisure), the northern white proletariat is often unsympathetic to the demands of Native People. Native People see the white proletariat of the North as being in many respects as colonial as the white bureaucrats, and successful implementation of the strategy would have entailed the wresting of some concessions from white workers (e.g., community enterprises would have replaced some workers in the forestry sector).

This kind of proposal would threaten the interests of white workers, especially since large privately owned resource firms in the province in some instances have seized upon the idea of community projects as a way of reducing their own production costs in terms of

---

24 "Immediate class interests constitute interests within a given structure of social relations; fundamental interests centre on interests which call into questions the structure of social relations itself." See E.O. Wright, *Class, Crisis and the State*, 88.

union labour and overhead. This emphasizes the reserve-army role played by Native People and points to the need for close cooperation between Native communities and labour unions with community employees, perhaps, becoming union members to ensure that community projects do not become a vehicle for raising the rate of exploitation in the North.

The fact is that the white proletariat and most Native People in the North do have a common experience of exploitation by nonresident (mainly U.S.) capital and hence their fundamental interests are not contradictory. Since organized labour in Manitoba is a much more potent political force than are Native organizations, some effort should have been made by the planners to generate support for the exercise among the white proletariat. This would not have been an easy task since, as stated previously, racism is widespread among white workers. But the leadership of northern unions has often been quite progressive and it is instructive that the president of the Manitoba Federation of Labour, himself a former leader of the mineworkers' union in Northern Manitoba, is attempting to link the struggles of Native People and unions. To this end regular meetings are held between the MFL and Native organizations.

For all these reasons, failures of the strategy exercise can be reduced largely to deficiencies of political conceptualization on the part of the planners. By accepting the strictures placed on their activities by the state, the planners failed to mobilize working class support for a strategy premised on such mobilization. In consequence they tended to withdraw into the technicalities of the exercise, producing a development plan totally divorced from, even if entirely sympathetic with, the social struggles of the people it intended to serve and which was, therefore, utopian. As such not only was the exercise bound to fail but to fail without even a murmur of protest from Native People. Yet the exercise was not a total failure. It did, after all, demonstrate the technical possibilities of an alternative, people-centred development strategy for the North and this had never been done before for any similar region in Canada.

The significance of this accomplishment began to be recognized by Native People only after the exercise had been shelved by the state; perhaps it took the rejection of the strategy by the state to convince Native People that it might, after all, be beneficial to them! Whatever the reasons, over the last three years the strategy has attracted a good deal of interest among Native groups in several different parts of Canada.[25] In Manitoba itself, a handful of progressive leaders have attempted to apply convergence principles to both individual reserves and to groups of reserves under the umbrella of a tribal council. Both the MIB and MMF have also expressed interest in the strategy. This shift in their position is the result of sharply deteriorating economic circumstances of Native People in the province due to general economic recession and to deliberate cutbacks in state expenditures. This has led to a more serious and more radicalized leadership being elected, to greater political pressure on the organizations from communities and to a corresponding relative decline in the influence of the state on the positions taken by the MIB and the MMF. They are, of course, still totally dependent upon the state for their finances and in this and many other respects, the organizations have not been transformed, but the heightening of contradictions of capitalism in Manitoba has shifted the political balance to the left and, in the process, has generated not only interest in, but also some support for, the convergence strategy.

This interest and support is still only embryonic, yet it holds out the prospect in the not too distant future of Native People themselves being able to confront both capital and the state in the North with a coherent, clearly articulated and internally consistent alternative development strategy to the profit-oriented resource export strategy which has typified northern development since the fur trade.

If this confrontation is to lead anywhere, Native leaders will need to be able to demonstrate that the bulk of Native People support them. Given the events of 1976–77 there can be little doubt that this support can be generated. More importantly, however, Native leaders will need to mobilize support among the white working class if they are to force major strategic concessions from the state. This will require profound changes in long-held attitudes on both

---

25 Interest in the exercise has been expressed by native groups in Manitoba, Saskatchewan, the Northwest Territories, and Northwest Ontario.

sides, necessitating a political focus on their shared fundamental interests and will be no easy task. Yet the recent initiatives by the leadership of organized labour and Native organizations in meeting to discuss a common response to the increasing politicization of accumulation in Manitoba and to the across-the-board cuts in state social reproduction and maintenance expenditures, seems to indicate that the potential for unity exists. At this stage it really is only a potential since the degree of overt working class opposition to state policies is itself quite minimal, and there is also a real question of the extent to which the position taken by the leadership of organized labour on this issue is consistent with that of the generally more conservative rank and file membership. Nevertheless, the joint meetings are certainly a step in the right direction.

The struggle of Native People for the adoption of a Thomas-type strategy in Northern Manitoba cannot, therefore, be divorced from the general struggle of workers against capital and it would take a pronounced heightening of these general struggles to force the state to depart significantly from its pro-accumulation policies in the North. In the meantime proselytization of the principles underlying the convergence strategy could be a useful means of raising class consciousness among Native People themselves and of generating white working class understanding of the problems facing Native People and the possible means of their solution.

The convergence strategy would appear to be a perfect complement to the various political movements for self-determination and self-government within Confederation among Native People in Canada. This movement is well advanced among the Dene in the Northwest Territories and among the Nishga in British Columbia, and has surfaced recently in Manitoba where its precise specifications are still a little vague.[26] The important point is, however, that Native People are beginning to recognize that their marginality can only be dealt with by capturing a degree of political power which, hitherto, has been denied them.

26 For the Dene see *No Last Frontier—Dene Nation, The Struggle of Canada's Internal Colony for Self-Determination* special issue of *Risk*, World Council of Churches (Geneva, n.d.). In Manitoba the issue of self-determination was raised by one of the candidates for the presidency of the MIB in July 1980.

The economic essence of the political struggles of both the Dene and the Nishga is that they wish to retain ownership of and control over their land. This would be vital for any successful convergence strategy for it would provide control over the resource base and, through it, in theory, enable them to regulate resource extraction industries in such a way as to minimize their negative impacts on the rest of the economy, essentially the renewable resource industries. Mel Watkins has gone so far as to propose that the Dene deliberately create a dual economy in which Native People concentrate on building a modern economy around a renewable base financed by taxing the rents of white-owned and -staffed non-renewable enterprises (Watkins, 1977: 94–9).

Whatever its attractions to the Dene and its practicability in the context of the N.W.T., which remains to be demonstrated in concrete terms, this particular strategy was not an option that presented itself as a politically or economically viable one in Manitoba in 1975–76. Outstanding Indian and Métis land claims were not presented in a way that challenged existing or potential resource industries. Native People were not claiming a share of the rents of these industries as redress for their loss of land or for the destruction of their resources base, except in the case of flooding caused by hydro expansion. At the same time, while the renewable resource base of Northern Manitoba could support a much higher material living standard than it does in terms of both direct production and production for exchange, the northern strategy exercise revealed that it still could not yield a satisfactory living standard for all Native People. This was not seen to be a problem since many Native People in Manitoba do wish to participate in the relatively more highly skilled and more highly paid jobs in the non-renewable industries and clearly should be allowed and encouraged to do so. For these reasons a modified convergence strategy seemed to be more appropriate in this context than a "dual economy" strategy as proposed by Watkins.

The Native People of Manitoba could, however, draw on the Dene example and the Watkins proposal by claiming the rent proportion of the surplus of northern resource industries as compensation for loss of land and destruction of the resource base. This would amount to a political statement about the consequences of their treaties and about the causes of underdevelopment, while presenting a specific proposal for redress around which Native People could mobilize. It would not preclude them from pursuing outstanding land claims but would emphasize the land-grabbing nature of past settlements. A central theme in any such political campaign would be the desirability of Native People freeing themselves, over time, from their financial dependence on the state.

Such an approach would be entirely consistent with a Thomas-type strategy and with struggles for some form of political self-determination within Confederation. All would represent powerful political issues around which Native People might be mobilized, indeed, must be mobilized if their appalling conditions of underdevelopment are ever to be eradicated.

CHAPTER 6

MANITOBA: THE DYNAMICS OF NORTH-SOUTH RELATIONSHIPS[1]

The purpose of this paper is to examine changing perceptions of the North and of North-South relations. It begins by looking at some of the views of the North as presented in the first reports on Northern Manitoba in 1916–18, but I should make it clear from the outset that I am not a historian. To paraphrase the premier, paraphrasing the Bruntland Commission economics is what I do.

1992 was the 80th anniversary of the northern territory being added to Manitoba, when 178,000 square miles (461,000 square km) were brought into the province. This marked the beginning of a profound change in how the region was perceived. To that point in time, the European view from the South was that the North was a "vast stretch of rock, water and muskeg" (Campbell, 1918: 13); "a back door and a closed one at that"; "a barren, inhospitable and practically worthless district"; "an obstacle in the way, one to be overcome in the shortest and most expeditious manner possible" (Wallace and DeLury, 1916: 39); "a hinterland" (Campbell, 1918: 13). By 1917–1918 this perception had changed completely. J.A. Campbell, the first Commissioner of North Manitoba, who was actually based in The Pas, observed that "North Manitoba is now beginning to have a really definite meaning to the people of Canada as a vast territory with immense possibilities just in the initial stages of its development. There exist there natural resources of great richness and variety" (Campbell, 1918: 13).

---

1 From "Manitoba: Dynamics of North-South Relationships," in G. Lithman et. al. (eds), *People and Land in Northern Manitoba*. University of Manitoba, Winnipeg, 1992.

Speaking of the mineral potential of the region, J.B. Tyrell remarked that "The people of Canada have began to realize that there is in Northern Manitoba a great country which is worth exploring and developing for the natural resources which it contains" (Tyrell, 1917: 25).

The North, then, was seen as the key to industrial development in the province as a whole and was referred to in those terms. It was argued that "in order to round off the industrial life of the community, new resources had to be tapped, and that the Northland, in all probability holds the key" (J.R. Wallace, 1918: 50).

The main instrument by which this would be brought about would be the railroad to Churchill, which was expected to do for the North what railroads had done for the South. It was already clear by 1917, therefore, what directions Northern Manitoba would take.

People were talking about mineral deposits and the development, in particular, of copper. They were envisaging forestry development; they were anticipating hydro development and were even specifying the major sites. With a few exceptions, what has followed was more or less predicted at that time, although obviously, the rich variety of mineral deposits was not outlined in any detail.

In addition to this mineral-hydro-forestry development of the North, there was a vision which included agriculture. People were enthusiastic about its prospects. They also had in mind a more balanced, integrated development of the North in which agriculture would play a key role even where the main emphasis was on minerals. As early as 1917, Tyrell speculated that: "If I should be alive twenty years hence and should have the good fortune to be able to revisit this country, which I have watched from its economic birth, I shall confidently expect to see in it towns and villages which will be centres of profitable mining industries and also a prosperous farming community which will not only be raising a food supply adequate for the use of the country itself, but also for export to assist in feeding those who live in cities or districts less favourably situated" (Tyrell, 1917: 25).

So there was this view of the North as an integrated economy, serviced by its own agriculture. There was also an early recognition of the potential of tourism (J.R. Wallace, 1918: 50). Thus, by the end of the First World War, there were already clearly economic visions for the North, some of which have dominated and continue to dominate North-South interactions.

The most striking aspect of this early report on the North's potential, though, was that with the single exception of a reference to the role of an Indian man in discovering a huge deposit of copper, Native People were singularly absent. And, indeed, in describing the North as a "hinterland," there was a suggestion of it being inhabited not only by a sparse population, but perhaps also by an inferior civilization.

The second theme was that as early as 1917–18, the main purpose of developing the North was considered to be resource extraction rather than improving the well-being of people who happened to live there. Implicitly, already, there was a suggestion that development of the North would be for the common good, meaning the good of the society beyond the North, i.e., that it would be driven by imperatives other than the needs of northern Native People.

Thirdly, the state was expected to play a key role in developing the North, focusing at that time, of course, on the railroad. And finally there was an emphasis throughout this report on large-scale production. This was the form that developments were going to take, with important implications for the Native inhabitants. Hendry, writing in 1918, already foresaw the hydro developments on the North River, and argued that such developments would all be large undertakings (Hendry, 1918: 28). People also thought at that time that large industries would move north, out of industrial centres and to the source of hydro energy (p. 28). They also spoke of lumber mills which would rival those of the East, again with an emphasis on large-scale production (Campbell, 1918b)

Some of these themes continue to dominate views of the North today. Production is concentrated on forestry, mineral, and hydro development, and is large scale. Tourism is also well established. We know, however, that the railroad did not lead to the North developing in quite the same way as did the South since economic integration has not developed the way that people thought it might after the First World War. In fact, production in the North is basically for export, while inputs required for production are imported, and profits themselves are exported. The North is, in essence, a classic case of an open economy. It is not an integrated economy, and with the exception of the Pasquia project and a few gardens, the agricultural potential of the North has not been realized.

In more recent times, perspectives on the North have changed somewhat. The 1963 Report of the Committee for Manitoba's Economic Future (COMEF) envisaged the North becoming more integrated with the South (COMEF, 1963).[2] This represented a move away from the idea of integrating northern industries more closely together, towards the goal of integrating northern and southern industries. The emphasis, therefore, was industrial amalgamation in the province as a whole, suggesting that this had not been a feature of past development (p. v-1-2). The explanation for this is that industrial enterprises in the North had been integrated with economies elsewhere through exports.

Native People were certainly not ignored in the COMEF report, which in many respects was a remarkably enlightened document for its time, but the development strategy proposed by the committee led inevitably, in my opinion, to the neglect of the needs of Native People. They saw resource development as the key to economic development, reiterating the theme of Campbell's Report in 1917–18—no effort must be spared to stimulate resource development in Northern Manitoba.

Secondly, they emphasized even more so than in the 1917–18 report the importance of scale. Large-scale production was important for competition and for engaging in trade in the world economy. There were numerous quotes which emphasized this in mining, forestry, and hydro. "The type and scale of investment required for major resource development will require investment by organizations who can manage large resources of technical knowledge, experience and capital...there is little hope for developing such resources to the full except in cooperation with enterprises which operate on a world-wide scale" (p. v-1-2).

A further theme in the COMEF report, absent in the 1917–18 report, was an emphasis on urgency; things had to be done quickly. Why? Because, if resources were not used to the full, they would be

2 COMEF. 1963. *Manitoba 1962–1975*. Report of the Committee on Manitoba's Economic Future. Winnipeg: COMEF.

wasted. "The power resources of Northern Manitoba are a good example of a resource whose potential economic value can be lost if left underdevelopmed too long" (p. v-1-3).

This is a theme which was prevalent in the Schreyer government in the late 1960s and early 1970s. Premier Schreyer was concerned, in particular, that there were huge quantities of free water running away to the sea whose potential was being lost. Hence the province should build large hydro dams. In the COMEF report a similar theme was applied to forestry. "The benefits to be reaped from the early development of what is now a wasting asset in Northern Manitoba offer adequate justification for government intervention" (p. v-3-12). There was, therefore, a feeling that any tree not cut down and made into a paper bag was a wasting asset.

The next theme in the COMEF report was one which obviously was not present in the 1917–18 report, but one that has come to dominate thinking on the North—that the traditional economy could not provide a living for the people of the North and that manufacturing industries were not likely to be established there (p. xi-3-3).

And, finally, once again the state figures prominently in the COMEF report. The State's function was to promote private foreign investment for large-scale industrialization and it would make things happen in the North because without state intervention the private sector would not participate.

Putting all these themes together, it follows logically that the COMEF report would recommend an economic strategy of integration for Native People. Native People ought to be made "productive" by joining the mainstream of white, urban, industrial society through migration. But also, putting together these various emphases on resource development, scale, urgency, and a contempt for other ways of life, it is not surprising that the goal of integrating Native People into mainstream life has been very difficult to achieve and, in fact, has not been realized.

By the early 1970s there was already widespread scepticism about this particular model of development, although at the same time, there developed a theoretical rationalization for the problems faced by Native People in the North. This rationalization, based on theories of dualism, now permeates literature on northern development, particularly the writings of fairly senior civil servants who moved from the province to the federal government, and who had significant influence on shaping economic development policy in Northern Manitoba. This theoretical influence is that not of geographical dualism but economic and social/cultural dualism. This approach argues that alongside a modern industrialized white society, which enjoys the good Canadian life, there is a Native society characterized by drunkenness, an inability to adapt, a lack of reliability, and an inability to participate in industrial society. It posits, therefore, a kind of cultural dualism which becomes racist in its connotations. This is not to say, by the way, that the civil servants I had in mind took it to this extreme, but their type of analysis was in fact carried to that extreme by the 1974 Report on Northern Transportation, which adopted a particularly crude form of dualism (Hickling-Johnston, 1975: Appendix 1, 2).

Dualism came to the fore in the Northern Working-Group Report of 1971, which recommended again, for the North, an emphasis on resource development (*Northern Manitoba—Northern Working Group*, 1971).[3] By this time hydro had become prominent, with mining and forestry continuing to play important secondary roles. There was recognition that the mining sector in particular had failed to integrate Native People—that it had failed to offer them jobs. But there was a view, at the same time, that these two Norths were quite separate, both physically and culturally. This taskforce report argued that "to a very substantial extent the development of the new North had left the old North comparatively untouched" (*Northern Manitoba—Northern Working Group* , 1971).[4]

One can immediately think of large sections of northern society for which this observation is patently not accurate, e.g., the Northern Flood communities, the people of The Pas and Churchill. Nonetheless, the report emphasized this dualism, the inability of Native People to adapt, and argued that the resource base was insufficient for community development, repeating a theme in the COMEF

3 Planning and Priorities Committee of Cabinet, Province of Manitoba. 1971. *Northern Manitoba—Northern Working Group, Internal Working Papers.* June.

4 Planning and Priorities Committee of Cabinet, Province of Manitoba. 1971. *Northern Manitoba—Northern Working Group, Internal Working Papers.* June.

report. The conclusion was again, inevitably, that people should relocate. But the working group did not feel that it was appropriate to continue existing policy, which encouraged the younger people to migrate. They felt that government emphasis should be, instead, on moving whole families.

By the mid-1970s in Manitoba, economic policy had shifted dramatically, at least on paper, with the adoption of the Northern Strategy for Development. This emphasized a commitment to the government's stay option—that, as far as possible, people ought to have the right to stay in their communities. The report attempted to develop a strategy which would converge the northern economy (i.e., one which would use northern resources to create employment and economic activities in the North, and would keep the benefits of resource utilization in communities). The emphasis was on small-scale and participatory approaches to development. The role of the state was still to be an important one, but the scale of its activities was reduced enormously. The state would facilitate, help plan, and subsidize. This policy was never fully implemented for a variety of reasons discussed in Chapter 5.

Contemporary approaches to economic development in the North can be said to be quite ambiguous. The emphasis is still put on resource development for export, particularly hydro, forestry, and mining development, given the Conawapa dam, the Repap project, and planned expansion of the Hudson Bay Mining and Smelting. The ambivalence flows from the continued view of a lack of alternative projects for small and Native communities.

The state plays a major role in promoting large investments and continues to do so in a variety of ways through direct investment, privatization at giveaway prices, and subsidization. But the state is also, now, much involved in smaller communities that rely on its assistance for welfare, job creation, infrastructure, local government, health care, etc., in some of which fields there have been improvements in recent years. The largest employer in these communities is, in fact, the state. What has not improved is the economic base, and so the ability to sustain these economies through their own taxes and incomes is simply not there. Most effectively remain, therefore, wards of the state. They do not own or even participate significantly in the massive resource projects of the North, although they are frequently adversely affected by them.

The current approach to development in the North is a reflection of how society at large lives in Canada, and indeed, in the industrialized world. There is an emphasis on limitless growth, and here I would disagree with the introductory remarks of the premier. The Bruntland Commission report contains some major flaws—the main one being that it assumes that continued growth and sustainability are compatible and that environmental effects of growth can be managed.

Secondly, our society has a throwaway mentality. We even throw away whole towns (e.g., Lynn Lake); once we are done with it, we depose of it. There is no attempt to think in creative terms how society might manage such single-resource towns beyond the life of the resource base. Thirdly, in a related point, resource development continues to be emphasized at the expense of community development. Fourthly, we accept consumption patterns as they are and we base our economic development on the notion that consumption growth is limitless. So, for instance, Manitoba is putting several billion dollars into the Limestone and Conawapa projects without thinking of how we might, for instance, reduce our consumption of hydro. It may well be that the many billions of dollars going into all the projects might be better spent reducing the national consumption of energy.

Finally, there is an assumption that pollution is a necessary price for meeting consumption needs (e.g., the notion that, in the case of the Repap project, bleaching paper is a good thing to do and it needs to be done). So, the problems that Native northerners face come partly from this general approach to development.

An alternative approach is needed, urgently, which would have entirely different implications for the people of both the North and the South. Such an approach would attempt to put people and the environment first, reduce scale, emphasize quality rather than quantity; it might even emphasize part-time work as opposed to full-time work, and it would emphasize conserving versus using resources.

This approach would not value the North only as a limitless deposit of resources. Indeed, it would have a different perception of resources. For instance, it would not automatically assume that resources are wasted if they are not dug out of the ground or chopped down. In this respect, it seems that new technologies might open up new possibilities for the North. These new technologies emphasize small-scale production and economy of scope, as opposed to economy of scale. They minimize transportation as a problem; they overcome remoteness as a problem.

These new technologies can be applied on a small scale and they are portable. There is, therefore, the possibility that the widespread adoption of these technologies in the North might open up new ways of living that do not threaten the environment and do not undermine or threaten the attachment that people still have to traditional ways of life. Whether or not this will happen, of course, will depend partly upon whether or not state policy can be adapted to move away from its emphasis on large-scale resource-based development and begin looking at more flexible and creative ways of meeting people's needs in the North.

RETROSPECTIVE ON CHAPTERS 5 AND 6

In reflecting on the Northern Plan exercise, issues of theory and empirical validity need some revisiting. To begin with, as acknowledged in Chapter 2, gender concerns needed to have been integrated into the social theory of the North and into the convergence approach. This was accomplished admirably in the contribution by Hari Dimitrakopoulou (1993) to the Northern Manitoba Economic Development Commission on women and sustainable development. Dimitrakopoulou drew heavily on the Northern Plan strategy and argued that "women not only want a strategy focussed on their needs, they are ready, willing, and able to identify exactly what needs to be done and how it can be done" (115).[1] Her review of women's participation in the northern economy is very comprehensive and there has been nothing like it since. Her use of the Northern Plan stands in stark contrast to the position of the commission as a whole, which was not to mention it at all! (see Northern Manitoba Economic Development Commission, 1992: 62–63).

In his influential book on the Micmac economy in Nova Scotia, Fred Wien (1986) commented on both the theoretical basis of my Northern Plan article as well as on its relevance for the Micmac. Wien cautioned about drawing too close parallels between conditions in Aboriginal communities and those in parts of the third world, because Aboriginal communities are surrounded by wealthy communities and the colonizers dominate. The reserves are merely remnants of a large land theft (113). The application of Marxist dependency theory and of a convergence strategy to the Micmac is

[1] Dimitrakopoulou also draws heavily on the typology of possible economic development strategies outlined in Chapter 2.

limited by their small and scattered numbers, by the absence of a bourgeoisie, and the dominance of public sector employment.

In reviewing various theoretical approaches to explaining Aboriginal economic development, Doug McArthur (1989) was quite critical of some of the formulations in "The Great Northern Plan" paper. Primarily, he felt that I'd confused surplus value, profits from exploiting labour, with resource rents and that Aboriginal People are hardly exploited in the Marxist sense since they hardly fit into the industrial wage model. They do not constitute an important element in the reserve army of labour, and the "formulation of new classes and new modes of production is largely a sterile effort in classification rather than explanation" (16). The relevance of the class structure of a typical First Nation community identified in that paper, in which some classes are immune from Marxian "exploitation," would be clearer if the analysis were placed within a contemporary framework (14).

There is much in McArthur's paper to commend it and, regrettably, it appears the paper was never published. On reflection, however, his critiques of the Northern Plan paper are not altogether valid. The estimates of surplus contained therein were exactly that: of surplus, not surplus value. They included Hydro rents, among others. The point being made was that lack of capital generated in the region could not explain Aboriginal poverty. The overall context here was theft of Aboriginal lands and lack of control of natural resources. The growing political influence of Aboriginal People in the North, the assertion of their land rights and their ability to threaten export sales to the U.S., has led to a major shift in the relation of Aboriginal People to the generation and use of surplus by Manitoba Hydro, as will be outlined below. This has been facilitated by the Provincial government being more representative of Aboriginal People and more sympathetic to their concerns.

The attempt in the Northern Plan paper to identify various classes on reserves was meant to dispel the myth of their homogeneity and to demonstrate their social complexity. This in turn reflects to some degree the articulation of various modes of production which continue to influence Aboriginal life. As such, it was, at the time, "contemporary" and, to some degree, probably remains so.

Yet the North has changed significantly in many respects over the past thirty years and there have been corresponding changes in the social structure of Aboriginal communities. These communities have much larger populations, in spite of migration to the cities, much higher aggregate incomes and employment, and much more responsibility for their governance and delivery of social services than they had. They have their own northern political organization and their own tribal councils. Aboriginal People are heavily involved in health and education services and, with the devolution of child welfare as a result of the Aboriginal Justice Inquiry in 1991, in the delivery of child welfare services. Levels of education and the number of people receiving education have both increased significantly. There is now a full university in the North with significant Aboriginal input. Communications have improved for many communities and all but a handful have hydro line service. The level of economic activity in the North, especially in the service sectors, is much higher now and some communities, such as Opaskwayak First Nation at The Pas, Split Lake, Norway House, and Nelson House have been highly successful in promoting community and business development.

At the same time, the North remains essentially a resource economy, subject to all the vicissitudes and trends of resource economies generally. This includes plant closures in mining towns such as Leaf Rapids; pulp mill closures, as in The Pas and Pine Falls; huge commodity price fluctuations and the long-term dispensing of labour. Thus, between 1986 and 2006, the number of people employed in the primary sector of the North fell from 4,820 to 3,295, or by almost a third. The North remains a staple economy and the linkages within the economy are few and far between (Freylejer, 2009).

The North also shows many of the signs of deprivation that were present thirty years ago. Average incomes and levels of educational achievement in the non-industrial towns remain well below those elsewhere. Levels of poverty, housing deprivation, and the incidence of TB, HIV/AIDS, diabetes, infectious diseases, suicides, violent deaths, and incarceration remain much higher (Hallet, 2006).

Perhaps the biggest single economic shift in the North is that concerning Hydro. Hydro's abysmal historical record (Waldram, 1988) to this day has negative effects on Northern communities. The Northern Flood Agreement of 1977 did provide some compensation to communities, in the form of cash and land, to offset the damage done to their livelihoods and their living environment and sacred sites. Four of the five communities involved (Split Lake, Norway House, Nelson House, and York Landing) signed the NFA, with Cross Lake holding out as late as 2010. Thus Nisichawayasikh Cree Nation, based in Nelson House, received $118 million in compensation from Canada, Manitoba, and Hydro; 55,000 acres or 17 acres for each one flooded (Primrose and Thomas, 2005: 6). These payments represented compensation for damage done without the consent of Aboriginal People by Hydro projects over which they had no control and from which they derived few if any employment or income benefits. As an approach to northern development, therefore, "flood first and discuss later" was highly problematic and very much opposed by Aboriginal People. It was also very expensive for Aboriginal communities and for Manitoba Hydro in terms of payments to lawyers and consultants.

A number of factors have combined in recent years to lead to a significant shift in Manitoba Hydro's approach to northern development. The first of these is that the negotiations around the NFA helped politicize Aboriginal resistance to Hydro, making it clear that future projects would require Aboriginal consent before they could proceed. Secondly, the presence of Aboriginal MLAs in the NDP government and the importance of northern seats for the NDP also helped shift the approach to northern development. Thirdly, Manitoba Hydro's shift in emphasis towards exports to the U.S. have forced it to accommodate powerful U.S. environmental and Aboriginal lobbies which insist on a changed approach. Their ability to obstruct state legislative approval for Hydro purchases have given greater prominence to Northern Manitoba Aboriginal concerns. For instance, the Potowatamin Band in Wisconsin has huge casino revenues and has thrown its support behind Manitoba First Nations insisting that their concerns be met before the state approves long-tern hydro purchases. Prompted by these developments, there has generally been a sea change in how both Hydro and the Manitoba government wish to proceed with northern hydro development.

The Limestone Project, completed in 1992, marked a significant departure from past practice by providing training to northern Aboriginal People and by providing business opportunities for them also. But more recent projects, Wuskwatim and Keeyask, go well beyond that and create a completely new model for hydro development in the North. They offer part ownership of the hydro projects to local First Nations, involvement in planning the projects and employment and procurement opportunities. Thus, the Wuskwatim project of 200 megawatts, to be completed in 2011, will be a joint venture of Manitoba Hydro with the Nisichawayasikh Cree Nation (NCN), whose members reside on three neighbouring reserves, Southern Indian Lake, Nelson House, and Nelson House B. The NCN will be able to purchase up to one-third of the $1.6 billion project and has already had an impact on environmental planning around the project (Freylejer, 2009). Peak total employment was around 1,000 and 44% of people hired to work on the dam have been Aboriginal (Manitoba Hydro, 2010: 24).

In addition to the NCN agreement, Hydro also entered business agreements with five other First Nations, the Manitoba Métis Federation, and the Manitoba Keewatinook Ininew Okimowin (MKO, a northern tribal council) to "benefit other First Nations not directly affected by this project" (Freylejer, 2009: 25).

Apart from Aboriginal employment and procurement preferences, training opportunities for skilled jobs are also offered through the $60 million Hydro Northern Training Initiative (HNTI), which is funded by Hydro, the province, and the federal government. This is, in turn, managed by the Wuskwatim and Keeyask Training Consortium (WKTC), whose northern Aboriginal partners are Nisichawayasihk Cree Nation, Tataskweyak Cree Nation, War Lake First Nation, Fox Lake Cree Nation, and York Factory First Nation, MKO, and the Manitoba Métis Federation Inc. Aboriginal People trained under this program would have skills which would be transferable to non-hydro projects. But they would also qualify for employment on other large hydro projects which are planned for the future. And this is where the new approach by Manitoba Hydro and the provincial government offers unprecedented employment and economic development opportunities for the next ten to fifteen years. The 695-megawatt Keeyask generating station is already under way and four Cree First Nations will have the option to buy 25% of the project, scheduled to be completed after 2018. The even larger 1,485-megawatt Conawapa station is in the planning stages, with five adjacent First Nations being involved. This would be completed some time after 2022. These projects offer reasonably firm long-term economic development possibilities in which northern Aboriginal People will not only have a say but through which they stand to gain skills training, long-term jobs, unique opportunities to supply goods, and a share in the long-term revenues of massive hydro projects. The contrast between the approach of Manitoba Hydro to northern development in the 1970s and the contemporary one could not be more striking. Current Hydro policy contains several features that could be described as being consistent with a convergence approach: involvement of local people in planning, some local ownership (although the source and terms of Aboriginal financing remains to be determined), local employment, local purchasing opportunities through Aboriginal preference, and retention of some of the surplus.

This is not to say that the approach of Hydro does not have its detractors. Kulchyski (2004a and b) has expressed concerns about the nature of the consultation processes involved, the types of jobs Aboriginal People are likely to end up with, and the risk to which communities might be exposed. He argues that ownership is risky and that dams undermine the potential for the building of a modern economy based on hunting. He cites the Peace of the Brave Treaty between the Cree of James Bay and the Quebec government as a preferred alternative approach. This guarantees land, supports traditional hunting, and also promises jobs and supply contracts for Cree businesses in new hydro developments, without joint ownership. Hultin (2004) argues that at the community level there are environmental concerns about the dams, their impact on traditional livelihoods and the likely debt burdens involved. These are all concerns that must be taken seriously and given the awful history of hydro development in the North, scepticism is both understandable and inevitable. But these arguments against Aboriginal joint ownership of hydro projects have been vociferously denounced by

Aboriginal leadership. Thus, Chief Jerry Primrose and Councillor Elvis Thomas of NCN have rejected Kulchyski's arguments, seeing their involvement in the Wuskwatim project as being consistent with exercising "sovereignty that sustains a prosperous socio-economic future" (Primrose and Thomas, 2005: 7). They also argue that the Peace of the Brave Treaty flooded an area almost 1,700 times larger than the likely Wuskwatim damage (less than 0.5 square kilometres) and therefore, called for a different approach, suggesting that NCN would not be able to negotiate the kind of deal open to the James Bay Cree. They accuse Kulchyski of being demeaning and paternalistic in suggesting that they are incapable of negotiating properly for themselves and deny that hunting and trapping can provide a modern lifestyle for many in their communities (ibid. 6–7). This debate was an important one but ultimately, it is Aboriginal People themselves who must make the decisions and in this case, joint ownership of hydroelectric facilities is their preferred option and does represent *a new* approach to northern development.

Nelson House or the Nisichawayasihk Cree Nation demonstrates how community-based economic development initiatives can be combined productively with both flood compensation funds and recent development agreements with Manitoba Hydro. The community used flood compensation to establish the NCN Development Corporation which in turn has set up a building supplies store, a construction company, a door and cabinet company, a window and frame company, a gas station, restaurant, radio and TV station, and a laundry. The construction company and laundry are joint ventures designed to supply Wuskwatim. NCN's unique Atoskiwin Training and Employment Centre of Excellence (ATEC), a 27,000 sq. ft. fully accredited, non-profit, community-based post-secondary training facility, has also played an important role in training community members to work on the dam project, in heavy equipment and trades. It also offers training in a wide range of areas of importance to the community (finance, business, health care, lifeskills, etc.) (Nisichawayasihk Cree Nation, 2010a). An unusual feature of these developments is the use by the community of franchises with other northern communities. Thus NCN sells franchises for the building supplies company, providing technical support, and it purchased a franchise from a Saskatchewan First Nation for the window/window frame company.

Other interesting aspects of the use of Hydro compensation by NCN was its purchase of the Mystery Lake Hotel in Thompson, 75 kilometres away, which now hires NCN members. NCN's construction company has also built houses in Thompson commercially. Its laundry partnership is located there and it has purchased land around the hotel which it plans to convert into an urban reserve (Nisichawayasikh Cree Nation, 2010b).

Annual earnings on the trust funds are allocated partly to the equity purchase of Wuskwatim but also to a variety of social purposes, including support to the elderly. They are used to finance a Country Food Program which promotes traditional ways of life by encouraging the harvesting of wildlife, fish, and berries, and community gardens. The food is distributed to those in need. The community has a camp in which members are trained in how to process meats and hides in the traditional way, and in equipment maintenance and safety. The trusts also provide subsidies for hunters and trappers. Hydro funds have been used, therefore, for a blend of modern and traditional ways of life and for the retention and strengthening of Cree culture (Nisichawayasikh Cree Nation, 2010c).

Only a handful of northern communities will benefit from Hydro's new approach and not all of these are likely to have the ability to take full advantage of it as NCN appears to have done. But the accomplishments of NCN demonstrate that with financial support, there are numerous economic development projects that can offer community members opportunities for a fuller and better life.

"The Dynamics of North-South Relations" reflected on the possibilities that new technologies might offer the North. Twelve years later, Duboff (2004) reported that 11% of northern communities did not have Internet access, that only three First Nations had high-speed satellite access and the rest had unreliable and highly problematical dial-up connections. Yet the demand for Internet services for health, education, community planning, and business development, employment and training services, purchasing of supplies, and finding financing opportunities, is immense (Cook et al., 2004). Since that time, it appears that rapid strides have been taken to rectify the situation.

Broadband Communications North Inc. (BCN), a non-profit community enterprise with input from tribal councils, First Nations, remote communities, and other stakeholders, has made great progress in providing high-speed broadband services and the Internet to rural, northern, and remote communities. Established in 2002, this company now appears to be able to service most northern Aboriginal communities using Manitoba Hydro fibre optic lines, MTS, and satellite infrastructure (BCN, 2010). Not surprisingly, NCN partners with BCN to offer high-speed Internet to homes and businesses in the community.

CHAPTER 7
ABORIGINAL ECONOMIC DEVELOPMENT IN WINNIPEG[1]

BACKGROUND

Although it is difficult to tell with complete accuracy, because of the limitations of the various censuses, it appears that there were remarkably few Aboriginal People living in Winnipeg from 1901 to 1951. In 1901 there appear to have been less than a dozen Indians and only about 700 Métis in the city of 42,340. In 1921 there were 69 Indians counted and by 1951 still only 210 in a city population of 354,000. The Métis were invisible.

In the early 1950s there were already concerns, however, about the living conditions of Aboriginal People in Winnipeg. The Provincial Council of Women noted the sub-standard living conditions of Aboriginal women, and that more than half of all the inmates of Portage La Prairie Jail for women were Métis. But the Welfare Council of Greater Winnipeg, which held the first of 15 Manitoba Indian and Métis Annual Conferences in 1954, concluded "it was seriously handicapped in any attempt to help these people, because very little was known about them" (Welfare Council of Greater Winnipeg, Annual Report, 1954: 1).

That began to change in 1958 with the first definitive study of the Aboriginal population in Manitoba since the 19th century. The Status Indian population of Winnipeg was estimated at 1,200 or 5.4% of the total of 22,077 Status Indians living in Manitoba (Lagasse, 1959: 31–37). Winnipeg's Métis population was estimated at

1 From "Aboriginal Economic Development in Winnipeg" in Jim Silver (ed.), *Solutions that Work: Fighting Poverty in Winnipeg*, Fernwood, Halifax and CCPA, Manitoba, 2000.

3,500, or 14.8% of the total Métis of 23,579 in Manitoba (ibid.: 58–75). The Métis figures were likely understated, perhaps by as much as 80%, since they did not include people of Métis ancestry who had "integrated to the point of not being recognized by their neighbours as Métis" (ibid.: 77). But if taken at face value, Aboriginal people appear to have represented just over 1% of the city's population.

Sample surveys revealed that about a third of Indians interviewed had lived in Winnipeg for less than a year, 58% for less than three. The figures for the Métis were 13% and 20% respectively. As many as 45% of the Métis had lived in Winnipeg for more than 10 years, compared with only 16% for the Indians.

The single most important reason for coming to the city for both groups was to find a job, and 83% of all men and 55% of all women who said they had come for work were actually employed at the time of interview (ibid.: 60). Just over 55% of all Aboriginal people were employed. A third of all Indians employed and 59% of all Métis had been in their job for at least a year, and 11% of Indians and 17% of Métis had been in their job in excess of 10 years. At the time of interview, only 13% of the Indians questioned and 23% of the Métis were receiving social assistance, but about a third had received it over the previous two years. Then, as now, social assistance rates were considered grossly insufficient.

The survey found that the educational performance of Aboriginal children was relatively poor. It identified a number of factors felt to be responsible: perceived cultural superiority on the part of the dominant society from which teachers were drawn; paternalist views of appropriate education for Aboriginal people; poor teachers and facilities; and prominence of religious schools with objectives other than education. A further factor was low attendance rates, felt to be explained by a low value placed on education, given the quality and pessimism about where it might lead in terms of worthwhile employment, discrimination by teachers and other pupils, poor diet, clothing, and housing, lack of school supplies, and the mobility of the head of household (ibid.: 117).

This report was remarkably enlightened for its time. It recommended that a Community Development Program be established by the province to "help people of Indian ancestry solve their own problems" (ibid.: 5). It argued that efforts should be made to take industry and jobs to rural and remote communities, and that systematic training programs be set up for Aboriginal people. It recommended far-reaching reform of the educational system and of social assistance. It argued for low-cost housing and the enforcement of housing standards. It pressed for services to assist people in settling into city life and to help them develop relations of mutual respect with those they were most likely to come into contact with, and face discrimination from—employers, landlords, school administrators, police, etc. It is perhaps no coincidence that the first Indian Métis Friendship Centre in Canada was set up in Winnipeg in 1959 to provide social services to migrants (Fulham, 1981: iii).

While the Manitoba Indian Brotherhood (MIB) had been established in 1946 (Daugherty, 1982, although it traced its origins back to 1871, see MIB, 1971), it had focused almost entirely on the needs of its reserve-based members. Finding an effective means of representing Status Indians in Winnipeg remains problematical to this day. A variety of organizations not affiliated to the MIB or its successor, the Assembly of Manitoba Chiefs, have sought to represent Status Indians and others in the city. In the late 1960s the Winnipeg Indian Council was very active (Damas and Smith, 1975: 11), to be replaced by the Winnipeg Council of Treaty and Status Indians and the Urban Indian Association, which amalgamated to form the Aboriginal Council of Winnipeg in 1990 (Aboriginal Council: 1993). The creation of the Manitoba Indian Women's Association (MIWA) in 1969 was another indication that Aboriginal people were beginning to replace well-meaning non-Aboriginal support groups in addressing pressing economic and social concerns, but it complained of being hampered by lack of funding (MIWA: 1973). The Manitoba Métis Federation was set up at this time too (1968), but the importance of having a representative structure in Winnipeg *was* recognized, and the city became one of six regions, each of which had a seat on the board (Sawchuk, 1978: 48). The prime concern of the Métis was, from the beginning, that of solving the acute housing problems faced by the community in Winnipeg, a problem which grew increasingly as population grew.

Most of the growth in the Aboriginal population in Winnipeg occurred after 1958, and that growth has been rapid. From 1958 to 1979, the number of Status Indians resident in Winnipeg rose almost fivefold to about 6,900, while the number of Métis and Non-Status Indians had risen more than threefold to 12,900 (Clatworthy, 1983a: 14). The total Aboriginal population in Winnipeg had grown, therefore, at over 7% per annum, to approximately 20,000 or 3.6% of the total population by 1979. (These numbers must be taken to be rough orders of magnitude only, given definitional problems and differences between the two periods.) Economically and socially, the community remained relatively deprived (Social Planning Council of Winnipeg, 1982; Stevens, 1982).

Our knowledge of the living conditions of Aboriginal people in Winnipeg in the early 1980s is substantial, due mainly to a number of excellent reports by Stewart Clatworthy (1981 a, b and c; 1983 a and b.). He found that migration into the City was proceeding rapidly, though more slowly than previously thought. The main reason for migration among males was economic and among women, social. Aboriginal families were much younger than average and the proportion of single parent families much higher. Unemployment among Aboriginal people was found to be more than five times that of others, and employment more irregular. Aboriginal household incomes were found to be only half those of the average urban household and most Aboriginal families were found to be dependent on transfers, mostly social assistance payments. Aboriginal families were four times more likely than others to suffer a combination of shelter poverty, poor housing, and overcrowding, and were highly mobile within the city.

ABORIGINAL DEMOGRAPHICS IN WINNIPEG IN THE 1990S

The 1991 census indicates that there were 44,970 Aboriginal people in Winnipeg: 6.9% of the total population of the city and 39% of the total Aboriginal population of Manitoba. By 1996 their number had risen to 52,500 or to about 8% of the total population. There were 2,660 more Aboriginal females in the City than males, an excess of 11%. This imbalance was greatest in the over-15 category where there were almost 2,800 or 18% more women than men. This imbalance reflects different motivations for migration between men and women. The latter leave rural communities for the city not only for better economic and social opportunities, but also to avoid social problems (Clatworthy: 1981b) including, presumably, violence.

The age composition of the Aboriginal population is quite different from Winnipeg as a whole. There is a much higher proportion of children in the Aboriginal population, with over 35% being 14 or under compared with only 20% for the city as a whole, and 13.5% being under four compared with only 7% in the broader population. Second, a significantly higher proportion of Aboriginal people are in the young working age category, 15–24, than is the case in the city as a whole; 18.4% versus 15.1% respectively. And third, there are a significantly lower proportion of people over 55 in the Aboriginal community, 5.9% versus 20.7% in the city at large. These demographic characteristics suggest that policy might need to look carefully at the educational needs of the community and the special problems Aboriginal youth might face in entering the job market. They also suggest that childcare needs are likely to be particularly salient in the Aboriginal community.

A comparison of the 1996 census figures with those of 1991 suggests that the Aboriginal population of Winnipeg has grown at a rate of 3.15% per annum, well in excess of the growth rate of the total population of the city, which was only 0.25% p.a. The Aboriginal population of Winnipeg also grew at a faster rate than that of Manitoba as a whole, suggesting that migration into the City has continued apace.

The 1996 census found that 13% of Aboriginal People had moved into Winnipeg within the previous five years. Perhaps even more important for social policy purposes, 45% of Aboriginal People had moved residence within Winnipeg during that time. This is consistent with a small survey of 144 inner city residents (84% Aboriginal) conducted for this study in 1993 (Loxley, 1996). This found a very high rate of mobility within Winnipeg, but suggested a much lower, though still high, rate of migration. Thus, 54% of Aboriginal People had lived at their current address for less than one year, while 10% had moved to Winnipeg in the past year. While 29% had moved into the city in the past five years, 58% of Aboriginal respondents had lived in Winnipeg for over 10 years. This suggests that population growth from migration is well in excess of natural growth and that this will have serious implications for the employment, housing, and service needs of Aboriginal People. It also suggests that the Aboriginal population is very transient within Winnipeg. This might have implications for the type of economic development strategies that are feasible for the community, perhaps making it difficult for neighbourhood-focused strategies, unless they are accompanied by efforts to stabilize the population.

EMPLOYMENT AND INCOMES

The 1991 Aboriginal Peoples Survey (APS)[2] reports that the participation rate of Aboriginal People in Winnipeg was 53.9% and the unemployment rate was 27.3% (Statistics Canada, 1993). By 1996, the participation rate had risen to 62% and the unemployment rate had fallen to 21%. While this suggests some progress has been made, these numbers are significantly worse than for those of Winnipeggers as a whole, which were 67% and 8% and go a long way in explaining urban Aboriginal poverty. They suggest that 59% of all Aboriginal adults in the city were without work in 1996.

Why are so few urban Aboriginal People in formal employment? This question has been examined for Manitoba by a number of writers (Clatworthy, 1981a, b and c; Falconer, 1985; Hull, 1984, 1991) and their explanations are remarkably similar to those advanced in other parts of Canada (Wien, 1986). Low participation rates and high unemployment rates are a result of Aboriginal People having much lower levels of education than the average in Winnipeg. Three-quarters of the Aboriginal population had less than Grade 11 education, the minimum level at which education has a significant impact on participation and employment rates. Aboriginal People also lack suitable training and have, in the past, not been captured by government training programs. Difficulties of gaining work experience are self-reinforcing, as employers usually demand experience.

2 The APS counted Aboriginal people on the narrower basis of self-identification, rather than ancestry or ethnic origin, on which the 1991 census was based.

Many employers are prejudiced against hiring Aboriginal people, as stereotyping and racism are widespread. Aboriginal People often do not have access to information about available job opportunities and are not plugged into networks where such information is readily available.

The high frequency of single mothers presents special problems. Childcare facilities are hopelessly deficient, and not just for Aboriginal children. The low-skill, low-entry jobs for which the majority of mothers might qualify pay wages so low that there is no incentive to leave social assistance, however inadequate it might be. Social assistance is at least reasonably predictable and allows the mother to spend time with her children; it therefore reduces some risks faced by single mothers. After some time living in poverty, however, it becomes increasingly difficult to break into the labour market because entrenched lifestyles are very difficult to change. And employers tend to look unfavourably at absence from the "formal" labour force.

Aboriginal culture is not, generally, seen as an obstacle to labour force participation. With time for adjustment and a supporting work environment, preferably one in which other Aboriginal people are present, Aboriginal People can and do fit quite readily into new work environments. But time and support are often not made available. Finally, Aboriginal People often find themselves competing for the same kind of limited job opportunities.

Reflecting the lower participation rates and higher unemployment rates which are the outcome of these circumstances, only 56% of Aboriginal adults reported employment income in 1996 compared with 67% in the population as a whole while 8.9% reported incomes of zero, compared with 5.4% in the population as a whole. Of those who earned incomes, 23% reported incomes of less than $5,000 per annum, compared with 14% in the city as a whole. Only 28% of Aboriginal adults reported total income in excess of $20,000, compared with 46% in the total population. A much lower proportion of Aboriginal women earned over $20,000, 22%, than did non-Aboriginal females (35.8%) or Aboriginal males (35%).

A major reason for the lower average levels of employment income among Aboriginal People is their concentration in relatively low-paying unskilled or semi-skilled jobs. Thus, the 1996 census indicated that, of the 16,640 Aboriginal People in Winnipeg over the age of 14 who had worked in 1996, 58% occupied clerical, non-supervisory sales and service or unskilled manual jobs compared with 45% of the population generally. Many of these positions are not unionized (Hull, 1991). While about 36% of Aboriginal employees occupied skilled, supervisory, professional, or managerial positions, the rate was 51% for the population generally. Furthermore, there was a higher proportion of females among the Aboriginal People employed (48.8%) than in the workforce generally (47.4%) and apart from being disproportionately represented in clerical and service jobs, there is an acknowledged tendency for females to receive less than males even in the same job. Three other possibilities are that Aboriginal People have less experience and have higher turnover rates and occupy more part-time positions than the average, but we have no evidence to confirm or reject these hypotheses. What we do know from earlier studies is that many Aboriginal People "hold jobs only on a periodic basis" (Falconer, 1985: 75), that there is no evidence of "significant upward occupational mobility" (Clatworthy, 1983a: 42), and that length of time in the city did not improve the chances of success in the labour market (Clatworthy, 1983b). Each of these propositions needs to be reinvestigated, however, in the light of the rapid growth of the Aboriginal labour force in recent years and, more importantly, in the light of what appears to be a significant increase in Aboriginal employment since 1986 (see Section VIII).

Just under a third (31%) of all Aboriginal adults reported reliance on social assistance payments in 1990, compared with 6.3% in Winnipeg as a whole (Social Planning Council, 1992), and two-thirds of these reported that such reliance lasted in excess of six months of the year. These rates of dependence on government transfers are extremely low compared with those found by Clatworthy (1981a) a decade earlier, which were in the 70–78% range. Clatworthy's figures included all types of transfers, but welfare dependence alone was more than double that reported in the APS. In our own survey of inner city households in 1993, 67% of Aboriginal respondents reported that welfare was their main source of household income, compared with 44% for the non-Aboriginal community. Unemployment Insurance was the main source for a further 7%.

The net result is that the incidence of poverty among the Aboriginal population of Winnipeg is much higher than the average (Luzubski, Silver, and Black, 2000).

The Aboriginal community is not, however, accepting of its poverty. Thus, only 13% of Aboriginal families report a monthly reliance on food banks, suggesting a discriminating use of these facilities. More importantly, the APS reports that well over half of those without jobs in 1990–91, and more than double the number formally unemployed, reported looking for work, while 18% of adults reported being involved in other activities for which they were paid money. Among those looking for work but not finding it, the most frequently cited reasons were that there were few or no jobs available (33%) or that their education or experience did not fit the jobs available (27%). An additional reason given (18%) was that there was not enough information about jobs which were available.

These findings by the APS are echoed in our own survey of the inner city mentioned earlier. This found that 72% of Aboriginal respondents want full-time work and 53% would take part-time work. Only 7% had a steady job (only 4% of Aboriginal women) but 42% expected to obtain one. Indeed, the survey found that a higher proportion of Aboriginal people wanted work than non-Aboriginal People (66%). A greater proportion of non-Aboriginal residents of the inner city, however, already had employment (38%). This demonstrates that even within the poorest neighbourhoods in the city, Aboriginal People fare much worse than others in terms of employment and that this has little to do with Aboriginal aspirations.

The reasons advanced in the survey for difficulty in finding work echoed those in the APS with one important difference; lack of childcare was given much more weight by respondents to our survey, with 26% seeing this as a major obstacle to their finding employment, compared with only 4.7% in the APS. This may reflect the preponderance of women in our survey (75%). Over 60% of both female and male respondents reported that they did not have any special problems holding jobs or looking for work.

Not only do Aboriginal residents aspire to paid employment and actively seek it out, they also engage in a wide range of economic activities best described as self-employment and direct production. Under the heading of self-employment, some 17% of people surveyed in the inner city make arts or crafts in the home for sale or engage in auto or electrical repair, while 35% provide services for sale, such as home childcare, cleaning, carpentry, etc. It is also apparent from the survey that Aboriginal people spend much more of their labour time producing goods for direct consumption (i.e., for consumption by them or their families) than they do working in either the formal or market-based informal economy (i.e., working for wages or in self-employment). The biggest absorber of time was childcare and supervision, followed by cooking, sewing/knitting, house cleaning, dish washing, laundry, and shopping.

The Aboriginal community is not homogeneous. Some 10% of the male population and 3% of the female population earn over $40,000 p.a.; some 1,300 now own their own business, while in the inner city survey, 24% report that they have a business idea they are working on. In 1996 there were over 4,100 Aboriginal People in the city occupying supervisory, semi-professional, professional, and managerial positions, and 51% of these were women.

A balanced view of the Aboriginal community must recognize, therefore, not just the prevalence of poverty, but also a desire to secure paid employment, both part-time and full-time, an active participation by many in informal sector activities, an unusually heavy workload in terms of household labour, contingent upon family size, and a diversified community in which many Aboriginal people are employed in reasonably well paying jobs and in business or, at least, have aspirations to enter business.

INSTITUTIONAL STRUCTURE AND CAPACITY
FOR ECONOMIC DEVELOPMENT

The three principal Aboriginal political organizations in Winnipeg are the Assembly of Manitoba Chiefs (AMC), the Manitoba Métis Federation (MMF), and the Aboriginal Council of Winnipeg (ACW). The first two are province-wide bodies headquartered in Winnipeg. The ACW was established in 1990, a product of the amalgamation of the Winnipeg Council of Treaty and Status Indians, which represented Status Indians, and the Urban Indian Association, which represented Status Indians, Non-Status Indians, and Métis.

Of these organizations, only the MMF has developed an institutional capacity for economic planning and development, backed up with financial resources. The Federation established the Manitoba Métis Community Investments Inc. (MMCII) in 1984 to undertake economic development initiatives essentially in rural Métis communities. In January 1991, the MMF established the Louis Riel Capital Corporation. It is capitalized at $7.6 million and has an annual operating budget of $0.27 million, employs three staff, two of whom are Métis. To date it has advanced $1.5 million in a range of economic sectors, from agriculture to retail. While none of the loans has so far been advanced in Winnipeg, there are no constraints on its ability to lend there except the viability of borrowers. The MMCII has also established the Métis Construction Company and an office/warehouse complex in Winnipeg. In 1998, the MMF–Winnipeg Region established the Winnipeg Métis Development Corporation to help Winnipeg Métis establish small businesses, initially by providing micro-lending.

The MMF, therefore, has a pool of capital, some economic and financial expertise and some office, storage, and construction capacity. While these resources are minimal and quite inadequate for a frontal assault on Métis and Non-Status economic problems, they constitute a base from which to start. The other political organs have no such base.

The Assembly of Manitoba Chiefs has no capital corporation, and only a tenuous attachment to a single position for an economic advisor. It suffered the elimination by the Filmon government of its core funding from the province, while the federal government first cut back and later abolished its Regional Opportunities Program (ROP), from which the economic advisor was financed.

The Chiefs have proposed the creation of a First Nations Economic Development Advisory Council, consisting of representatives of Tribal Councils, unaffiliated reserves, urban Indian organizations, and women's groups. Assisted by a small technical secretariat, the Council would operate at arm's length from the AMC and would be responsible for developing and advising on economic development policy. In this way the Chiefs, as politicians, would retain some distance from the technical aspects of development, while the Advisory Council would service the broad needs of the community for economic development and not merely be a creature of the federal government.

The refusal of the federal government to make resources available to the AMC for this purpose suggests the government is not really interested in developing the capacity of the First Nations Indian community to shape their own economic development agenda. Rather, the government has a narrow preoccupation with involving First Nations organizations in its economic programs, but on its terms, and in a purely advisory capacity. The Chiefs are concerned about being co-opted into structures which duplicate their own and over which they have little control, and about being seen by their constituencies as being party to decisions which may often be unpopular. The end result is a stalemate. The situation remains one in which the Status Indians have no central economic development institutions and no source of capital over which they have control.

Once they leave the reserve, Status Indians find themselves in an ambiguous position. Since the federal government does not accept the principle of portability of treaty rights, and since bands have no incentive to transfer funds to urban areas to provide services to migrants, their own funding being hopelessly inadequate, urban Indians find themselves in a netherworld. They have no obvious representation and by and large, the AMC has not, until recently, directed its attention to their predicament because it does not have the resources to do so. Yet there are some urban Status Indians who believe that the tribal council approach is not the way to further their interests and these have tended to throw their support behind the Aboriginal Council.

The Aboriginal Council has the backing of numerous Aboriginal institutions in Winnipeg and of some very prominent urban Aboriginal activists, Status, Non-Status, and Métis alike. Its position is that Aboriginal people should have the right to self-determination regardless of place of residence. In those urban neighbourhoods where Aboriginal people are a majority, they might exercise a degree of territorial jurisdiction. Otherwise, since urban Aboriginal People have no land base, they will have to exercise jurisdiction through the development of self-determining institutions. ACW believes that "status blind" institutions would best serve the interests of urban Aboriginal people, to deliver services regardless of legal distinctions between Aboriginal People (Aboriginal Council, 1992), but at the same time is careful to point out that it does not believe in a "melting pot" approach to urbanization. Rather, it respects the diversity of the different groups and believes in the portability of treaty rights.

The Council also suffers from a lack of resources, receiving only $45,000 in core funding from the province. It has no in-house economic development capacity, but it does have a huge volunteer base and close ties with numerous inner city Aboriginal organizations, and it draws on these to leverage resources from government agencies for specific development projects.

A number of non-urban Tribal Councils have their headquarters physically located in Winnipeg (though legally based on reserves for tax reasons). The largest and most significant of these is the Southeast Resource Development Council, Inc., which represents nine bands in southeastern Manitoba. This Council owns two extremely profitable buildings, a parking lot, and a junior hockey team in the city. It also provides significant educational supports in Winnipeg for students coming into the city. It has an economic development capacity through its Economic Development Division, which employs seven staff, four of whom are Aboriginal, but this focuses entirely on community development on the reserves. Southeast has, however, discussed plans to set up a fast food outlet in the centre of the city and has, in the past, discussed establishing a travel agency and a cheque-cashing facility. The council has a number of economic ventures designed to service its reserve members, such as a building supply store, an electrical contractor, and an airline, but all of these are based outside of Winnipeg.

Aboriginal women have felt the need for their own political organizations for some years, and with the emphasis they have been putting in recent years on male violence, their organizations have become very prominent. In Winnipeg, the main women's bodies are the Aboriginal Women's Unity Coalition, the Original Women's Network, and the Indigenous Women's Collective. None of these has the resources to develop its own economic decision-making capability but the first two work closely with the Aboriginal Council and all contain women with considerable experience in building development projects from the ground up. What is clear is that any efforts to strengthen the institutional capacity for Aboriginal organizations to formulate economic policies and plans and to implement them must also involve making resources available to women's organizations so that their particular experiences and insights can be given full expression, and so that their particular problems and needs can be addressed.

STRATEGIES OF ECONOMIC DEVELOPMENT PROPOSED BY THE ABORIGINAL COMMUNITY

One of the most influential statements on economic development for urban Aboriginal People in Manitoba, dating back to the early 1970s, comes from Stan Fulham (1981). Fulham proposed the creation of a Native Economic Development and Employment Council (NEDECO) appointed by representatives of Aboriginal organizations and senior levels of government. The Council would establish a Native Development Corporation (NDC) which would operate a number of subsidiary companies, offering them financial and administrative services. The NDC would set up a Native Industrial Centre, a business complex to house companies. The Council would negotiate contracts with government, Crown corporations and private business for Corporation subsidiaries to supply goods and services employing Aboriginal people. It would concentrate on labour-intensive activities, would work with government to set up appropriate training schemes, and would maintain an inventory of Aboriginal people, their skills and employment experience so as to maximize their employment opportunities, both within the Corporation and elsewhere.

The Native Industrial Centre would house a credit union for staff and businesses, and several other personal service enterprises, such as a café/restaurant, barbershop, hairdresser, and shoerepair shop. By sharing premises, both subsidiaries and other businesses would economize on costs (subsidized where justified), and would have ready access to managerial expertise and a source of finance.

Fulham also advocates the "setting aside" of government purchasing of supplies and services to benefit specifically Aboriginal businesses. While relying heavily on government resources, for purchasing and for training, and while drawing on community input for the Council and the Corporation, Fulham sees the aim of his proposal as being, primarily, "to establish and promote a private business sector for Native People" (74).

Fulham poses this strategy in opposition to affirmative action, which he views as a "negative approach" (75) and, in this respect, his views are quite at odds with those currently held by Aboriginal groups in the city. Also at odds with contemporary thinking in the Aboriginal community is the degree of state supervision of the quite cumbersome institutional structure which Fulham envisages.

Some of Fulham's thinking embraces ideas put forward initially in 1969 by the Indian and Métis Friendship Centre for a Native community in Winnipeg. The proposal was fleshed out in some detail between 1972 and 1975 as Neeginan—a Cree expression which can be translated as "Our Place" (Damas and Smith, 1975: 10). This envisaged the creation of an ethnic quarter in Winnipeg for Aboriginal people to serve as a transitional milieu for those moving into the city. It would have its own housing, social service, and economic facilities and would be run by Aboriginal People. It was seen as a more enlightened alternative to a proposal being put forward at that time by Kahn-Tineta-Horn of an urban reserve to be located 10 miles outside of Winnipeg (ibid.: 6). A 1975 report went into considerable architectural detail for the community services centre which would be the focal point of the community, housing social service agencies, shops, schools, residential accommodation, and Aboriginal political organizations. The report also examined alternative locations in the inner city.

The Neeginan proposal was quite thoroughly developed, therefore, and had considerable support both inside and outside the community. For many years, however, governments were not prepared to fund it and, after much frustration, its proponents simply lost steam (Krotz, 1980: 60).

Though formulated over 20 years ago, Fulham's views, and related proposals such as Neeginan, have a remarkable currency and continue to surface. Thus, the centrepiece of *An Economic Strategy for The Manitoba Métis Federation*, prepared by Thunderbird Consulting (1992), and endorsed by the MMF, is the proposal for government "setting aside" markets for Métis businesses. The incubator proposal (or "franchise" as Fulham would have it) also surfaced again in recent years, albeit in modified form, in the proposal to establish the Aboriginal Centre of Winnipeg in what used to be the Canadian Pacific Railway station which is located in the heart of the core area.

The idea behind the Aboriginal Centre was that it would bring under one roof a variety of Aboriginal organizations providing services to the community. Existing organizations would be encouraged to move their offices there. It would house an Aboriginal Institute which would deliver existing and new employment- and training-related services. Attempts would also be made to bring in public sector agencies providing services to Aboriginal people. A restaurant and childcare facility would be set up to cater for those working or being trained in the building. Finally, there was provision for light industrial activities, such as catering, printing and publishing, etc., and for conferences in the huge, 146,000-square-foot building.

Considerable progress has been made in realizing this plan, which contains many elements of the Neeginan proposal, especially the community service centre component, without the emphasis on building a separate neighbourhood as such. The building was purchased in December 1992, initially by means of the CPR taking back a mortgage, and later by means of loans from the Assiniboine Credit Union. Since March 1993, several Aboriginal organizations have moved in. As a National Historic Site, the Centre qualifies for special funding for restoration and maintenance from the federal government, but provincial, civic, and other forms of federal funding were pursued too, while a charitable organization was established to accept public donations, needed to leverage government grants.

By 1999, the Centre had 25 tenants and was fully occupied. Aboriginal firms which have established there include a security company, a woodworking enterprise, a printer, an auto body shop, a restaurant (which is in part a training initiative), and an art gallery. Many other tenants provide important services to the community, such as counselling, employment advice and training, and health and wellness. The Aboriginal Council of Winnipeg is also located there as are a number of non-Aboriginal entities which provide services to the community, such as the post office, legal aid, and human resources organizations of government and the Aboriginal Business Development Centre, a federally funded organization which offers counselling to small businesses in an "Aboriginal friendly" environment.

This represents a considerable accomplishment for the Aboriginal community of Winnipeg. The Aboriginal Centre will undoubtedly become a focal point for the community and represents the realization of an idea long in the making, having been envisaged by the Urban Indian Association which the Aboriginal Council replaced.

The Centre is not, however, without some potential dangers. First of all, due to its large size, it may expose Aboriginal tenants to a degree of risk they might not otherwise carry. Thus, failure to obtain the break-even occupancy level might put pressure on tenants to raise rents and/or associated fees. Occupancy problems were in evidence until 1999 when, after successfully creating a high school campus in the Centre, the space was fully rented out. Annual rents now bring in over $700,000 a year.

Secondly, the project is likely to remain highly dependent on state funding for rental income. This is not, of course, unusual for Aboriginal institutions, but the centrality of that funding to the ongoing commercial viability of the Centre is, perhaps, somewhat unique. Diversifying the tenants helps reduce risk in this regard, as does diversifying the types and sources of state funding. In late 1999, there were 25 tenants drawing funding from the federal, provincial, and city governments, as well as Aboriginal educational authorities, so one could argue that this risk has been recognized and addressed to some degree.

Thirdly, the *geographic* concentration of Aboriginal organizations in one building limits the extent to which they can be incorporated into holistic community development based on "balanced growth" within neighbourhoods. It could be argued that this is a necessary structural weakness of the incubator approach.

Fourth, the incubator concept has been only partially successful with regard to commercial businesses. The ones listed earlier are important initiatives but are not highly integrated, sharing little but a common roof. Some of the services which might have accomplished this and which were originally in the plan have not materialized, e.g., the credit union, perhaps because of scale problems. Finally, the large concentration of Aboriginal institutions, each with a different mandate and agenda, will call for a high degree of diplomacy in the handling of problems and disagreements among tenants and between tenants and the Centre. Initially, there were grounds for optimism that the key institutions behind this proposal, the Aboriginal Centre and Ma Mawi Wi Chi Itata Centre, an Aboriginal child and family services organization, would be equal to this task, as both are the product of broad alliances within the community. Unfortunately, the board of Ma Mawi pulled the organization out of the Centre in the mid-1990s, ostensibly on the grounds that the building was unsafe because of the presence of asbestos-lined pipes. Since local regulatory agencies had declared the building safe, one has to question what the real motivation for the move was, but the net result at the time was a huge hole in the operating revenue of the Centre of some $100,000 per annum (Inner City Voice, January, 1994), and the resignation of the Executive Director of Ma Mawi, who was also the Chairperson of the board of the Centre. This most unfortunate development cast a large question mark on the viability of the Centre until alternative tenants were found. As a result, the Centre experienced financial problems for most of the decade. Only in 1999 was full occupancy accomplished and a net profit on operations earned. This helped reduce an accumulated loss on operations of some $350,000 to that date (although it has net assets of over $5.5 million, on account of the building) and the Centre entered the 21st century with its financial prospects looking better than ever. The importance of diplomacy and a process for managing disagreements, cannot, however, be overstressed.

The biggest success of the Aboriginal Centre may prove to be that of resurrecting the Neeginan concept and pushing it through to implementation. The serious problems of the inner city became apparent in the late 1990s with extensive Aboriginal gang activity, a rapidly deteriorating housing stock and an outbreak of arson. In 1999 the Pan Am Games were held in Winnipeg and the politicians decided that Main Street needed a facelift. Proceeding with the Neeginan concept was felt to be a way of meeting several objectives at once: clearing up derelict hotels on Main Street; replacing them with an impressive structure celebrating Aboriginal strength and culture; placating the Aboriginal leadership and offering financial support (over $6 million) to the community's own solutions to the economic and social problems it faces. Neeginan seemed to offer all of this.

Construction of the Thunderbird House, Neeginan's home, was completed in early 2000. This strikingly impressive building was designed by Douglas Cardinal who sees it as "a place of rebirth and vitality; a place of healing and sharing" (Cardinal, undated). It will have several components: a place for Aboriginal art and culture, a youth complex, and a "commercial complex/business incubator." The incubator component is exactly the same as that envisaged for the Aboriginal Centre and Harold Cardinal describes it thus: "In this village, we will provide stores which will offer an assortment of goods and merchandise such as: food, clothing, gardening equipment, leather goods, and other necessities. We will have banks, bookstores, video stores, pool halls, movie theatres, arcades, and restaurants" (ibid.). It remains to be seen, however, whether or not Neeginan will have more success in this regard than the Aboriginal Centre, which is located just across the street.

Perhaps the most clearly articulated approach to community economic development for the Aboriginal population of the inner city of Winnipeg is that put forward by members of the Neechi Foods Co-op Ltd. (a community store) in their *It's Up To All Of Us* guide (Winnipeg Native Family Economic Development, February, 1993). They lay down 10 community development criteria by which to assess proposed or actual community initiatives. The first three of these essentially advocate a "convergence" approach to economic strategy as they provide for the use of local goods and services, the production of goods and services in the local economy and the reinvestment of profits locally. The point here is to emphasize the potential of the inner city market to sustain economic livelihoods. This means that income *earned* in the inner city should, as far as possible, be spent there, and preferably on goods and services which are actually *produced* there. This contrasts with the current situation in which substantial inner city income leaks away in expenditures elsewhere in the city on goods and services which are not produced in the inner city. Neechi encourages both Aboriginal residents and non-Aboriginal residents and others earning incomes in the core to use their purchasing power to benefit the local community. The idea is to spend in such a way that leakages from the inner city economy are minimized and economic linkages within it strengthened. This would reduce dependence on outside markets and build greater community self-reliance.

The fourth principle is to create long-term employment for inner city residents, so as to reduce dependence on welfare and food banks, enable people to live more socially productive lives, and to build personal and community esteem. In the process, of course, more income would be available for spending in the community (Hunter, 2000). Related to this, the fifth principle calls for the training of local residents in skills appropriate for community development.

The sixth principle or guideline is the encouragement of local decision-making through local cooperative forms of ownership and control and grassroots participation. The aim would be to strengthen community self-determination as people work together to meet community needs (Hunter, 2000).

Principles 7 and 8 recognize the importance of community development promoting public health and a safe and attractive physical environment. The ninth principle stresses the centrality of achieving greater neighbourhood stability by providing more dependable housing, encouraging long-term residency, and creating a base for long-term community economic development.

Finally, the whole approach is premised on the safeguarding and enhancement of human dignity. While there is a personal dimension to this, in the form of promoting self-respect, much of the emphasis is social: recognizing the need to generate community spirit, encourage equality between the sexes, and respect for seniors and children. The Neechi criteria also call for the promotion of social dignity regardless of physical or mental differences, national or ethnic background, and colour or creed. Above all, community development should promote Aboriginal pride.

This is an exhaustive and demanding set of criteria by which to evaluate community development proposals. Underlying it is a definite vision of both the process and the goal of community economic development.

The Neechi approach to economic development is not merely an intellectual one. It is rooted in and shaped by practical experience. Its origin can be traced back to the Northern Plan exercise in the mid-1970s (see Chapter 5). The 10 principles evolved during two training programs conducted in the early 1980s for Métis and Indian economic development and finance officers. Sponsored by the MMF and the All-Chiefs Budget Committee of the AMC, but run independently, these programs have produced over 50 well trained Aboriginal staff, most of whom are now employed by Aboriginal organizations in the Province (see Métis Economic Development, 1986). Out of these courses, which combined rigorous classroom work with practical on-the-job experience, came a series of community planning meetings in the summer of 1985, run by the trainees. Four projects were identified in these meetings as being high on the list of priority needs in the community in Winnipeg: a food store, a housing co-op, a commercial daycare, and a crafts shop, and the trainees proceeded to appraise each, working in conjunction with project working groups. All but the last of these has now been implemented and, in the early years, were loosely "federated" under the umbrella of the Winnipeg Native Family Economic Development (WNFED), a mutual support group.

Neechi Foods Co-op is an Aboriginal workers' co-op operating a grocery store and Aboriginal specialty shop in the inner city. The objectives of the co-op are to offer Aboriginal people a better selection of food at better prices, to promote community health, which it does in a number of ways (e.g., by not selling cigarettes and by subsidizing sales of fruit to children), to promote Aboriginal pride and employment, to keep money circulating in the community, to foster sharing, cooperation and local control, and to create capital for new projects. The store employs four full-time and five part-time employees, all Aboriginal, and annual sales are now in the region of $0.5 million.

The housing operation affiliated with WNFED is the Payuk Inter-Tribal Co-op, which has a 42-unit apartment block and five duplex units. One of its aims is to provide a safe and supportive environment for Aboriginal women and children (e.g., alcohol is prohibited in the building). Rents are tied to ability to pay. The Nee Gawn Ah Kai Day Care is located in the Payuk building, has space for 30 children and employs six people.

The Ma Mawi Wi Chi Itata Centre, Canada's first major urban Aboriginal child and family support service—which now employs 55, largely Aboriginal, staff—was also associated with WNFED. This organization was the outcome of efforts by the Winnipeg Coalition on Native Child Welfare, which also worked closely with the Economic Development Training Program, underlining the holistic, integrated approach to economic and social reform subscribed to by an influential section of the community.

The Neechi approach has clearly influenced the thinking of the Aboriginal Council in its formulation of an economic development strategy for Aboriginal People in the city. It argues for "a community economic development planning process geared towards developing a convergent, self-reliant local economy based upon community economic development principles: maximizing income retention, strengthening and promoting economic linkages, and maximizing community employment" (Aboriginal Council, 1992). It argues for the development of linkages between the urban Aboriginal community and reserves and rural Métis communities, but it would also like to see treaty administration centres established in Winnipeg to meet the needs of off-reserve Indians. The Council puts a major emphasis on the Aboriginalization of the staff and control of the social service delivery system catering to Aboriginal clientele. They see Aboriginalization as an important component of community economic development and extend it to education (with calls for an Aboriginal school board and control over all aspects of urban Aboriginal education), health, services to women, seniors, youths, and ex-inmates; in short, to all sections of Aboriginal society. This "decolonization" would be based on the principle of participation by all sections of Aboriginal society and would be accomplished, ideally, in cooperation with the other political organizations. This strategy has, therefore, some unique features, but at root, as a convergence strategy, it is essentially that proposed by Neechi.

The Neechi/WNFED approach to economic development shares some things in common with the Fulham approach. They both recognize the importance of Aboriginal organizations in the process; they both stress the importance of developing linkages and mutually supporting economic initiatives, both within Winnipeg and between the city community and Aboriginal communities outside; they both recognize the importance of having support services available to Aboriginal businesses, and especially of appropriate training; both argue the importance of providing decent long-term housing; and both admit the social desirability of non-Aboriginal support for Aboriginal ventures even when more lucrative investment outlets or cheaper purchases could be had elsewhere.

There are, however, crucial differences between these two approaches which need to be highlighted. First of all, the Neechi approach is much more clearly grounded in grassroots community activism than is the Fulham model and its variants, and envisages a much less significant role for Aboriginal political organizations in the economic development process. Secondly, the Neechi model attaches a much greater importance to community ownership and control than does Fulham, who is more wedded to the promotion of private Aboriginal business. In this respect Neechi appear to have strong community support for their views. In a survey of 144 inner city households conducted for this report, 69% of households responded that community ownership of business would be best for the neighbourhood and only 7% said private ownership. Thirdly, the Neechi approach is a much more holistic one, in which economic development is seen as one aspect, albeit a very important one, of healthy communities, in which economic opportunity, health and educational development, and social and environmental stability go hand in hand. It is not that Fulham et al. would necessarily disagree with this, but they do not articulate their philosophy in such a comprehensive, holistic fashion. Fourthly, a related point, Neechi would attach less importance to the physical aggregation of economic enterprises under one roof, preferring more spatial balance and securing supportive services and economies of scale in other ways. Finally, the Neechi model promotes restoring economic balance and community self-reliance through economic restructuring which in some ways challenges the logic of the market economy. Fulham's approach, on the other hand, accepts the dominant market on its own terms and seeks to break into it with state assistance.

In its most recent variant, the Neechi Principles now include support for other CED initiatives. These principles have been adopted by the Community Development Business Association (CDBA) and its more than 25 members.

The Assembly of Manitoba Chiefs has taken an eclectic approach to economic development in Winnipeg. It is supportive of both the "incubator" concept and of community-based initiatives of the kind advocated by Neechi. It also argues for aggressive employment equity initiatives in the public sector, and for the opening up of employment opportunities in the private sector. The AMC has been particularly insistent on greater accessibility to mainstream employment opportunities and has developed a close working relationship with some large-scale private employers, such as the banks. Over the years, the AMC and its forerunners have also advocated a much greater Aboriginal presence in those governmental institutions dealing directly with Aboriginal people. This emphasis has paid off in one or two federal departments in Winnipeg having fairly high rates of Aboriginal employees, but the AMC would argue that there is a long way yet to go in the federal civil service as a whole, and has, in fact taken up the matter of the general lack of progress with the Canadian Human Rights Commission.

The Chiefs of Manitoba have argued also for the creation of funding vehicles to promote Indian economic development in the city of Winnipeg, as well as in the reserve communities. As early as 1969, the Manitoba Indian Brotherhood argued for the creation of a Manitoba Indian Development Inc. which would serve as a development bank to give financial and other supports to First Nation economic ventures. This idea surfaced in somewhat amended form in the mid-1980s as the Manitoba Indian Development Association, MIDAS (All-Chiefs Budget Committee, 1984). Eventually, however, the Chiefs decided to pursue the capital corporation approach, with the Tribal Council, or associations of Tribal Councils, as the focal point. The result of this has been the institutional development outlined earlier and a situation in which, while new capital corporations are empowered to lend money in Winnipeg, there is no institution set up specifically to cater to First Nations people in the city. This is being recognized as a problem now, as there is insufficient funding to cater to the needs of reserve communities which is where the existing capital corporations must first focus their attention. Thus, consideration is being given to how best to rectify this problem. Had the Winnipeg Tribal Council emerged as a viable entity with strong grassroots support, then this could have been a vehicle for launching a new financial institution for First Nations People in Winnipeg, but this does not appear to be the case and an alternative approach will likely be needed.

In November 1998, the AMC, MMF, and ACW participated in a Round Table on Aboriginal People in Winnipeg's Urban Community (Human Resources Canada, 1998). They agreed on the need for an economic development strategy which would create 2,000 jobs every year. They proposed the adoption of a common vision which would promote community-level ownership of economic ventures. The need to break away from dependence on welfare and government services was acknowledged, as was the necessity to move from non-profit to for-profit activities. While much was made of building "partnership" among the three groups, the AMC argued its case for the portability of treaty rights into the urban setting while the MMF advanced its claim to be the legal representative of all the Métis in the province and asked for funds so that they could be properly enumerated. The superficial cooperation hides, therefore, some deep political divisions and these became apparent when Neeginan was announced, the AMC and MMF withholding their support on the grounds that they had not been part of the decision-making process.

Thus, a variety of approaches to economic development in Winnipeg are to be found within the Aboriginal community. The supporters of these different viewpoints coexist quite amicably and even with some degree of cooperation, although some struggles have been waged within organizations over the preferred approach. There is so little happening in the field of Aboriginal economic development at this time, relative to the problems of Aboriginal need, that there is ample room for eclecticism and disagreement over strategy.

THE CORE AREA INITIATIVE

The most significant policy intervention in the city of Winnipeg in the recent past was the Winnipeg Core Area Initiative. All three levels of government shared equally in providing funding to improve the "economic, social and physical conditions" of the core, where the majority of Winnipeg's Aboriginal people reside. The first phase of the Initiative was 1981–86 and the total direct funding involved was $96 million; the second was 1986–91 and the cost $100 million. Since many projects "leveraged" funds from elsewhere, the impact of the Initiative was much greater than these figures indicate and it dominated urban policy during its lifetime.

In the first agreement, $4.4 million went to administration, evaluation, and information (Sector 3); $11.0 to industrial development and small business assistance and $35.4 million to large-scale physical redevelopment of the city (Sector 2); $12.9 million to housing, $14.7 million to employment and affirmative action and $16.5m to various community initiatives (Sector 1). In the second agreement, $4.0 million went to administration, etc. (Sector 3), $8.4 million to industrial and entrepreneurial support and $49 million to large scale redevelopment (now transposed as Sector 1); $10.5 million to housing, $12 million to employment and training and $16.2 million to neighbourhood and community development (now transposed as Sector 2). It was the Sector 2 category of program funding in WCAI 2 and Sector 1 in WCAI 1 that had most relevance for Aboriginal people.

The evaluation of the Employment and Affirmative Action component of the first agreement documents quite carefully its impact on the Aboriginal community (Clatworthy, 1987). Over 500 residents of the core were trained and placed in both public and private employment. Over 200 of these were Aboriginal, of which 25% were single parents and 26% were youths. The unemployment rate of graduates fell from 83% before training to 12.5% after; their total incomes rose, on average, by two-thirds and earned income tripled, while dependence on government transfers had declined by 80% in cash terms (ibid.: 41). Although no new jobs were created by this program, inner city residents, including Aboriginal people, gained opportunities to work which they would otherwise not have had. The cost of training each graduate was, however, almost $31,000.

Two other parts of this component trained nurses and social workers, again with great success. Of the 93 people trained, over a half were Aboriginal. By March 1987, 41 people had been placed in employment and about half were Aboriginal.

While the evaluation found that this component had, by and large, met its objectives, it also found that there was a failure to integrate the training component of the WCAI with its other job creation components (21). This would help explain why the Economic Stimulus programs (Sector 2) and the Industrial Development Program failed to hire Aboriginal people (Epstein Associates, 1987: 48, 51)

Although WCAI did not reduce the overall unemployment rate in the core, it has been argued, "conditions would have been significantly worse in the absence of the CAI" (Working Margins, 1991: 36). For Aboriginal people in the core there was, in fact, a large rise in the unemployment rate between 1981 and 1986 from 27.7% to 31.5%, due to a huge (67%) increase in the Aboriginal labour force in the core in those years (for which the CAI was, of course, partially responsible). At one level, the initiative was successful yet, given the demographic trends, it was not equal to the task of stabilizing, leave alone reducing the Aboriginal unemployment rate.

Data on employment creation appears to be a little more comprehensive for the second agreement. A total of 1,968 jobs not directly connected to CAI construction projects were created by all components of the agreement. Of these, 298 or one-third, were Aboriginal. Most of the jobs, 72%, were in the private sector: 28% of the total were in manufacturing, 15% in finance and 10% in construction. Two-thirds of the jobs paid under $20,000 per annum which, according to the evaluation, suggests that most were to entry level or lower level positions (Working Margins, 1991: 20) but 60% of the jobs paid more than $15,000 a year, or much more than the average Aboriginal worker would earn in Winnipeg.

A total of 2,241 individuals benefited from training programs. Aboriginal people represented 43% of all trainees and about a half the number of Aboriginal people unemployed in 1986 received training during the five-year period (Working Margins, 1991: 26–27). Some

250 Aboriginal trainees were placed into employment. In contrast to the first agreement, training and affirmative action were not only aimed at the private sector, NGOs and other sections of government, but were firmly integrated into Core Area Initiative projects themselves. The average cost for graduates placed in employment, at $14,394, seems to be under a half that of the first agreement.

A major problem with CAI placements, however, appears to be a high turnover rate, especially in manufacturing and construction. A survey of employers in all sectors including the public found that only 41% of those placed were still working with their original employers (Working Margins, 1991: 23).

In contrast to Sector 2, it appears that Sector 1 and related initiatives, accounting for 57% of all funding, provided little if any benefit to the Aboriginal population of the core. Most of this money went into financing high-profile real estate and property development transactions such as the Forks project, North Portage Place and the Exchange District improvement.

The overall assessment of the impact of WCAI II on employment creation would be similar, but less favourable in relative terms, to that of WCAI I. About the same number of jobs were created but the Aboriginal labour force continued to grow significantly in the 1986–91 period. The Initiative itself also raised labour supply by more than it did demand.

Apart from training and job creation, the WCAI was important to Aboriginal people for the funds it provided for improvements in housing and community infrastructure. A total of $12.9 million was earmarked for housing under the first agreement, and $10.5 million under the second. The first upgraded over 6,000 houses and helped build in the region of 500 new houses. Most assistance was to individual homeowners, but $2.0 million was put into non-profit housing (Epstein and Associates, 1987). The second added 327 units to the housing stock and renovated just over 1,000 or 5% of the core's total housing stock. Many more houses were inspected and their owners forced to undertake repairs. It was not possible, however, to assess the effect of these on "stabilizing the area's population base and neighbourhood" (Winnipeg Core Area Initiative, 1992: 94).

Under the heading of Neighbourhood and Community Development, WCAI 2 provided over 300 grants totalling more than $14 million to community facilities and services. These were taken advantage of by most agencies operating in the core area. Some projects were specifically aimed at the Aboriginal community and Aboriginal organizations received $1.8 million for a whole variety of projects. The largest of these were the $216,000 received by Ma Mawi Wi Chi Itata Centre's New Directions Project to promote self-identity and self-esteem among Aboriginal youth; $161,000 for the Manitoba Association for Native Languages; $236,000 for the Native Women's Transition Centre for a new facility and programming, and $98,000 for background studies related to the Aboriginal Centre.

Very little funding under the Neighbourhood and Community Development component was aimed at community economic development "per se." Indeed, of the $14 million assigned to this envelope, only $667,000 was earmarked for economic development projects in the community; $341,000 was actually invested in community ventures, of which there were only three in total. Most of this, $201,000, went to Neechi Foods, $107,000 went into a greenhouse project for the mentally handicapped, and $33,000 into a cooperative laundromat. This failure to more aggressively promote community economic development was recognized by the community as the most glaring weakness in the WCAI.

We have a very clear idea of what the community, including the Aboriginal community, of the core area actually felt about the WCAI because in 1990 a Community Inquiry into Inner City Revitalization was held, prompted by the impending expiry of the WCAI 2 and the anticipation of future government initiatives in the city. What the Inquiry found was that inner city residents and groups recognized the value and accomplishments of the tripartite initiative, had benefited greatly from it and wished it to continue, but with certain improvements in direction and focus (Community Inquiry Board, 1990: 4).

The Inquiry found that residents wanted a much greater role in planning and decision-taking, a much greater emphasis on promoting ownership, self-help and self-determination, and a much greater focus of capital expenditures on housing, infrastructure, and community facilities (as opposed to the grandiose town planning gestures). Concern was expressed that many innovative programs and services would disappear along with the WCAI and that no provision had been made for their long-term funding. This was related to the critique of the WCAI for its lack of emphasis on community economic development. Without such development, the core area would not be able to build the financial base of the community and make it less dependent on state funding in the longer run. The Inquiry called for a closer link between education and economic development and a greater commitment to affirmative action hiring by companies benefiting from government finance.

The Inquiry called for the drawing up of an economic development strategy for the inner city by the Aboriginal community in conjunction with the WCAI and governments. It also supported the idea that priority should be given to Aboriginal business development and diversification, generally, and to the establishment of the Aboriginal Centre, specifically. There was support for easily accessible loans for small and micro-businesses and for earmarking a portion of available funds for community groups to undertake development initiatives. There should be greater community control over Aboriginal education and training and more emphasis put on training Aboriginal women.

The Inquiry revealed that improving both the quality of housing and Aboriginal access to the ownership of housing are considered crucial to stabilizing the core. A variety of financing schemes were proposed including sweat equity, rent-to-own, deferred mortgage loans, and the redirection of social assistance funds for rents. There was strong support for cooperative and non-profit housing and for using housing to encourage community-based economic development through worker cooperatives for building and renovation.

What emerges from the Inquiry report, and what is clearly evident in recent community initiatives, is a very clear recognition of the problems facing inner city residents and a strong desire to rectify them. This is not a community given over to fatalism or one trapped, irrevocably, into some "culture of poverty." On the contrary, it is a community with an impressive depth of leadership which has shown resolve and creativity in building institutions to serve the needs of Aboriginal people. It is a community full of ideas and energy but one also starved of resources and one which meets severe institutional obstacles when it attempts to give concrete substance to its creative ideas.

Unfortunately, the three levels of government were unmoved by the Inquiry recommendations and the WCAI was replaced by a city-wide Winnipeg Development Agreement. While this has given important financial support to a number of specific initiatives, such as the Aboriginal Centre, Neeginan, SEED Winnipeg, and Just Housing, these account for only a small proportion of the $75 million to be spent between 1995 and 2000.

SEED WINNIPEG

SEED Winnipeg is a development loan scheme for micro and community businesses overseen by a volunteer board. It facilitates three loan programs: a micro-loan scheme, a lending circle scheme, and a community project loan scheme. In its micro-lending it advances start-up capital in the form of loans up to $10,000 to economically disadvantaged people, who are usually unemployed or on welfare. Special consideration is given to Aboriginal people, members of visible minority communities, people with disabilities, ex-offenders, or inner city residents. Borrowers typically cannot meet the requirements of mainstream institutions for collateral and require training in business planning and management. All would-be applicants must first attend a three-hour orientation session. The credit circle program consists of groups of 10 or so borrowers, who take it in turns to borrow, support each other, and act as a pressure group for loan repayment. Community projects are larger, collective ones requiring more development work and larger sums of finance. SEED provides experienced mentors to assist borrowers. It has little capital funding of its own, and draws mainly on funds from an inner city credit union which has earmarked them specifically for this purpose and which works with SEED in evaluating applications. Operating funds are provided by the Community Education Development Association (CEDA), the Mennonite Central Committee (MCC), various charitable organizations and, as SEED has developed a track record, from government. Mentors are drawn from the Mennonite Economic Development Associates (MEDA). These various organizations, the Aboriginal community, and the provincial government are all represented on either the board or the advisory committee to the board. While SEED is a relatively small institution, it is important as a model and it underscores the point made by members of the Aboriginal community that there is indeed a scarcity of start-up capital for small businesses. Its average loan size, and credit cost per job, is under $5,000, or only 15% that of the Aboriginal Business Development Program. The mentor dimension of SEED is also something which has proven invaluable to clients and could usefully be emulated elsewhere. Finally, SEED has been successful in negotiating the continuation of social assistance payments during the initial period of business activity, thereby reducing pressure on the borrowers until break-even is achieved. More recently, it has assisted CEDA in helping realize the creation of a development corporation in one of the poorer sections of the city. The North End Community Renewal Corporation was created in 1999 and will offer a full range of community economic development services.

SEED also administers the Christmas Lite campaign which started as an adjunct to the Christmas Cheer Board, raising funds for Christmas hampers but buying food, etc., from Aboriginal inner city businesses so as to help create permanent jobs in the community donors are seeking to help.

OTHER DEVELOPMENTS

In addition to the initiatives discussed above there have been numerous efforts to increase Aboriginal participation in the Winnipeg economy through business development, training, affirmative action, and employment equity. Many of these were outlined and assessed in Loxley (1996). The training scene, in particular, has evolved rapidly since the mid-1990s with significant Aboriginal "ownership" (both figuratively and literally) and staffing of the schemes themselves. Elements of the private sector, including the Winnipeg Chamber of Commerce, have also recognized the need to strengthen the Aboriginal business and employment presence in the city and have committees which encourage purchasing from Aboriginal suppliers. The Royal Bank, among others, has also actively promoted Aboriginal employment and business development.

Social organizations within the inner city have for many years pressed for private and public support of community economic development projects that would benefit Aboriginal people. The most persistent and most successful in this regard has been CEDA, which in 1999 brokered a proposal for a housing trust fund that would see a mix of financial contributions from the three levels of government and the community to buy, repair and sell inner city housing. The Assiniboine Credit Union has also been actively supporting CED initiatives in recent years, including SEED, housing, and a variety of community business projects.

Finally, many Aboriginal people enter the labour market in Winnipeg without any form of special assistance and a number of Aboriginal businesses are also formed and operated entirely on their own initiative.

WHAT HAVE THESE INITIATIVES ACCOMPLISHED?

There are indications that Aboriginal employment in the city increased significantly between 1986 and 1996. The 1986 Census data suggests that 7,974 Aboriginal People were employed in that year (calculated from Census data contained in Social Planning Council, 1989). The 1996 census records 16,640 Aboriginal employees, an apparent growth rate of 7.6% per annum. over the decade. There may, however, be problems with these numbers in that some of this increase might reflect not new employment but simply the capturing in the data of people not previously described as Aboriginal in 1986. One should be extremely cautious, therefore, about these findings. Whatever the accuracy of the 1986 base, however, there is other evidence of high growth rates in Aboriginal employment. On the basis of estimates of Aboriginal employment in 1991 in Loxley (1996), it appears that Aboriginal employment grew by about 6.4% per annum between 1991 and 1996, a remarkably strong performance.

If these numbers are anywhere near to being accurate, they paint an encouraging picture of Aboriginal employment growth in the city. The total number of people employed in Winnipeg rose by only 1.7% between 1986 and 1991 and by 1.3% between 1991 and 1996. This means that the proportion of those employed who were Aboriginal People rose from about 2.7% in 1986 to about 4.0% in 1991 and 5.1% in 1996. This increase undoubtedly owes something to the initiatives described above, but how much is impossible to tell.

At the same time, because the Aboriginal labour force itself doubled, the number of *unemployed Aboriginal people* also rose over this period, from 2,197 to possibly 4,000 in 1991 and to 4,445 in 1996, or at about the same rate as employment grew over the same period, *in spite* of the numerous economic development, employment equity, and training initiatives. One can only speculate how bad the situation might have been without such programs. The numbers suggest then, that the growth of the Aboriginal labour force in Winnipeg is so rapid that a whole new *scale* of intervention is required if the unemployment rate and the total number of unemployed in the Aboriginal community are to be reduced. This will mean building on what appears to have been successful in the past, and modifying or replacing initiatives which have had less success. It may also suggest that government initiatives are not equal to the task of coping with the rapid growth of the Aboriginal labour force, and that the time is ripe for an entirely new *approach* to Aboriginal economic development drawing, as much as possible, on the strategies proposed by Aboriginal People themselves.

RECOMMENDATIONS

A number of proposals to strengthen *institutions* emerge logically from the above. First, the main representative Aboriginal organizations in Winnipeg need resources to build up an economic development planning, policy, and advisory capacity. If self-government is to have any meaning, then governments must be prepared to transfer to Aboriginal organizations not just responsibilities but also resources. The strengthening of economic capacity should apply as much to the organizations of Aboriginal women, where they express a desire for it, as to the three main political bodies or their technical arms. The main purpose of these staff would be to work with the local community to promote and support economic development initiatives and to ensure a coherent approach to economic development.

There is also a pressing need for *a pool of capital* controlled by and used to the benefit of the Aboriginal community. The MMF has an institution in place, and perhaps all that is needed there is additional funds earmarked specifically for urban Métis. Status and Non-Status Indians have no such institutional structure. Theoretically, the mandates of Tribal Council capital corporations do extend to Winnipeg but, institutionally, this is an unwieldy way of addressing the capital needs of city residents which, if resorted to extensively, might face opposition from the constituent bands. There seems to be a case, therefore, for the creation of at least one new capital corporation with representation from the different communities or, if that cannot be agreed upon, one institution for First Nations People and one which would be status-blind, to *complement* any urban activities of the existing capital corporations. The main point is that there is a lacuna in the city which needs to be filled quickly.

This pool of capital would be available to promote and support all forms of initiative in the community, be it small-scale business or *community development initiatives*. Lack of funding for the latter is particularly acute, and yet the Aboriginal community in Winnipeg has a strong preference for community ventures.

There are no shortages of ideas in the Aboriginal community, at the level both of strategic approaches to economic development and of specific projects. There is, however, a need for resources to be made available at the neighbourhood level to enable people to develop and realize their ideas. *Education for community economic development* is currently conducted essentially on a voluntary basis, with two notable exceptions. The Community Education Development Association (CEDA) has long been active in this area, but it operates on a tight and vulnerable budget. The Crocus Investment Fund, a labour-sponsored venture capital fund, has also contributed on a sporadic basis by bringing in practitioners to speak to Winnipeg activists. To involve the Aboriginal community more fully in the development process, additional funding for community development education is essential, as is more explicit encouragement and funding of community development projects. One without the other is unlikely to work for, as Neechi have pointed out, inner city development projects must rely for their long-term viability on a commitment from local residents and those earning their incomes in the inner city to help retain local incomes in the local community. The Neechi/WNFED approach also requires the local community to consider the development potential of all activities taking place in the community, from house building to medical services, and even to food banks. Such an approach is quite alien to the way governments and those working and/or living in the inner city tend to think and behave (Rothney, 1992). To transform current patterns would require a good deal of community activism and the availability of resources to work out in detail how alternatives might be developed.

Some of these resources ought to be channelled into *training programs for community economic development officers*, with strong business and planning skills, specifically for the inner city. There is a model on which to build, namely the All-Chiefs and Métis training programs of the mid 1980s. These officers could be sponsored and later hired by the economic arms of the Aboriginal institutions, revamped according to the first recommendation, and/or they could be attached to CEDA, SEED, or directly to neighbourhood organizations. The absence of this capacity in the city is particularly striking.

More attention needs to be given to *stabilizing the urban Aboriginal population*. This is important not only in building a sense of geographic community, but also for improving the educational accomplishments of Aboriginal children. More quality housing at affordable prices is needed and should be attainable. This may mean diverting the housing component of social assistance into innovative housing schemes, be they privately or cooperatively owned, for the Aboriginal community and others. It may mean giving greater weight to sweat equity in calculating down payments for CMHC loans. It will certainly require a commitment of financial resources by all three levels of government, along the lines of the housing trust fund proposal put forward by inner city groups. However it is accomplished, it ought to be possible to increase or improve the housing stock in ways which involve little or no net drain on government resources since the indirect returns from improvements in housing should more than offset the direct cost.

Economic development initiatives by the Aboriginal community must be complemented by bolder and more systematic efforts at *employment equity and affirmative action* (Loxley, 1996). At all three levels of government, employment equity programs are encountering serious problems. The number of Aboriginal recruits is too low, their turnover is too high, they are concentrated in junior and impermanent positions, and they tend to be ghettoized in certain occupations or departments. If significant progress is not made in the immediate future, the Aboriginal community should press for legislative changes to make employment equity targets mandatory and to impose sanctions for non-compliance.

Our preference is for Aboriginal capital corporations, with boards which are representative in terms both of gender and age, to ultimately replace *funding agencies* of the federal and provincial governments to which Aboriginal people apply directly. These should be funded adequately to cover overhead costs and a reasonable level of inevitable bad debts.

Addressing the poverty of single-parent families will require action on a number of different fronts at once. Clatworthy's three-pronged approach still has relevance (Clatworthy, 1981b). This combines longer-term occupational training programs with increased access to stable relatively high-paying jobs, facilitated by a relaxation of the barriers to participation in the labour force. The principal barrier is, of course, adequate childcare facilities (Loxley, 1993). The state ought also to "recognize the productive work of parenting" (Falconer, 1990: 205) and adjust transfer payments so that they provide a decent "wage" to those who choose to stay at home and care for their children. Finally, as the movement to self-government proceeds, it is vital that Aboriginal institutions be fully representative of single-parent women, of women generally, and of all age groups, including youth and the elderly, so that the particular economic concerns of these groups will not be overlooked or given insufficient weight, and so that the community can draw to the fullest on their talents and experience.

Funding for the Access Program and New Careers ought to be restored. Both levels of government could link some aspects of the programs more explicitly to their own employment equity goals and to the needs of Aboriginal self-government, but the programs have a much wider rationale than this. The provincial government should also reinstate social assistance payments for youth returning to school to complete their education.

Ultimately, however, it will be the extent to which the Aboriginal community can be mobilized to draw on its inner strengths and abilities which will determine the pace of Aboriginal development in Winnipeg. State resources will have an important role to play but Aboriginal pride and determination to be self-reliant in the long term will be more important. It is for this reason that the holistic approach of Neechi, with its emphasis on using available resources as fully as possible to meet the needs of the community, and its recognition that one cannot separate *economic development* from *social and cultural development*, appears to offer the most coherent way forward for Aboriginal economic development in the city of Winnipeg.

CHAPTER 8

FINANCING COMMUNITY ECONOMIC DEVELOPMENT IN WINNIPEG[1]

This chapter reviews the literature on the financing of Community Economic Development (CED) and examines how the system of financing CED in Winnipeg has evolved in recent years. There has been rapid institutional growth with a plethora of organizations offering credit and support for individual and collective CED ventures, most supporting a "convergence" approach to CED. At the heart of these developments have been the Assininboine Credit Union and SEED Winnipeg. Most institutions are, however, heavily dependent on state funding and finding ways to reduce that dependence while meeting the constraint of inadequate funding for equity or grant investments will require innovative solutions.

The infrastructure for community economic development (CED) in Winnipeg has developed markedly in the last decade. Before, there was little in the way of support for individuals or groups that might have had ideas for CED projects and those projects that did materialize had great difficulty gaining access to both technical assistance and funding. Prior to 1991, the Winnipeg Core Area Initiative (WCAI), phase 1, 1981–86 and Phase 2, 1986–91, a tri-level agreement between the federal, provincial, and civic governments, had been an important source of funding for community organizations but only a small portion of its funds had been devoted to CED (Loxley, 2000: 100–103). Thus, out of a total WCAI package of $100 million in Phase 2, only $341,000 was earmarked for economic

[1] From *Économie et Solidarité*, Vol. 34, No.1, 2003.

development projects in the community. Of this amount, Neechi Foods, an Aboriginal workers' co-op retail store and an important model of CED in the city, received $107,000 and had to supplement it by raising loans and grants from sympathetic individuals in the community (Loxley, 2000: 102).

In 1990 a Community Inquiry into Inner City Revitalization called for the renewal of the WCAI but with more emphasis on CED and guaranteed, longer-term funding for community organizations. It also called for a clearly defined strategy for economic development to be drawn up in conjunction with the Aboriginal community and for easily accessible loans for small and micro businesses. Improving the housing stock of the inner city was considered a priority need and a promising foundation for CED initiatives (Loxley, 2000: 102–103). In the event, the WCAI was not renewed but instead replaced by a citywide Winnipeg Development Agreement (WDA). Nonetheless, some progress has been made in implementing the major recommendations of the inquiry. The object of this paper is to examine how has this happened and what has it meant for funding CED projects in Winnipeg. It begins by r eviewing the literature on financing of community economic development. This is followed by an overview of different approaches to community economic development in Winnipeg. A brief overview of the methodology employed then serves as a prelude to the main body of the paper.

FINANCING COMMUNITY ECONOMIC DEVELOPMENT

The need for community economic development is often justified in reference to the shortcomings of the dominant private enterprise system. CED is seen as necessary either, in a reformist vision, to fill in gaps left by capitalism or, more radically, as a viable alternative to capitalism as a whole. In either version, some degree of collective intervention is necessary to allow CED activities to gain access to financing or, as Gunn and Gunn (1991) put it, to allow them to share in the social surplus. Two types of funding are required by community economic development organizations. The first is to cover the overhead costs, salaries, and administration of organizations that promote CED. The second is financing of the business activities that such organizations promote. Neither type of finance is typically available from private banks in Canada because banks see them as being too unprofitable or too risky. Moreover, private banks have tended to withdraw their physical presence from those geographical locations where most CED activities tend to be located: inner cities, rural, and remote (especially Aboriginal) areas (National Council of Welfare, 1998: 13). As a result, CED literature stresses the need for cooperatively owned financial institutions to fill the financing gaps left by banks. The literature is unclear about how CED overheads will be funded.

In Canada, the most important cooperative form is the credit union or the caisse populaire, which are member-owned cooperative banks. In 2001, there were 1,772 of them throughout the country (1,069 caisses populaires, 703 credit unions), with 10 million members and assets in excess of $120 billion. Credit unions/caisses populaires are particularly strong in Western Canada and Quebec, often reaching 60% of the population and accounting for as much as 40% of the total domestic assets of all deposit-taking institutions combined (Department of Finance, 2002).

Contrary to the views of their more uncritical proponents (e.g., Fairbairn et al., 1995), cooperative ownership of these financial institutions does not necessarily mean that they will, in practice, operate much differently from privately owned banks. Their mandate is still to earn a rate of return for members and in large centres, they are required to compete with banks for deposits and loan business. Indeed, these pressures can often lead to community organizations avoiding lending to local CED activities because of their perceived high risk and acting as a conduit for the export of capital to other, larger centres (Gunn and Gunn, 1991: 61). The Vancouver City Credit Union (VanCity) has resolved the dilemma of the riskiness involved in some CED lending by putting aside a portion of its earnings to finance grants, loans, and technical assistance to community economic development ventures, such as "affordable housing, employment and nonprofit enterprises" (Driscoll, 1996: 7). In doing so, it has become a model for others across the country.

Community loan associations or community development loan funds are another collective form of financial assistance to CED ventures and low-income earners. As non-profit entities, they borrow from individuals or institutions (such as churches, foundations, corporations) sympathetic to their aims, often at less than market rates, and lend, again at favourable rates, for purposes consistent with their aims (Jackson and Pierce, 1993: 225–227). The Montreal Community Loan Association is a prime Canadian example, combining direct financing with leverage financing, technical assistance, and education (Mendell and Evoy, 1993). The majority of such funds in Canada are, in fact, to be found in Quebec, where more than 250 of them operate (some at regional as well as local level), many with state financing (Ninacs, 2000: 14–15).

Community development corporations (CDCs) can also act as sources of finance for CED. These are again not-for-profit organizations often set up in distressed areas to promote economic development. Owned by the community, CDCs can help fund individuals or businesses and may even own their own enterprises. They obtain funding, both for overheads and for investment/lending purposes from the state, from foundations or from sympathetic individuals and organizations. They often play an active role in attracting businesses, and in offering training and technical assistance. In the U.S., they can be constituted as development banks, taking deposits from the public (Gunn and Gunn, 1991: 69–73).

Micro-lending programs have become very popular throughout the world as a source of funding for small-scale community economic activities, with an estimated eight to 10 million households being served (Morduch, 1999). Internationally, the Grameen Bank has been held up as the model to follow, with a 97% repayment rate and women constituting 94% of the membership. It operates as a credit circle in which peer pressure replaces normal types of loan security. It obtains its capital from government and international aid sources. In Canada, the Calmeadow Foundation has operated similar schemes in First Nations communities, obtaining its funding from banks but offering them guarantees and contributions to overhead costs (Jackson and Pierce, 1993: 224–225). Though these schemes are very fashionable, recent literature has begun to look more closely at them, raising important questions, in particular, about the extravagant claims made for the Grameen Bank, in terms of its repayment record, its economic impact, its sustainablity without subsidies, and the precise role played by women in the loans they obtain (see, for instance, Neff 1996; Rahman, 1998; and Morduch, 1999). Similar issues have been raised in the Canadian context, as well as questions about the dangers of dependency on the state and the link between credit circles and CED philosophy (McMurtry, 1993).

Operating on a micro level, there are a variety of asset-building programs in Canada and elsewhere in which poor individuals are encouraged to save for education, housing, business investment, or acquisition of personal assets through Individual Development Accounts (IDAs). The sponsoring organization, funded by government, charitable foundations, or donations from individuals or businesses, matches, doubles, or triples the funds saved over a period of time. These schemes are also becoming popular, with the Department of Human Resources, Canada, sponsoring learn$ave, "the largest demonstration project on IDAs in the world" (Robson-Haddow, 2002: 16).

A variety of funding arrangements which can potentially benefit CED owe their existence to the favourable tax treatment of charitable donations or contributions to retirement savings. Several charitable foundations, from the United Way to those that handle the bequests of families or private individuals, are willing to put money into CED initiatives, often as core funding for staff but sometimes also for the provision of loan capital (Gunn and Gunn, 1991: 73–79). Likewise, labour-sponsored venture capital funds, contributions to which receive generous provincial and federal tax credits, may be willing to assist CED ventures (Jackson and Pierce, 1993: 219–223). The earliest and now largest of these is the Solidarity Fund of the Quebec Federation of Labour, but similar organizations now operate in many parts of Canada. A case can also be made for regular pension plans investing a portion of their funds in CED activities (Usiskin, 1996) but, as will be argued later in the paper, the riskiness of much CED activity is not a good fit for pension funds.

APPROACHES TO CED IN WINNIPEG

There are a number of clearly identifiable approaches to CED in Winnipeg, three of which seem to dominate. The origin of two of them lies clearly in the Aboriginal community (Loxley, 2000).

The first, which can be traced back to the writings of Stan Fulham (1981), is the incubator approach. This advocates the bringing together under one roof of a variety of social and economic development agencies and business ventures, as well as Aboriginal political organizations. The idea is they would each gain from being close to the others, sharing rent, bookkeeping and financial services, customers, and marketing facilities. So far, there are two such physical entities, the large Aboriginal Centre in the former CP railway station, and the newer Neeginan or Thunderbird House, currently a beautifully designed cultural centre but with plans of also offering incubator facilities. In practice, the Aboriginal Centre has been a success in attracting government agencies and Aboriginal services dependent upon government funding. Both buildings themselves absorbed huge government subsidies. The Aboriginal Centre has been less successful in building up a private business or commercial base.

The second approach is that of community-based economic development (CED), or the Neechi approach, named after a worker-owned Aboriginal cooperative retail store which developed the following principles of CED (referred to below as the Neechi Principles): production of goods and services for local use; use of local goods and services; local reinvestment of locally generated profits; long-term employment of local residents; local skill development; local decision making; improved public health; improved physical environment; neighbourhood stability; human dignity and solidarity among communities and businesses following these principles. The idea of this approach is to build a strong, inward-looking, self-reliant economy which is based on goods and services consumed by people who live or work in the community. In theoretical terms it is a convergence strategy of economic development (Thomas, 1974). It favours cooperative ownership, small-scale production, and popular control over economic decision-making. It is a holistic approach, in which the safety, health and self-respect of residents are of paramount importance (Loxley, 2002). These principles have formed the basis of a number of Aboriginal initiatives apart from Neechi; the Payuk housing co-op,[2] an Aboriginal day care centre, an Aboriginal child welfare organization, a cooperative making star blankets. Aboriginal women figure prominently in each of these. Many non-Aboriginal organizations have also adopted these principles.

The differences between these two approaches are that the latter is more grassroots-oriented and more neighbourhood-focused, whereas the incubator approach tends to centralize activities spatially under one roof. Political organizations, notoriously unstable in the Aboriginal community, play a prominent role in the incubator approach, but not in the Neechi approach. Neechi has a more holistic philosophy and tends to fight against market ideology rather than be dependent upon it. While, given the lack of capital in the community, both approaches require government financial input, the scale of dependence in the Neechi approach is likely lower and the prospects for long-term self-reliance somewhat higher.

A third identifiable approach is one which places the individual at the centre of CED activities. Assisting individuals to become small entrepreneurs is at the heart of much micro lending, business development, and asset building activity. Governments tend to be very supportive of this approach and hence willing to fund these initiatives.

Finally, there is an emerging school of thought that locates itself within the CED paradigm but which emphasizes the workplace community rather than the residential or cultural community. This stresses worker or cooperative ownership of relatively large-scale operations which can compete with the private sector and which are able to pay wages competitive with those of the private sector. At this stage, this is more a philosophy than a concrete experience in the city.

2 Housing is a crucial priority for community economic development (Mendell and Evoy, 1993: 47). Each approach to CED in Winnipeg has a housing component appropriate to its own philosophy, but housing is a particularly appropriate sector for the convergence approach to CED, given that it is a basic need, it has huge potential linkage possibilities, offers training and employment prospects, and can be organized collectively.

METHODOLOGY

The literature on financing CED in Winnipeg is almost non-existent whether it pertains to funding the overhead needs of CED organizations, the capital requirements of CED lending, or investment activities or, as is the case here, both. The main approach of this paper, therefore, is to reflect on the experiences of the author and of other CED activists within the city over the past 10 to 15 years. Interviews and discussions with those activists and, where possible, reference to annual reports and other documents of the institutions with which they are involved, form the basis of what follows.

THE GREENING OF THE ASSINIBOINE CREDIT UNION

In 1992, a group of social activists in Cho!ces, a Winnipeg coalition for social justice, organized a campaign to elect a more progressive board of directors of the Assiniboine Credit Union, the largest credit union in the city. They formed a group called The Greening of the Assiniboine which gradually took control of the board and began to steer the credit union, gently and, after a while, with the active support of the senior management team, in more socially responsible directions. This development has probably been the single most important development in the area of CED funding since 1990, since Assiniboine figures prominently in almost all current CED initiatives in the city.

Assiniboine has assets of over $650 million and a membership base of 51,000. Since its "greening," it has systematically developed services and products designed to promote CED. In 1995 it established a Community Loan Centre with four loans officers, a loans clerk and a CED project manager (Assiniboine Credit Union, 2002). The CED manager has a long track record of working with the Aboriginal community in developing successful CED projects and his appointment has been instrumental in moving ACU's CED agenda forward and in building community confidence in the ACU. The loan centre provides almost $50 million in credit to 550 small businesses, micro enterprises, cooperatives and non-profit organizations. But more than that, the ACU is involved, one way or another, with almost all CED initiatives in Winnipeg and with almost all financing initiatives, even when it is not the principal source of funding. Its importance in underpinning and promoting the CED movement in the city cannot be overemphasized. This was recognized in 2001 when ACU was selected for the 13th Annual Credit Union Community Economic Development Award (Assiniboine Credit Union, 2002).

SEED WINNIPEG AND THE ACU

The second major development in the early 1990s was the launching of SEED Winnipeg Inc., an independent, non-profit agency designed to promote micro and community enterprise development for low-income people. Originally set up in 1988, it was not until 1993 that SEED (Supporting Employment and Economic Development) got off the ground. Again, the appointment of an executive director who had the energy, the right mix of abilities and the insight to turn the concept into a practical reality was crucial. SEED provides a whole range of services vital to business development: from planning and evaluation, business management training, organization development, consulting, networking and advocacy. While it has the ability to provide small amounts of financing, it works closely with the Assiniboine Credit Union to provide access to capital to community-based businesses. The ACU has representation on SEED's board and since 2001 a senior staff member of SEED, who has been pivotal in helping consolidate and develop SEED's activities, has been a member of the board of ACU. The synergies created by this cooperation have been vital in the development of a whole range of new financial institutions and facilities in Winnipeg.

SEED was initially founded on financing micro-enterprises through its Micro-Enterprise Development Program, now called the Build-a-Business Program. This is a training based program in which clients develop a business plan. If the plan suggests the business is likely to be viable, clients can borrow up to $10,000 in startup loans. The loans are provided through Assiniboine and a joint ACU-SEED credit committee evaluates loan proposals. Since the program's inception, a total of 160 loans, or about $540,000, have been advanced. Since 1998, some of the funding for this comes from the ACU-Western Economic Diversification Micro-Loans Fund which finances businesses which are deemed to be high risk in terms of their collateral. To date, the Micro-Loans Fund has approved 250 loans totalling $3 million, of which 80 have been disbursed for a total of $1.3 million.

SEED also operated an 18-month Credit Circle pilot project, based on the Calmeadow model, in conjunction with Women's World Finance Manitoba Association, and funded by the United Way and the ACU. Women who had no credit history or little collateral were encouraged to form credit circles to gain access to credit to set up small businesses. First-time loans could not exceed $1,000 and additional loans could be secured only after all members were up to date on servicing existing loans. As mentioned earlier, the idea behind credit circles is that the social ties between members would act as a gentle incentive for each member to repay their loans, so that collectively, the risk is much less than it would be if individuals borrowed on their own. Five credit circles were formed consisting of 30 women. After a 12-week training program, members of each circle assessed and approved each others' loan applications before submitting them to a management board for approval. Early indications of success led to expanding the program to single parent women on social assistance through cooperation with the province's Taking Charge project (SEED, Annual Report, 1998). The credit circle program was frozen in 1999 and then abandoned. The problem was that the circles were put together somewhat artificially, especially those under the Taking Charge program, so that members had few if any ties with each other beyond the credit circle, with the result that collective responsibility for loans and defaults was lacking. Few businesses were created under this program and, when faced with the choice of program, those interested in forming businesses chose the micro-enterprise program (Source: Discussions with program officer responsible and direct experience as board member of SEED since its inception and Chair of SEED Winnipeg for the past four years).

Credit circles had been envisaged as a logical step in the progression from encouraging and supporting micro enterprises to developing a third main type of business, larger community enterprises. Indeed, the original conception of SEED in the mid-1980s, by the Community Education Development Association (CEDA), which has played a key role in many of the CED developments in Winnipeg, was that it would concentrate on collectively owned community ventures. Micro-business development, though useful in and of itself, was seen mainly as a necessary step towards achieving this goal, as funding was more easily attainable for this purpose and SEED needed to build a track record to gain credibility before moving on to sponsor larger, more collectively based undertakings. The collective element in credit circles was seen as the link in this progression. Unfortunately, with hindsight, the circles were not developed carefully enough or slowly enough to ensure that their collective foundations were solid.

Building a community enterprise program also required sufficient core funding and prior to the election of the New Democratic Party provincial government in 1999, there was no money for this. One of the achievements of SEED's two executive directors has been that they have painstakingly put together core budget funding which is now stable enough and large enough to allow SEED to take community enterprise development seriously. Core funding for SEED initially came from the United Way, which has been a vital and consistent supporter, the Thomas Sill Foundation, the Mennonite Central Committee (in kind), and a modest amount from the ACU and the Crocus Investment Fund. Later, contributions were received from a local progressive philanthropist and the Winnipeg Foundation (the largest philanthropic organization in the city). A significant scaling-up became possible in 1999 when government funding was received from the Canada/Manitoba Economic Partnership Agreement, bringing in $100,000 a year from Western Economic Diversification and $100,000 from the province. The big breakthrough came, however, in 2001 with a provincial government commitment of $235,000 a year for five years. With this size of funding in place for operations, serious attention can now be turned to promoting community enterprises and a Community and Worker Ownership Program has been established for this purpose. A small operating surplus in 2001 has allowed SEED to designate $30,000 for equity contributions in this area on a pilot project basis. Staff has developed a policy manual and timing guidelines for enterprise development and have been working with a number of existing and planned enterprises, helping develop business plans, assessing markets and fleshing out ideas. The goal is to develop two to four new businesses a year (SEED Annual Report: 9).

LITE

The ACU and SEED have played a crucial role in helping develop what was originally Christmas LITE, now called simply LITE, Local Investment Towards Employment. Established in 1994, LITE raises tax-deductible donations from the public and purchases food for Christmas hampers from community-oriented inner city businesses. The hampers are distributed through the Christmas Cheer Board, but by channelling money through LITE, charitable donations help strengthen permanent jobs in the inner city. In recent years, some portion of donations has been devoted to community-based ventures not involved in Christmas hampers. In 2001–02, LITE had a budget of $175,000 and made purchases of about $50,000 while giving grants of about $47,000. The beneficiaries included Neechi Foods, an Aboriginal worker-owned retail co-op, North-End Housing Aboriginal Youth Training Project, Native Women's Transition Centre, Northern Star Workers' Cooperative, Andrew Street Family Centre and seven other projects, including the Winnipeg IDA Project. The annual fund-raising campaign of LITE is a major educational tool for CED in Winnipeg and has the support of churches, trade unions and many other NGOs. 2001 marked a watershed for LITE in that it received grant funding from the Winnipeg Foundation enabling it to hire a full-time staff person for the first time.

ACU contributed to developing LITE by supporting, and persuading all other credit unions in Winnipeg to support, the annual appeal, and by providing technical advice and assistance. SEED assisted LITE initially by providing staff and office accommodation, helping with bookkeeping and issuing tax receipts on its behalf. Recently, LITE has secured its own charitable tax status and is now able to operate independently of SEED.

ALTERNATIVE FINANCIAL SERVICES COALITION (AFSC)

The ACU, SEED, the North End Community Ministry, the United Church Conference Office (Manitoba and Northwestern Ontario), and community residents have formed the Alternative Financial Services Coalition (AFSC) to increase opportunities for residents of low income areas. The AFSC has created the Financial Foundations Resource Centre to help fill the financial vacuum left by the departure of nine commercial bank branches in recent years. A study conducted by AFSC of pawnbrokers in the area showed that they were charging interest rates as high as 280 and 420% (*The Times*, Winnipeg, May 29, 2002). The Centre will encourage people to save, facilitate access to affordable loans, and provide financial training and education. Under the leadership of SEED, the Centre has introduced three asset-building programs. The first is the Winnipeg Individual Savings Account Pilot Project, which encourages participants to save for designated goals such as housing, education, or business capitalization and, after financial training, receive matching funds for each dollar saved in the ratio of 3:1. Since inception, 35 participants have deposited $34,400, averaging $77 a month (as opposed to the $25–$35 originally projected) and received matching funds of $97,600. 80% of the participants are women, 14% Aboriginal and 14% visible minority, and almost all have incomes well below the poverty line. Close to $30,000 has already been released, about half for housing and half for education. The pilot was funded by the Province of Manitoba, the Thomas Sill Foundation, the United Way, and two anonymous donors (SEED Annual Report 2002: 14). Based on the success of this pilot to date, a Saving Circle Individual Development Account Pilot Project has been launched with 25 members saving up to $720 for consumer durables such as furniture, disability aids, and education. This is funded by the United Way and the Investors Group. Other plans are in the works to extend the IDA program in Winnipeg and the Financial Management Training curriculum on which the original pilot was based is in high demand for other purposes (SEED Winnipeg, 2002b).

The third asset building program initiated by SEED and the Alternative Financial Services Coalition is the learn$ave program, for which Winnipeg is one of 10 designated national demonstration sites. learn$ave operates pretty much along the same lines as the IDA with participants saving for education or for starting a business and with savings being matched 3:1 up to a maximum of $4,500plus $1,500 or $6,000 over three years. The national partners in learn$ave are Social and Enterprise Development Innovations (SEDI) and Social Research and Demonstration Corporation (SRDC) and the program is funded by Human Resources Development Canada. The Winnipeg project will recruit 150 participants over two years. As of October 2002, there were 103 participants, with an average monthly deposit of $61, a total deposit of $19,000, and a matching amount accrued of $51,000.

People can also access SEED's Build-a-Business Program, the micro lending program, out of the Financial Foundations Resource Centre, which is located closer to the North End than the SEED office proper.

URBAN ENTREPRENEURS WITH DISABILITIES PROGRAM

The ACU and SEED also play a major role in the Urban Entrepreneurs with Disabilities Program, initiated by the Independent Living Resource Centre (ILRC). The Centre offers services for, advocates on behalf of, and is run by people with disabilities and has an impressive 20-year record of accomplishments. The Urban Entrepreneurs with Disabilities Program was initiated in 1999 and is financed by Western Economic Diversification through a special fund held in the ACU, though fully controlled by ILRC, with SEED providing training support. Both SEED and ACU are represented on the ILRC Loan Committee. To date, six businesses owned and operated by people with disabilities have received loans totalling $350,000 and have used these to leverage other monies from the ACU Community Loan Centre.

THE JUBILEE FUND

The Jubilee Fund Inc. was established by a coalition of faith groups to promote community economic development in Winnipeg, aimed at low income people and distressed inner city neighbourhoods. It was launched in 2000, the Jubilee Year, with technical support from the ACU. The fund raises money by offering Jubilee Investment

Certificates at 2% less than regular term deposit rates. ACU administers the fund, sits on its board, credit committee and project identification and support committee. It helped the Fund obtain charitable tax status, is helping it gain RRSP status and provided it with office space in the early days. So far, the Jubilee Fund has loaned eight projects a total of $350,000 and these have leveraged three times that from the credit union movement. Jubilee Fund deposits now stand at $450,000.

COMMUNITY OWNERSHIP SOLUTIONS (COS)

The most recent potential source of finance for CED projects is Community Ownership Solutions (COS), a not-for-profit development corporation with charitable tax status. This was created by the Crocus Investment Fund, a labour-sponsored investment fund, with the mandate of "the alleviation of poverty and structured unemployment in Winnipeg through the creation and transformation of market driven enterprises" (Community Ownership Solutions, 2002: 1). Its start-up costs were funded by Crocus which has committed to providing $90,000 a year for the next four years. The provincial Department of Intergovernmental Affairs and the federal Western Economic Diversification have each provided $250,000, spread over four years. COS will focus on two main activities: i) enterprise creation and incubation and ii) enterprise transformation through employee empowerment, participatory management and worker-ownership (Community Ownership Solutions, 2002: 1). COS views low-income joblessness (i.e., poverty) as being caused by "a lack of effective market relationships" and proposes sectoral development strategies, "which leverage existing market forces," to deal with this (Community Ownership Solutions, 2002: 2).

The first start-up enterprise supported by COS is the Inner City Renovations (ICR), established in June 2002 in conjunction with four other local development corporations, and building on earlier initiatives, to provide construction and renovation services in the inner city. ICR employed 20 full-time workers at commencement and expected to add 18 others by the end of its first year. It is, therefore, a significant project, both in terms of helping meet acute housing needs and in terms of training and employing local residents. This project has recently won a Social Enterprise Business Plan Competition run by Social Capital Partners of Toronto,[3] consisting of $15,000 for the business plan and $50,000 in financing, giving it a substantial boost.

Initially, there were misgivings in the CED community when COS was formed, because it appeared not to be sufficiently acknowledging of, or integrated with, the efforts of those who had struggled for so long to promote CED in the city.[4] It has been suggested that there was also perhaps a clash of cultures, language, and values with COS coming essentially out of a business background whereas much of Winnipeg's CED movement comes out of a social services background. There is certainly a need to bridge these gaps if CED is to advance and working together is probably the only way this will happen. These early misgivings about COS have been allayed by the appointment of a general manager who had been seconded by Crocus to assist in the formation of the North End Community Renewal Corporation and who, in the process, built up an excellent reputation for being able to work effectively with people on the ground. COS also has a board consisting of people with considerable CED experience both in Manitoba and elsewhere. With the successful launching of ICR, COS is now a welcome addition to the CED scene.

3 Social Capital Partners is "a venture philanthropy organization created to invest in and support revenue-generating social enterprises that employ at-risk populations outside the economic mainstream in Canada." It was formed in 2001 and expects to invest at least $5 million by 2007 in ventures which it hopes will eventually be financially self-reliant. (Press release, Social Capital Partners, Toronto, September 19, 2002).

4 The way in which COS appears to define the causes of poverty is also quite different from the dominant view in the Winnipeg CED community. A lack of effective market relationships as a cause of poverty overlooks the fact that the market can be both a creative force in the evolution of a neighbourhood as well as a basis for its loss of self-determination; witness the fate of many company towns (Mendell and Evoy, 1993: 49). Eric Shragge has also commented on the irony of the state withdrawing from social programs designed to rectify the inadequacies of the market, only to turn around and call upon poor communities to use the market as a means of ameliorating local economic and social conditions (UNDP, 2002: 12). Whether defining the problem in the way COS does will lead to any practical problems in implementing CED remains to be seen.

REFLECTIONS ON THE FINANCING OF CED IN WINNIPEG

The last 10 years have seen a blossoming of CED financial institutions in Winnipeg, the product of the vision and the hard work of a relatively small but dedicated number of activists whose goal has been to improve living conditions for poorer residents of the city. Anchoring these developments has been the ACU, the "greening" of which was the product of concerted, strategic political action. Without the "greening," progress elsewhere would have been much slower and much more difficult. But the ACU is a commercial undertaking which must compete for business with other financial institutions, including other credit unions, and the prime responsibility of the Board of Directors is not and cannot be support of CED at all costs. By and large its loans must be commercially viable and the larger and more profitable its commercial loan and related business, the more ACU can afford to put resources aside to subsidize CED projects either directly or in terms of potential losses and the relatively high transactions costs entailed. Almost by definition, CED projects are at best marginal ones commercially; otherwise the need for CED would not be there, as the gap it is filling would not be left by the private sector. This means that CED projects must have access to sources of funding other than the ACU, for equity, project preparation and evaluation, business and market development and so on, and it is this which explains both the need for a variety of financial institutions working on CED and the need for capital from government, foundations, donations, etc.

Reliance on government is clearly important for most of the financial institutions mentioned above, and even some of the ACU lending activities are government-funded. Most of SEED's core funding is from the federal and provincial governments and its charitable tax status is what allows it to be eligible for funding from the United Way. Both LITE and the Jubilee Fund rely heavily on tax-deductible charitable donations. The Urban Entrepreneurs with Disabilities Program is state-funded as are the individual asset building programs of the AFSC. The core funding of the COS is partially raised indirectly from tax-deductible RRSP contributions through Crocus and partially from direct government funding.

Government funding therefore underpins almost all the CED funding initiatives in Winnipeg, except for the basic business of the ACU.

Government funding also underpins the activities of the neighbourhood development or renewal corporations which have emerged in recent years. For example, the highly successful West Broadway Development Corporation has its own land trust, promotes house building and repair, provides education, training, and job services, offers environmental services, and a whole host of outreach, art, and cultural activities. In many ways it is a model for other development corporations. In 2001–02 it had a budget of $1.1 million and fully $0.95 million was funded by government, $0.5 million by the province alone (West Broadway Development Corporation, 2002). Its success, therefore, is based very much on its ability to mobilize state resources. This is almost certainly true also of other neighbourhood development or renewal corporations[5] and is highlighted not as a criticism, but rather as a situation which needs careful consideration in terms of its implications for future stability.

Dependence on government funding has enabled a marked increase in CED activity in recent years, especially after the 1999 election. It was something the CED community pushed hard for, on the basis of a clear set of CED principles—the Neechi Principles outlined above—which almost all CED institutions in the city have agreed upon. These principles have been accepted as the lens through which the provincial government will evaluate the contribution of its own activities to furthering CED. Thus, the community has had an impact on government policy even as it heightened its dependence on government funding. Influencing policy in this way has certainly made the financial dependence more palatable, as has the multi-year financing approach of the provincial government. Yet there is still some uneasiness about that dependence as a change

---

5 Certainly it is true of the North End Community Renewal Corporation (NECRC). SEED obtained government funding to help establish this corporation but initially it had only project money and resources it was able to generate, creatively, through CEDA, the Mennonite Central Committee, the Jubilee Fund, the Canadian Community Economic Development Technical Assistance Program (CEDTAP), the United Way, and the Crocus Investment Fund. In 2000, it received a core operating grant of $200,000 from the province. See Perry, 2001)

of government sometime in the future might potentially destabilize the financial infrastructure that so recently and painstakingly has been constructed.

There are a number of ways of minimizing the potential instability of this dependence on government funding.[6] The first is to establish a CED trust or endowment fund, or a series of such trusts or funds, into which government(s) would make lump-sum contributions. The earnings on this fund would provide annual capital and operating funds for CED institutions and would be administered by an arms-length body representing the community, though undoubtedly with some government representation. In effect the government(s) would be capitalizing future contributions and paying them, one-time, up front. The attraction to the CED community is obvious, as this arrangement would remove the uncertainty surrounding government budgeting and regime changes. It would not likely remove all uncertainty, as the government resource allocation process would be replaced by an alternative allocation process in which personal, ideological, and jurisdictional disputes might still prevail. But the CED community would take their chances on this.

From the government's perspective, however, the advantages are much less clear. Funding CED operations to the tune of, say $1 to $2 million a year (i.e., excluding capital and housing funding but covering operating costs) would require an endowment of $17 to $40 million up front with interest rates in the 5–6% per annum range. Funding housing or equity finance for businesses in this way would require much larger endowments. Under existing balanced budget legislation, the provincial government is not allowed to borrow this and finding this kind of money would not be easy. At the same time, government would also lose flexibility in determining the allocation of CED support and discretion over CED priorities. While this might be a good thing from the community's point of view, the political attractions to government are less obvious. Nonetheless, one could argue that a trust arrangement would test the government's commitment to CED and its confidence in existing CED institutions.

---

6 The Canadian CED Network is also examining sustainable funding strategies, but what follows are suggestions currently under discussion in Winnipeg.

Certainly, this proposal is alive and well in Winnipeg and the government will continue to face it.

There are four other proposals for dealing with the issue of potential instability in relying on state funding, each of which involves diversifying funding sources. The first two of these are not incompatible with the trust or endowment proposal. The first advocates relying more on charitable foundations. While some continue to consider this money "tainted" because much of it comes from profits amassed by private enterprise, others as Gunn and Gunn (1991: 73–76) have pointed out, see nothing special in the origins of this particular form of "social surplus." Like other sources, its ultimate origin is people's work, past or present "and as much of that money should be returned to poor communities and people as can be wrung from the foundations" (Gunn and Gunn, 1991: 76). Since the basis of foundations is tax deductibility of donations, the state still plays a major role in determining their size and scope of activities and it can still create uncertainty and instability by its actions.[7] But, once a foundation is up and running, the extent of state intervention is likely to be much less than it might be under directly state-funded operations.

The Thomas Sill Foundation was definitely ahead of its time in supporting CED efforts in Winnipeg, funding SEED before any other foundation was prepared to. It has also supported CEDA, the North End Community Renewal Corporation, the North End Housing Project and others. It helped pave the way for other foundations to support CED in Winnipeg. Since the early 1990s, the United Way has played an increasing role in helping build CED institutions. Before that, it more closely resembled Gunn and Gunn's generic description of United Ways across North America, as being "cautious" and "elite controlled," favouring the charity model approach as opposed to the CED approach. Now, the Winnipeg organization is more "forward looking and innovative in meeting community needs" than it used to be, realizing a potential that is inherent in the "local structural form" of all United Ways (Gunn and Gunn, 1991: 76).

7   For instance, it took SEED and LITE two years of negotiating with Canada Customs and Revenue Agency (CCRA) before LITE's activities were accepted as being consistent with CCR's definition of "charity."

At the present time, the Winnipeg United Way, in conjunction with the ACU, has established a committee to study gaps and needs in the operations of CED institutions in Winnipeg, as a means of determining its future possible contributions in this area.

The other major development on the foundation front in Winnipeg is the entry into CED financing of the Winnipeg Foundation. This foundation had already begun to support CED in the city by helping fund SEED and LITE. In December 2001, it received a $100 million donation from the Moffat family in Winnipeg, owners of a successful TV station and related activities, taking the total size of the foundation to $315 million. The annual income from the Moffat donation alone will be $6.6 million and 80% of this will be available for "programs giving children and families an equal chance in our society" (*Winnipeg Free Press*, December 14, 2001). Some portion of this will be available for funding CED projects. Most significantly, the Winnipeg Foundation has hired the former Executive Director of CEDA to take care of this, a community activist who has perhaps played a larger role than any other single individual in developing the institutions of CED in the city.

The CED activities of foundations in Winnipeg are, therefore, likely to grow in the immediate future and to provide an important complement to state funding.

The second proposal for diversifying the funding base of CED activities is that of extending tax credits to business for donations in cash and in kind (staff, materials, services). This model is used in the U.S. where tax credits are sometimes extended for companies providing long-term jobs for people on social assistance. In Winnipeg, the main proponent of this approach, which is designed to "develop long-term relationships" between community groups and business, is the President and Chief Executive Officer of the Crocus Fund (*Winnipeg Free Press,* September 26, 2002), but it is also being advocated by the Canadian CED Network. The advantages over other approaches would be that there might be more stability than direct government funding and companies might identify more closely with the CED projects they are supporting than they would if their donations were channelled through a foundation. There might also be benefits to CED projects, other than the financial, from being close to companies.

On the other hand, from the point of view of the budget's bottomline, a tax credit is no different from government spending but government has less control[1] over both the total and the allocation of funds inherent in the tax credit. For that reason, governments might want a more hands-on approach. Business would undoubtedly have its own view of what constitutes appropriate CED and there might be less chance of the CED community influencing that than if the funds were mediated through a foundation, or even allocated directly by government. At this point in time, neither the Crocus Fund (directly or through the COS), nor the major foundations in Winnipeg, has endorsed the Neechi CED Principles. This may suggest ideological differences in approach to CED, and certainly Crocus appears to be much more optimistic about the benefits of working closely with private business and through the market than do the majority of CED actors in Winnipeg. At the same time, the one project so far supported by the COS is a partnership with community organizations, including the North-End Housing Project, which do subscribe to those principles and the project itself is perfectly consistent with them. In the case of the foundations, they also seem quite happy to fund CED institutions committed to the Neechi Principles without openly adopting those principles themselves.

The issue of what we mean by CED is one which goes beyond the particular mechanisms adopted to raise money for CED. At the moment, there are at least three quite separate activities being funded by the institutions described above: i) micro-business development, ii) individual asset-building and iii) community- or worker-owned larger-scale business projects. All of these have legitimate CED components and each can be designed to reinforce or complement the others. The last is, however, qualitatively different from the first two in a number of ways. First, the scale is different. The problems of poverty and unemployment in the inner city of Winnipeg are too large to be dealt with by micro-businesses alone or by subsidizing individual savings, important though these might be for the individuals involved. Not every poor person aspires to be or has the qualities to become a successful micro-entrepreneur and the scope for micro-businesses is quite limited. The idea of providing people with a house, an education, and furniture and appliances through subsidizing their savings in a 3:1 ratio is a fine one but it cannot be generalized to all the poor of the city, simply in administrative and budget terms. (Though even modest efforts in this direction could be designed to support more collectively based, larger-scale housing or business projects, while educational advancement is clearly imperative for all CED initiatives). Creating community- or worker-owned businesses faces its own constraints, in terms of requiring a higher level of technical assistance, larger amounts of equity and legal or administrative barriers to cooperatives raising money,[8] but it nonetheless seems to offer more employment possibilities and a lower demand on administrative resources per job created. It also provides explicitly for collective activities and decision-taking, not allowed for in the other options, although there are plans to establish an IDA to assist co-op members with equity financing.

The link between the approach to CED and the method of raising money to finance CED might become much more apparent if community- or worker-owned enterprises grew in such number and size that they became competitors with privately owned businesses. At that point, the drawbacks of corporate tax credit or foundation financing might become readily apparent. As things stand, there is so much that needs to be done to promote CED in Winnipeg that these dangers are more intellectual than real at this point in time.

Tax credits need not be confined to businesses. In Nova Scotia, the province offers residents provincial tax credits equal to 30% of eligible investments in Community Economic Development Investment Funds. These funds raise money by an RRSP-eligible limited public offering and credits are capped at $9,000 per person. The government of Nova Scotia guarantees 20% of the amount invested in community economic development entities (information provided by Department of Finance, Province of Nova Scotia).

---

8 If cooperatives wish to raise more than $500 per member in loans or shares, an offering statement must be prepared which can be quite time-consuming. Also, the Self-Employed Assistance Program, SEA, when run by the federal government, used to be prepared to consider "group SEAs," but since the province took over the program this option appears to have been closed off (Source: Personal communication with Blair Hamilton, CED consultant, October 18, 2002).

This has helped keep savings in the province, whether RRSP-related or not, and has been a boon for CED activities. In the early days the credits were directed to specific businesses but are now increasingly being deposited in blind trusts, or pools, from which more than one business is financed. In these kinds of programs, provision for exit is important, especially when retirement funds are involved, and this presents its own design problems.

Personal and corporate tax credits are being examined in Manitoba but there is a feeling in the provincial government that other levels of government, especially the City of Winnipeg, need to become more actively involved in these kinds of incentive programs. Thus, the province has changed the City of Winnipeg Act to give the City power to allow companies to retain for a number of years any property tax increases which might come from a business expanding as a result of investment and to use them for reinvestment purposes. The thinking is that CED activities might benefit from this type of scheme (interview with Minister of Finance, Province of Manitoba, April 20, 2002).

The third approach to diversifying the funding base of CED does not necessarily face the potential conundrums raised by corporate tax credits. This is the grow bond approach, currently in operation in rural and Northern Manitoba. Grow bonds are used to raise capital for corporations and the attraction is that their principal is guaranteed by the provincial government. They are overseen and issued by a local Grow Bond Corporation, formed for that purpose, and governed by their own legislation (Statutes of Manitoba, 1991). Proceeds can be invested only in the corporation for which they were issued, but must not exceed 40% of the total capital of the company. They are available in $100 denominations, subject to a limit of $50,000 per person, and can be held only by residents of Manitoba. There have been proposals to extend this type of financing to projects in the inner city of Winnipeg, but the provincial government has resisted this on the grounds that for the program to work there as it does in the rest of Manitoba, the City of Winnipeg would have to become much more involved in inner city business development than it is now. It is also not clear who actually buys such bonds and if, in rural areas, the main investors are local, as opposed to being provincewide, this might limit the transferability of this approach to the inner city, where such capital is lacking.

The fourth proposal for diversifying the funding base of CED is for neighbourhood development or renewal corporations to undertake business ventures, such as property development or property management. In decaying areas of town this will call for a mix of commercial and non-commercial activities and the private sector is not likely to be interested. Neighbourhood corporations may, however, be able to leverage non-market financing to undertake this task and build up financial capacity in this way.[9]

In any event, interviews with leaders of CED organizations suggest that, at this time, funding for the overhead of CED ventures does not appear to be a critical constraint in Winnipeg. The institutional structure that has evolved in recent years can handle the demands being made upon it and the funding for the operations of that structure is not, by and large, preventing it from performing the functions it is designed to perform. If asked, the leaders of all CED institutions would admit they could use more funding if it were available, and new ideas are constantly being generated by activists (e.g., SEED is attempting to reach out to immigrant women interested in forming a business), but there is a general feeling that the structure is in better shape now than ever before. The availability of loan financing for projects also does not appear to be a problem, given the availability of the Assiniboine Credit Union. The one financial constraint that might bite if larger, collectively owned projects were to be developed in any number, is equity (or grant) capital. This exists only for micro-enterprises and asset-based schemes. It does not exist in an organized fashion for community- or worker-based enterprises. Currently, there are two important review exercises taking place in Winnipeg; one is being conducted by LITE and covers the structures within which CED operates in Winnipeg,

---

9 Garry Loewen, the first Executive Director of SEED and the first Executive Director of the North End Renewal Corporation, brought to my attention the fact that the North End Community Renewal Corporation sees a need for this on Selkirk Avenue, once a major commercial centre in the North End of Winnipeg and now a distressed area. Here, there is an important "development gap," as he calls it, in the property development and management field.

including the funding structure; the second is being conducted by the United Way in cooperation with ACU and is aimed primarily at what role it might play in CED, although it is branching out into other areas. It is almost certain that these reviews will highlight the equity gap in current arrangements and make recommendations to address it. There should be a role here for both government and foundations and a special fund, if not a trust or endowment, should be designated for that purpose. Some thought needs to go into how best to raise capital for this.

While there is tremendous potential for worker-influenced pension funds to contribute towards expanding CED operations (Usiskin, 1996), there are also dangers given that such funds must earn a reasonable rate of return to secure members' pensions. It is possible to segregate a portion of pension fund investments for social objectives which, while needing to earn a return, need not return the commercial average, but this can only be a small portion. Going beyond that raises concerns about pension fund viability. As Stanford has argued (1999: 377–378), "It is politically and strategically risky to require them to adhere to a higher ethical and social standard (which, if we are honest, implies some sacrifice in terms of financial returns) when the other 88% of the stock market is allowed to run roughshod over the social and economic landscape." This suggests, on the one hand, that creative ways have to be found to guarantee those returns and, secondly, that equally creative ways must be found to bring other actors—individuals, companies, churches, and NGOs—into the picture. In the process, all options, including guarantees of principal and/or rates of return, tax credits, and charitable tax receipts, need to be examined in detail.

In what is a crucial area of CED activity, housing, the issue of equity capital has not proven to be as constraining as it appeared to be a few years ago. All three levels of government have suddenly woken up to the implications of the acute shortage of housing and the poor condition of much of the housing stock. CED approaches to upgrading or in-filling houses have many attractions, in terms of community involvement and pride, ability to train local residents for full-time permanent jobs, and putting public dollars to better use. A number of institutions, such as Just Housing, North

End Community Renovation Enterprise,[10] North End Housing Project and housing associations in West Broadway and Spence, and the land trust in West Broadway, have been set up with success in recent years, drawing in part on the model established by Quint in Saskatoon, which has an excellent track record (Caledon, March 2001). It is through these and similar community organizations that a recently announced tri-level housing program, costing in the region of $70 million and creating 2,500 affordable housing units, will be delivered (Winnipeg Real Estate News, September 27, 2002). There is an obvious tie-in here also with the asset-building schemes and it is interesting to note that the Canada Mortgage and Housing Corporation (CMHC) is looking into the possibility of launching a national housing IDA pilot project, with Winnipeg as a possible site (Source: correspondence with the SEED IDA project officer). It is in sectors other than housing that the equity/grant financing constraint may become critical. The development of commercial and semi-commercial space in rundown areas of the city, and even erecting or renovating buildings which might be occupied partly by educational and other services, will require significant amounts of equity/grant funding. Finding this will present a real challenge.

CONCLUSION

Much has happened since the Community Inquiry in 1990 and many of the demands of the community are now being met, in one degree or another. Loans for small businesses and micro-enterprises are more accessible than they were at that time, the housing stock is being improved, and many key CED actors have subscribed to the Neechi Principles which, while not constituting a development strategy, lay out clearly the basis on which such a strategy should proceed. No serious observer of the Winnipeg CED scene would argue, however, that enough is happening to radically change the incidence of poverty in the city. The steps taken so far are impressive but still halting and marginal given the size of the problem being

---

10 Just Housing and North End Community Renovation Enterprise no longer exist, the latter having been replaced by Inner City Renovations.

faced. "Scaling up" current efforts is seen to be essential and this will require many more resources than provided so far. The key to scaling up will lie in addressing the binding constraint of equity or grant financing.[11]

---

11 There is perhaps an even greater constraint to CED in Winnipeg, that of human resources, to replace existing leadership and to allow the movement to grow. This is currently being addressed by a number of initiatives designed to strengthen the training of all types of CED workers.

CHAPTER 9

THE STATE OF COMMUNITY ECONOMIC DEVELOPMENT IN WINNIPEG[1]

The main purpose of this chapter is to reflect a little on the nature of the momentum in the CD/CED movement in Winnipeg and on what lies behind it. I will also suggest some of the measures that might be needed to maintain and strengthen that momentum.

It seems to me that Winnipeg is rapidly becoming a major focal point in Canada for community economic development and I think there are eight reasons for this.

1. CED in Winnipeg is guided by a clear set of principles, the Neechi Principles, to which almost all groups and activists adhere (see Chapter 7). These are clear, unambiguous, and demanding. They have received national attention and were developed in Winnipeg by an Aboriginal workers' cooperative.

2. Activists in Winnipeg have demonstrated a willingness to engage with people across the country in promoting the philosophy and practice of CED. There has been an eagerness to learn from what others have done across Canada and internationally and we have benefited from activists being willing to come to Winnipeg to share their experiences. The annual conferences of CCEDNET, CED-TAP, and of workers' cooperatives, which were held in Winnipeg in 2002, provided us an excellent opportunity to connect constructively with both theorists and practitioners from elsewhere. Our own practitioners are also actively involved in these national organizations. For some years now, a regional representative of CCEDNET

---

[1] From John Loxley, Jim Silver, and Kathleen Sexsmith, (eds.), *Doing Community Economic Development*, Fernwood Books, Halifax, 2007.

has been appointed to Winnipeg and is based in the office of the Canadian Centre for Policy Alternatives-Manitoba.

3. We now have a very strong institutional base for CED in Winnipeg, with several institutions now having a long track record. For animating both CD and CED, there is the Community Education Development Agency (CEDA), which celebrated its 25th anniversary in 2003. For financial support there is the Assiniboine Credit Union (ACU), which has won national awards not only for its CED work but also for its progressive human resource policies, SEED Winnipeg, LITE, the Alternative Financial Services Coalition, the Jubilee Fund, Community Ownership Solutions, and the Urban Entrepreneurs with Disabilities Program (these are described in more detail in Chapter 8). We also have a growing number of delivery agencies on the ground which are maturing and making an impact, notably the development corporations in West Broadway, Spence, and the North End (see Chorney, 2003). The number of CED-based housing institutions has proliferated (see Cates, 2003), such as Inner City Renovations (which replaced Just Housing and the North End Community Renovation Enterprise), the North End Housing Project and housing associations in West Broadway and Spence, and Ogijiita Pimatiswin Kinamatwin (the Aboriginal Youth Housing Renovation Project, for ex-inmates). Housing is, in my opinion, particularly important to CED because it clearly fulfils a crucial basic human need, it provides opportunities for the acquisition of skills by local residents, it offers opportunities for well-paying jobs, it potentially helps create linkages with other service and production ventures (e.g., training and building supplies), and it can play an important role in helping promote neighbourhood stability which is crucial for long-term CED. Winnipeg also has a multitude of employment and training agencies and social service agencies and it also has an embryonic social enterprise sector (see papers by Loewen, 2003a and 2003b). It also has a social purchasing portal established by SEED, which directs businesses via the web to suppliers of goods and services that create employment opportunities for individuals or groups "that face multiple barriers to employment" (<sppwinnipeg.org/>). This creates jobs in inner city and social purpose businesses while enabling purchasers to be socially responsible.

4. Since 1999, government support of CED has improved markedly. The election of an NDP provincial government in that year has led to a substantial increase in support for CED, in a number of different ways. First of all, the creation of a Community and Economic Development Committee of Cabinet (CEDC) has elevated CED policy to an unprecedented level in the province. Secondly, and through CEDC, a CED policy lens has been introduced through which the contribution of all government activities will be evaluated. This lens is unique in Canada and is based on the Neechi Principles which, clearly, now have the support of the provincial government (see Sheldrick, 2007, for an elaboration as well as a critical assessment). Thirdly, provincial financial support for CED has been increased markedly through the Neighbourhoods Alive! Program, which provides core funding for many of the institutions mentioned earlier. The NDP government has also brought in legislation enabling financial contributions to CED to be eligible for tax credits and is the first government in Canada to introduce tax increment financing which enables municipalities to reinvest property tax revenues into CED initiatives. It has also taken steps to support CED projects, both Aboriginal and otherwise, through its procurement policies (these and other initiatives supported by the province are described more fully in the Manitoba Budget, 2006). While many within and outside the provincial government would like to see it do more, this is an impressive record. The federal government has also made an important contribution to CED in Winnipeg through Western Economic Diversification (WED) which, for instance, was instrumental in helping SEED Winnipeg get off the ground. The Winnipeg Partnership Agreement, between all three levels of government, has given CED a significant boost in the city, and will invest $75 million over five years into CED and urban renewal (Winnipeg Partnership Agreement, 2005).

5. Winnipeg CED has also benefited significantly in recent years from the active involvement of a number of charitable foundations. The Thomas Sill Foundation and the United Way have provided important strategic assistance to a number of local CED organizations, with the latter assuming an increasingly important coordinating role in the CED movement generally. Most recently, the

Winnipeg Foundation has joined them, funding a large CED initiative in the hitherto relatively neglected Centennial neighbourhood. That these foundations would depart so significantly from a narrow charity model of assistance represents a remarkable transformation in approach over the last decade or so and is a great credit to their boards and leadership.

6. There is also a very supportive academic environment for CED in Winnipeg. All three universities have an interest in CED and a good track record of research in the field. The approach to research is both interdisciplinary and participatory. Research findings and non-academic participants in CED are brought into the classroom to strengthen teaching and to bring the subject alive for students. Many academics are actively involved in CED ventures. In 2002, the three universities cooperated with the Canadian Centre for Policy Alternatives-Manitoba, a number of community organizations, and the provincial and federal governments to form the Manitoba Research Alliance and obtained an $895,000 SSHRC/INE grant to conduct research into CED and the new economy, one outcome of which was the volume in which this paper originally appeared (Loxley, Silver, and Sexsmith, 2007). This was a unique project, led by a non-academic community-based research organization and supported by such CED agencies as the North End Community Renewal Corporation, the West Broadway Development Corporation, and SEED. This alliance was based on cooperation between academics and non-academics interested in CED and has helped push back the frontiers of knowledge, examining what works and what does not and what are the best practice opportunities for promoting CED. It gave unprecedented opportunities for a number of young people to become involved in CED through research and, in the process, has been important in helping create the next generation of CED activists and intellectuals.

7. Winnipeg is fortunate to have a fairly large number of remarkable people involved in promoting CED. Many of these have slogged away in the trenches for years when there was little to show for these efforts. Some have stayed involved with early CED initiatives, such as Neechi or SEED, over many years, through thick

and thin. Many have cut their teeth in CEDA. For over a decade now many have hung in with ACU, watching it grow from strength to strength. Many more have sat as volunteers on CED boards, receiving little thanks or acknowledgement for their efforts. Without such people, and my sense is that Winnipeg is unusually well endowed with them, CED would not be as well developed as it is.

8. There is, therefore, a strong cultural foundation of CED in the City, underpinned by a widely held view of the need for and importance of collective action to improve social well-being. It is based on irreverence towards the establishment and a willingness to challenge it to address issues of poverty, deprivation, and exclusion. It is also based on mutual respect for fellow CED activists, even though they may often draw their inspiration from quite different ideological perspectives. It is quite pragmatic, building on what works, working with the establishment where it helps, and doing what it takes to get things done, but all generally within the framework of the Neechi Principles.

It is this combination of factors that makes Winnipeg such a dynamic place for CED today. Many of them are difficult to replicate elsewhere because they originated, uniquely, in the history, politics, and sociology of the city. Nonetheless, we can expect interest in our CED experience to grow as successes in the city are consolidated. This is not to denigrate or belittle the CED experience elsewhere in Canada or to suggest that the Winnipeg experience does not borrow from and build on those experiences: quite the opposite. The Winnipeg CED community has benefited enormously from lessons learned in Quebec, B.C., Saskatchewan, Nova Scotia, P.E.I., and elsewhere, bringing in visitors from these provinces to help shape our policies and approaches. Without this input, which is greatly appreciated, CED in Winnipeg would be much less developed than it is.

This description of accomplishments is also not meant to suggest that there are no problems facing CED in Winnipeg. On the contrary, if the momentum of the CED movement here is to be maintained, then some important challenges have to be met. Among them are the following:

THE TRAINING AND REPLACEMENT OF PEOPLE

The challenge here is one of succession and growth; to produce a sufficient number of people trained in CED to provide both for the replacement of current practitioners and for the inevitable growth in CED activities in the city. This challenge was recognized some time ago and provision was made for coordinating existing and developing new CED training programs. This was a cooperative effort involving many CED groups in Winnipeg and led to the establishment of a CD/CED Training Intermediary, a partnership between the community and provincial government, with associated courses at Red River College. This, however, has been beset with problems and has not worked well. There have also been problems of accreditation with Red River. Skills shortages, especially in finance and bookkeeping, appear to be a significant problem in existing institutions and staff need to have the opportunity to upgrade.

Succession needs more careful planning as well as provision of financial resources for a smooth transition. Especially in leadership positions, there is too much reliance on a few skilled individuals.

STABILIZING AND DIVERSIFYING THE FUNDING OF OPERATIONS

It is generally acknowledged that the success of CED in recent years in raising grant funding from the government for operations also contains the seeds of a potential vulnerability should government or government policy change (Chapter 8). It is one thing to recognize this danger, quite another to address it. Three possibilities are a) reducing dependence on any single grant source by diversifying funders as much as possible, b) seeking to build an endowment or trust approach which, in effect, means obtaining funding upfront for use in future years, and c) building up personal or corporate donations through the new tax credit program. Each of these presents its own challenges, but pursuing them is worthwhile given what is potentially at stake.

FUNDING CAPITAL EXPENDITURES

It is also generally acknowledged that there is currently a crucial gap in CED financing in Winnipeg: capital spending. There is a need to build an equity fund or to secure grant financing for long-term capital expenditures if the development of social enterprises, in particular, is to be achieved. There are tentative beginnings in Community Ownership Solutions (COS), a non-profit development corporation which promotes market-based solutions to CED <communityownershipsolutions.com/about/index.html> and, to a smaller degree, in SEED and the issue has been studied systematically. COS suffered a big setback with the recent collapse of the Crocus Investment Fund, which sponsored it.

THE PROMOTION OF SOCIAL ENTERPRISES

There is a widely held view in Winnipeg that for CED to make a big impact, we must move aggressively into building commercially viable social enterprises. It is recognized that this is not an easy challenge, as suggested by the cautious progress of social enterprises in the city to date; it is, nonetheless, a necessary one if CED efforts are to be scaled up significantly. There have been a number of unique opportunities which could have been, and some could still be, pivotal for social enterprises in the city, but which appear to have been missed to this point in time. The Winnipeg Floodway extension is now in progress, the largest civic infrastructure project by far. A new Hydro building is being constructed downtown, presenting potential social enterprise opportunities for both construction and maintenance. A new spate of hydro dam building is about to start in the North, in which some provision has been made for partnerships with local First Nations communities. There may be logical extensions to social enterprises in Winnipeg. A new wave of infrastructure spending is under way in the city, funded in part by senior levels of government. There are proposals for building a road up the east side of Lake Winnipeg and, again, the potential spin-off benefits for companies in Winnipeg are huge. Momentum is also building for expansion of programs to provide accessible housing, especially for recent immigrants and possibly on a cooperative basis. Each of these presented and may still present potential economic opportunities for social enterprises.

There is also a growing interest in alternative delivery mechanisms in the social service area which might be ideal for social enterprises. Finally, the Winnipeg Partnership Agreement cries out for fresh ideas on community economic development and could help finance pursuit of social enterprises in areas outlined here.

Each of these opportunities offers the possibility of pursuing social enterprise on a scale large enough to promise viability, the possibility of decent wages and salaries, the potential of significant linkages among a number of social enterprises, and a degree of stability which can only be envied by existing social enterprises that struggle for survival in the highly competitive and fickle commercial service sector.

It is apparent, however, that the CED community lacks the organizational capacity to make inroads into most of these areas using social enterprises, despite a sympathetic and supportive government policy environment. What is needed is an organization which has roots in the community which can respond to economic opportunities by mobilizing people, putting together a business plan and having the capability to establish and run, or find others to run, competent social economy enterprises. This need was acknowledged in the CED symposium held in Winnipeg in April 2006 and meetings designed to rectify the situation are planned for the fall of 2006. It remains to be seen what is left of the above employment opportunities by the time such a vehicle is up and running.

The most successful forms of social enterprise in Winnipeg appear to be cooperatives, in the form of a co-op gas company which is both large and, with the rising price of gasoline, rapidly growing; credit unions, which are becoming the daily banking vehicle for an ever greater proportion of the population as banks scale back retail operations, and housing co-ops of which there are several successful examples and for which there is a large unmet demand. In the past, retail grocery co-ops have had some success and the Neechi Foods and Mondragon restaurant worker co-ops continue to survive, if not thrive. To me this suggests that co-ops are seen to be a suitable organizational form for social enterprise in Winnipeg[2] and, secondly, that there is interest in having the goods and services of daily life provided by social enterprises, in the form of co-ops. Perhaps a major concern of the planned CED social enterprise facilitation vehicle could be not just to foster participation in megaprojects, but also to encourage the provision of cradle to grave goods and services, such as childcare facilities, housing, transport, consumer durable goods, groceries, cafés, and funeral parlours. Perhaps also, some consideration could be given to help meet the technical needs of existing CED organizations through the creation of self-supporting, non-profit social enterprises in the fields of finance or human relations.

THE ABORIGINAL CHALLENGE

Some 50,000 Aboriginal people currently live in Winnipeg and by the year 2016, one in five children in Winnipeg will be Aboriginal (Loxley and Wien 2003). An atrociously high proportion of Aboriginal people in the city live in poverty—almost two-thirds—and that rises to over 80%, four out of five, in the inner city (Lezubski, Silver and Black, 2000). If this outrageous situation is to be addressed, CED must also play a part. Solutions will call for early childhood interventions, educational reform, improved housing and recreation, and greater neighbourhood stability, a larger training and apprenticeship initiative, and training geared more directly to future employment needs. CED can play an important role in many of these areas and the Aboriginal factor must be built into all CED approaches and recognized in the opportunities outlined in 4 above. The issue of whether Aboriginal needs should be met through separate Aboriginal institutions or through integrated ones is a tough one to deal with. The needs are so great that a mix of both

---

2 In principle, there are numerous organizational forms through which social enterprises can be operated and, if the situation is right, any one can be as effective as any other. If co-ops have an edge at all, it would lie in the clear legal framework, including that of democratic decision-taking, profit-sharing, and taxation, in which they operate. See Loughran (1985) for a detailed comparison of community development corporations versus cooperatives in CED.

is probably needed. This will require changes in the way several CED institutions operate. It will require greater attention to recruiting, training, advancing, and retaining Aboriginal staff and a greater say by Aboriginal people in the definition of their priorities for and strategies of CED (see Silver, Ghorayshi, Hay, and Klyne, 2007). It will also require a greater Aboriginal presence on boards of directors. Each CED institution probably needs to develop an Aboriginal Advancement plan dealing with these questions.

THE COMPLEXITY OF POVERTY IN WINNIPEG

While the specific needs of the Aboriginal community in Winnipeg requires special attention, because of its unique historical and cultural origins, care must be taken to recognize that poverty in the city is multi-ethnic, multi-dimensional, and non-static. Thus, most Aboriginal people living in the inner city are poor, but most poor people are not Aboriginal. Indeed, recent inflows of refugees come from a diversity of backgrounds and many are, in fact, African. Unidimensional anti-poverty strategies which do not take into account the varied backgrounds, problems, and culture of the poor are, therefore, unlikely to be successful.

HUMANIZING THE MANAGEMENT OF CED ORGANIZATIONS

If CED is to truly offer a more socially acceptable, people-centred, alternative approach to development, then we must address the issue of management of CED institutions of all types. We cannot replicate the top-down autocratic management styles of the private sector, driven by the bottom-line pursuit of profit. We must demand the highest standards of honesty and integrity, financial or otherwise, of managers. We must allow and encourage democratic structures of management with genuine worker input and horizontal decision-taking structures. We must seek out and promote democratic, participatory management styles. We must change the way several of our organizations deal with staff, governing through intimidation, unilateral direction, arbitrary control, and the threat of dismissal.

Even where union agreements are in place, they are often unilaterally abrogated. These approaches promote insecurity and fear. They should be replaced by a more nurturing and supporting style of management and staff difficulties should be addressed more compassionately and more constructively. There should be clear representative structures for dispute resolution and the provision for mediation. Staff should be encouraged to join trade unions.

The kind of autocratic management behaviour referred to should be condemned wherever it occurs. In this respect, Aboriginal organizations or those with Aboriginal leadership have, on occasion, been as guilty as non-Aboriginal ones.

Now that CED has reached a degree of maturity in Winnipeg, we must begin to pay more attention to these issues and be more demanding of management. We should also begin to pay more attention to the provision of adequate salaries, benefits, and terms and conditions of service. We should pay particular attention to working hours and pension provisions. We cannot allow CED to become just another source of cheap labour. We should also begin to judge CED workers by what they accomplish, and not just by the hours they put in. This points to developing and encouraging flexible working arrangements.

RESPONSIBILITIES OF BOARDS

Boards of directors have a crucial role to play in CED organizations. That role must be clarified and board involvement must increase if the other challengers outlined above are to be met. Boards have a responsibility to ensure that organizations are managed efficiently and that funds are spent wisely and as approved. They must ensure management honesty and accountability, whatever management system is in place. In relatively small organizations they must also maintain contact with staff to ensure that all is well. Ideally, this could be done through having staff representatives on the executive committee and/or board. The issue of management accountability is a complex one which, potentially, can be made more difficult with participatory management structures, but it needs to be addressed. The fact that managers often play an important role in recruiting board members also complicates the accountability question and helps explain why arbitrary management styles are sometimes not held in check by boards. Ultimately, it is the board which is accountable to funders and clients for the performance of CED organizations and we need to rethink the role of boards in Winnipeg to ensure that they are performing this function satisfactorily. This may, necessarily, lead to constraining the influence of some executive directors.

IDENTIFYING WHAT WORKS AND WHAT DOES NOT

We need a forum in which honest assessments can be made of experiments tried in CED, both in Winnipeg and elsewhere. We need to know, more clearly, what works and why and at what cost, and what does not work or can be improved upon. There is literature on this based on what has been tried elsewhere in Canada, but it is not used widely (see, for instance, Ninacs, and Favreau, 1993; Lewis and Lockhart, 1999; Community Resilience Team 1999; Richard, 2004). These lessons must be made available to all those who are active in CED and drawn upon in their daily work. We must apply the same analytical frankness to our own experience in Winnipeg and in Manitoba generally. This means being brutally honest, even if some people are upset in the process, for only by being so can past errors be rectified and avoided in the future. Such lessons should be drawn not only from projects but, more importantly, from policies and strategies that have been attempted.

CED MUST GO BEYOND POVERTY

While the immediate concern of much CED activity in Winnipeg is that of poverty alleviation, this must be considered only a necessary attribute of CED and not a sufficient one. CED is about much more than poverty, especially in its transformative version. Other goals of CED are a more equal distribution of income and wealth, greater gender equity, the sensible use of resources between generations, a more balanced spatial pattern of development, and greater social inclusion. CED also furthers democratic decision-taking and participatory empowerment. This will require transforming the nature of the state and would require political mobilization of both the poor and the non-poor. The CED movement would become part, therefore, of a much broader movement for economic, social, *and* political transformation. While poverty eradication would remain an important element in the CED agenda, it would be but one element. This would necessitate CED activists becoming involved in broader social movement politics and mobilization, integrating the values and insights of these movements into the CED movement while promoting the fundamental values of CED among the broader movement, and pressuring the state to be supportive of them.

These are the main challenges as I see them and they can and must be addressed if the remarkable progress of CED in Winnipeg is to be sustained and if the alternative vision of society that CED offers is to be fully realized.

RETROSPECTIVE ON CHAPTERS 7 TO 9

The Neechi Principles of CED now shape the activities of almost all actors in Winnipeg, as well as those of the NDP provincial government. This is perhaps the most important legacy of the "Great Northern Plan," as those principles are based on the convergence theory which underlay the plan. CED activities in Winnipeg, and in Manitoba more generally, are based on a theory which was applied to the North in the mid-1970s but which, in turn, owes its origins to both Tanzania and the Caribbean through the work of C.Y. Thomas (1974).

The Aboriginal institutional framework in Winnipeg continues to evolve, but only the major developments will be touched upon here. Child welfare services have been devolved as a result of the Aboriginal Justice Inquiry and First Nation and Métis agencies are active within the city. Aboriginal capital corporations are well established. The Louis Riel Capital Corporation and the Tribal Wi-Chi-Way-Win Capital Corporation (TWCC) are the most prominent. Both were established under the Canadian Aboriginal Economic Development Strategy (CAEDS) of the federal government in the early 1990s. The TWCC has grown significantly, from three employees in 1993 to 120 in 2010 (*First Nations Voice*, October 2010: 6) and from a starting capital of $7 million, it has provided around $35 million in loans to 45 First Nations communities in Manitoba. It is owned by five tribal councils and five individual First Nations. In 2010 it challenged the decision of the federal government to give guarantees to five non-Aboriginal banks and credit unions (including the Assiniboine Credit Union) through the Loan Loss Reserve (LLR) designed to stimulate lending to Aboriginal businesses. TWCC argued that it had expanded its own business without subsidy and that Aboriginal capital corporations should have been invited to participate in the LRR (*First Nations Voice*, October 2010: 7).

The Aboriginal Centre continues to thrive and has a number of businesses under its roof, from a printer to a restaurant, as well as the highly successful Centre for Aboriginal Human Resource Development Inc. CAHRD is a non-profit organization that delivers education, training, and employment services to the urban Aboriginal population of the city. The Aboriginal Centre is said in 2010 to be investigating the promotion of social enterprises.

Neechi Foods is still going strong and is establishing the 49,000-square-foot Neechi Commons on Main Street, comprising a supermarket, various retailers, and office tenants. The new store will be double the size of its present location on Dufferin Street and provide a much higher profile to drive-by traffic. This development will cost $5 million, much of the funding coming from Assiniboine and the Jubilee Fund, with some from government, and is expected to provide a major boost to this area of the city.

A fairly recent development is that of urban reserves in Manitoba. There are currently four of them (INAC, 2010): the Opaskwayak Cree Nation (adjacent to the town of The Pas), Swan Lake First Nation (in the Rural Municipality of Headingley but adjacent to the City of Winnipeg), Roseau River Anishinabe First Nation (also adjacent to Winnipeg), and Long Plain First Nation (adjacent to the city of Portage la Prairie). In 2010, the Long Plain First Nation made an agreement with the City of Winnipeg to establish an urban reserve close to Polo Park in Winnpeg. The plan is to move the First Nation's Yellowquill College there, set up offices and retail outlets and a supply store that would sell goods tax-free to First Nations (Kusch, 2010).

Typically, First Nations either buy the land on a willing-buyer willing-seller basis or have it transferred to them through a Treaty Land Entitlement process. Then a First Nation requests the federal government to give reserve status to that land. Negotiations then take place with the relevant municipality on a service agreement covering issues such as "tax-loss compensation, levies, bylaw application and enforcement, and dispute resolution procedures" (INAC, 2010). First Nation leaders complain about delays at the federal level over adding to their reserve lands and the time taken to complete the Treaty Land Entitlement process (ibid.).

A major development in CED in Winnipeg took place in 2006 with the creation of Building Urban Industries for Local Development (BUILD), an organization designed to help low-income people reduce their energy and water bills while at the same time creating employment and training for inner city residents. Initially set up as a pilot project in the Centennial neighbourhood with funding from the United Way and the Winnipeg Foundation, BUILD now works in 16 poor neighbourhoods partnering with four neighbourhood renewal corporations (BUILD, 2010). The retrofits pay for themselves and BUILD now works mainly on Manitoba Housing Authority houses, providing steady work for 50 staff. It is funded by the government of Manitoba (Loney, 2010).

The Pollock's Hardware Co-op Ltd. is also a major development in CED in Winnipeg. It was created in 2008 after the owners of Pollock's Hardware Ltd., a North End landmark since 1922, had retired and closed the store after failing to find a buyer. A group of North End Winnipeggers, meeting over a beer in Lisi's Ranch House, decided to try to save the store and reopen it as a co-op. They were successful in doing this, raising significant sums of money in both membership dues and in investment share sales. The latter are supported by the Province of Manitoba's CED tax credit, which gives holders a 30% tax credit in the first year. These, together with funding from Assiniboine and the Jubilee Fund, and some technical help from SEED and Inner City Renovations Inc., were key to the success of the co-op. This is an excellent example of what a community can accomplish when it throws its weight behind an initiative it considers important, and there are important lessons here for others wishing to form a co-op in Manitoba (see Board of Pollock's Hardware Co-op Ltd., 2010).

SEED Winnipeg has expanded considerably, mainly in the area of asset-building programs in which low-income earners save for education, housing, or a business and after reaching a certain level of savings, receive matching funding in the ratio of three from SEED to one saved. This program has proven to be very popular by the over 1,700 people who have used it over the past 10 years, although it is not without its critics who see it taking away from social enterprise activities (Simms, 2010). SEED also continues to fund micro-businesses and social enterprises. In the latter category it has recently helped create Diversity Foods at the University of Winnipeg, a home care co-op and an urban garden co-op and is looking into a funeral co-op (SEED, 2010). SEED provides a wide range of other services, increasingly catering to Winnipeg's ethnic and culturally diverse communities. It has strong leadership, has developed very good staff relations and has a high proportion of women on both staff and the board.

Financing of CED in Winnipeg, including that through SEED, continues to benefit importantly from Assiniboine Credit Union, which remains both active and creative in most CED initiatives. Its importance to the CED scene in Winnipeg cannot be overstated.

The NDP provincial government has also retained its commitment to CED and in 2010 steps were being taken to streamline and coordinate the activities of the various arms of government supporting the same CED project. This helps reduce duplication and multiple forms of reporting. It has attempted to maintain CED funding despite the expiry of the tripartite Winnipeg Partnership Agreement, which was an important source of support for CED in Winnipeg and which drew on widespread volunteer support from CED groups for its implementation.

There are still concerns about the availability of equity and longer-term financing and fears about what might happen to funding if the provincial government were to change. The Manitoba branch of the Canadian Community Economic Development Network (CCEDNET) has put a lot of thought into this issue and especially on how social enterprises might be funded (CCEDNET, 2009). CCEDNET has gone from strength to strength, undertaking important consultative and partnering arrangements, providing policy-focused research and taking over CEDTAS, the provider of technical assistance to CED groups, from SEED.

CHAPTER 10

WHY NATIVE BUSINESSES FAIL AND HOW AGENCIES CONTRIBUTE[1]

The aim of this chapter is to see what lessons may be learned from the experience of small business failures of the past and from specifically Native experience. An attempt is made to identify broader environmental contributions to what often appear on the surface to be weakness internal to small business. Then, drawing on personal experiences of funding agencies in Manitoba, Saskatchewan, and Third World countries, an attempt is made to identify the types of shortcomings on the part of funding agencies which often contribute to the failure of clients' businesses. Finally, we end on a more positive note with a review of factors that have been offered as explanations for why community projects, both narrowly business-oriented and otherwise, have succeeded in the past. It is to be hoped that some useful lessons can be drawn from this.

WHY BUSINESSES FAIL

The most common reason cited for small business failure is *inadequate management*. This catch-all explanation covers a variety of sub-explanations such as managerial incompetence, lack of experience, or imbalanced experience which, together, are said by Dunn and Bradstreet to explain almost 90% of all small business failures in the U.S. (Strang, 1972). Similar conclusions have been arrived at in explaining business failures in black ghettos (ibid.) and in Native communities in Canada (Fulham, 1981).

[1] From Chapter 4 of *The Economics of Community Development*. Report prepared for Native Economic Development Program, DRIE. January 1986.

The main aspects of business activity in which poor management reveals itself are *marketing* and *finance*. A lack of marketing ability is held by Dunn and Bradstreet to explain both inadequate sales and competitive weakness, factors which they identify as being responsible for two-thirds of all business failures. Minority businesses in the U.S. suffer the same problems, and although no data is available, the same can be said of Native enterprises in Canada.

Often, Native enterprises are started on the basis of lucrative short-run contracts with little consideration being given to the longer term. Also, some small communities sometimes end up with two or more enterprises competing for the very limited local business, with the result that each fares badly. This may be the outcome of poor planning or of overoptimism about competitive strength.

On the financial side, two major problems can be identified: lack of capital and inadequate controls. As a sign of management weakness, lack of capital can take a number of forms. Attempting to start a business without adequate long-term capital usually means that the owner ends up continuously struggling to refinance short-term borrowings which are being used to finance long-term assets. This may also mean incurring exorbitant interest charges if these borrowings are from finance houses (e.g., vehicle or machinery financing). Lack of equity finance may result in excessive borrowing of all types—short *or* long—with interest payments absorbing most of net earnings. This renders the business very vulnerable to even minute fluctuations in gross earnings or sales.

A second form of financial problem is inadequate working capital. All too often, insufficient provision is made to finance normal cash holding, the excess of receivables over payables and an adequate inventory of raw materials, goods in process and finished products. Yet working capital is vital to any business and must grow with that business. In a very real sense, therefore, working capital is permanent capital, notwithstanding the fact that it turns over regularly. Small businesses frequently underestimate these needs, and their costs.

Insufficient cash flow from operations is the third form of financial problem which can be traced back to poor management. This is the "bottom line" of business operations (even more so than accounting profit) and hence is a reflection of all the various factors making for business failure or success. The *timing* of these flows requires careful planning so that commitments can be met as they fall due. Often with Native enterprises, creditors may not be prepared to be flexible if payment dates are not met and this can lead to closure (see Fulham, 1981). Hence total cash flow over time is not the only consideration here.

Inadequate internal controls are cited as being over twice as important in minority business failures as in small business failures in the U.S. as a whole (Strange, 1972: 127). This explanation is certainly an important one in Native business failures. The starting point is usually a weak business plan and hence a poor idea of what future activity levels and their associated cost and revenue implications are likely to be. From this, a poor budget follows. Weak financial skills and lack of familiarity with record-keeping systems allow problems to go unidentified. Lack of controls frequently lead to proprietors making excessive salary or "surplus" draws from enterprise funds, to the granting of excessive credit and the failure to collect outstanding receivables; they lead to excessive overhead expenditures in the form of office, entertainment, utilities, travel, and other non-directly productive expenditures; they may also lead to the acquisition of fixed assets or inventories beyond what the business can carry or require. They may even permit unsustainable wage payments either because too much labour has been hired, wage rates are too high, or productivity performance is being measured incorrectly. It seems essential, therefore, that someone in the enterprise possess a working knowledge of planning, bookkeeping, and elementary control techniques.

HOW AGENCIES CONTRIBUTE

Many of these apparent shortcomings of management reflect, however, a negative broader environment in which small business ventures must operate. A major element in that environment for Native businesses is the behaviour of state funding agencies on which Native ventures are usually heavily dependent for both finance and technical assistance. They have responsibilities which go well beyond those of commercial funding agencies because their clientele are recognized as needing special supports on non-commercial terms; otherwise there would be no need for their existence. But in many cases the agencies themselves lack the necessary business expertise to assist Native businesses properly. Often, their staff have essentially social work or administrative backgrounds and little or no training or experience in business or economics (Fulham, 1981, makes a similar point). They are not in a position, therefore, to give clients the management support they need so badly. Frequently, they make no provision for upgrading client skills through practically oriented training programs, nor is similar provision made for upgrading the skills of their own staff.

Funding agencies themselves are often underfunded and in turn this constraint is passed on to clients, with working capital bearing the brunt. Native People constantly complain about basically sound businesses being undermined by chronic working capital shortages relatively early in the life of the project. Funding of activities is often erratic and unreliable (Thalassa, 1983: 114; and D.E.C., 1983: 192–193). This would suggest that these agencies might attempt to do *less* with the resources that they have, but do what they do *properly*.

The financing mix made available by agencies to Native enterprises is also often a problem. Long-term loan finance with interest rates at or above commercial rates, as in the case of IEDF, is "incompatible with development initiatives" (DIAND, 1980). Debt financing in a conservative, risk-averse manner is also not appropriate as the dominant type of finance in businesses which are high risk and developmental in nature.

Agencies are sometimes accused of demanding too high an equity input by Native clients. Thus, IEDF has been criticized for requiring a 20% equity involvement (Thalassa, 1983: 49). The issue of equity participation is a tricky one. On the one hand Native proprietors (private or communal) must have a financial as well as an emotional "stake" in the business if they are to bring to it the strong motivation that most studies believe is essential for success (e.g., Strang, 1972: 126). On the other hand, that stake should not be prohibitive. In this respect, a guideline of 10% is a reasonable starting point, recognizing that it is a minimum which some communities might be able to exceed, and that for very poor communities the 10%

might still be achievable through sweat-equity provisions. The key here is flexibility to respond to differing individual circumstances.

Native People complain that state agencies contribute to business failure by being isolated from the communities they are designed to serve, and because they deal inadequately with a whole range of cultural and attitudinal problems that inevitably arise between Native People and white institutions and staff. Racist and paternalistic attitudes, subtle or otherwise, on the part of agency staff serve to erect barriers between client and agency—barriers which are reinforced by different social values, different languages, and by an unequal power relationship. Where this happens the agency will be incapable of assisting Native enterprises properly, whatever the level of its expertise and funding.

It follows that state funding agencies dealing with Native communities must attempt to recruit Native staff themselves and provide them with required technical skills if they do not already possess them. Non-Native staff must be screened for sensitivity to and awareness of Native conditions, values, aspirations, and viewpoints. Native language training for agency staff is an area that is, sadly, rarely ever considered important or useful.

Agencies sometimes contribute to business failure by not evaluating proposals properly in the first instance. The underestimation of fixed and working capital requirements and the overoptimistic assessment of market potential are common errors. Failure to insist on proper bookkeeping and control arrangements and to provide clients with the necessary skills to operate them means, in effect, that agencies are subsequently incapable of monitoring performance properly because regular and accurate reporting cannot be enforced. Lack of monitoring and follow-up may result in problems being detected only after it is too late to rectify them. Once problems have arisen, funding agencies are often notoriously slow in responding to them.

Part of the reason for procrastination when businesses do encounter problems may be that to a degree staff of agencies do not *expect* Native businesses to succeed. Fulham (1981: 57–69) would go so far as to argue that many state agencies "program" Native businesses for failure because their bureaucratic agenda is quite different from that of the enterprises they are supposed to serve. Also, he argues affirmative action goals are often confused with business development goals, which makes it difficult to demand performance. It is this apparent lack of commitment to success that leads some to conclude that "the most successful Indian economic ventures appear to flourish in spite of rather than because of DIA policies" (Thalassa, 1983: 116).

Even those not holding this extreme viewpoint would have to admit that coordination between government agencies, or between different wings of the same agency, often leaves much to be desired and that this weakness can be very detrimental to Native projects. Stories abound of projects failing or encountering difficulties because required infrastructure was not in place, because different funding agencies disagreed on viability and on appropriate types and degree of control, because market support was not forthcoming from government, because access to raw materials was denied, or because training programs were not organized in time (see D.E.C., 1983 for some of these). What this underlines is the need for an integrated and comprehensive approach to planning which recognizes the complexities of launching even a "single" project. The reality is that to move on a single business project usually requires communities to move on several other supporting fronts if the project is to be successful in the long term.

THE BROADER ENVIRONMENT

One cannot, however, pass the blame for the high failure rate of Native businesses entirely onto government agencies. The general environment in which most Native enterprises function is not a healthy one for business; if it were, we would not be discussing the problem of the economic backwardness of Native communities. The very essence of that backwardness continues to render it very difficult to identify business potential in most Native communities, leave alone realize that potential. Restricted market, acute social problems, lack of infrastructure, and a limited resource base are not ideal breeding grounds for business development.

On top of this the very circumstances in which many Native businesses arise and are operated leaves much to be desired. There is often a clear link between access to political office in Native organizations and access to government funding for development projects. Political entrepreneurship is often the springboard to personal wealth regardless of business experience or ability and regardless of community needs. While fitting in with state plans to create a Native middle class, this robs communities and organizations of political leadership and may, accordingly, impede the development of communities as a whole.

Because state funds are often dispensed as political largesse in this way, often to silence potential or real critics, success in business is a distinctly secondary consideration to both parties. Corruption is not unknown and where this involves the construction phase of the project, this too reduces both the prospect for long-term viability and the interest in it of the proprietor. One must also consider, therefore, as an "environmental" factor, the fact that not all Native leaders or "would-be" business people have in mind the best interests of the community or of the project.

THE REQUIREMENTS FOR SUCCESSFUL NATIVE ECONOMIC DEVELOPMENT

There is an emerging consensus in the literature that "economic development succeeds best when carried out at the local level by (Native) governments accountable to the community" (Thalassa, 1983: 116). This presupposes a leadership committed to the community (D.E.C., 1983: 210–211) and significant community involvement in and control over the planning and implementation of development activities (DPA, 1982). The community, or a representative proportion of it, must actively participate in identifying needs and setting priorities and its leadership must be able to "identify and mobilize the community's own sources and strengths" (ibid.). These are, of course, fundamental requirements of the convergence strategy, modified or otherwise, outlined in Chapter 2.

An important aspect of "participation" when that term is used to mean not merely "consultation" (as it often does when used by government, see Loxley and Rothney, 1983), but effective "control" is accountability to the community. Accountability presupposes not only formal community structures in which progress of CED can be monitored and evaluated, but also systems that provide regular and accurate flows of information in a manner understandable to the community and/or its representatives. The design and implementation of these data systems is vital to the success of CED, and their rationale goes well beyond the requirements of management. They should be simple and non-bureaucratic, not voluminous or too technical, but they should be effective.

Projects that meet a variety of community needs at once (as convergence projects almost invariably do) and those which are sensitive, in their design and operations, to the interrelationship of social, economic and cultural views have a greater chance of achieving community support. The recognition of non-monetary values such as human dignity, good working conditions, the sense of ownership and involvement, is often cited as being responsible for successful community initiatives (e.g., D.E.C., 1983).

Where possible, projects should be such as to generate a local pool of capital which can then be drawn on for further development initiatives. In this connection, taking over the local store from the Bay has been a key factor in the success to date of some communities (e.g., South Indian Lake, King Fisher Lake). The explanation for this is that the store is often the *only* major source of capital in some communities. Ploughing back profits in support of a more comprehensive development plan is necessary if the community is to generate further surplus while providing employment and meeting a variety of other social needs.

Other requirements of successful CED are the training *and* retention of staff who will provide technical and managerial input into projects. A training component should be central to all community plans and ideally should also encompass the needs of boards elected by the community to oversee the operations of projects. Once staff (and boards) have received training it is important that they be retained for a length of time to provide continuity to the project. A similar point can be made about funding agency staff; there should be some continuity in officers assigned to projects, otherwise the monitoring and advisory functions of the agency will be undermined and communities will become disillusioned and discouraged.

It follows from what has been discussed earlier in this chapter that successful Native community economic development will also need i) clearly defined and reasonably stable and secure markets, ii) adequate funding for both fixed *and* working capital, iii) appropriate technical assistance in the form of advice and training facilities, iv) the coordination of the plans, budgets, and activities of government departments and agencies and, above all v) support and encouragement to communities to do as much as possible for themselves. In the long term, the success of community economic development initiatives will be measurable by the extent to which local capabilities have been built up in the areas of planning, management, and government generally. Without the creation of this local capacity, it is unlikely that funding agencies themselves will be properly accountable for the public monies they disburse.

CHAPTER II

THE ROLE OF SUBSIDIES IN CED[1]

Underlying most approaches to CED is a philosophy of self-reliance and community independence. In reality, however, CED ventures have to compete with other, often monopoly producers; CED initiatives often have to accept the prices these more powerful competitors fix, which are based on much larger scales of production and wages close to or below subsistence levels (a prime example being the well-known retailer Walmart). In contrast, in CED projects the scale of production is usually very small, overhead costs are relatively high, wage levels must be socially acceptable, and workers are often in need of training and facing social problems not necessarily experienced by the general labour force. For all these reasons, and until prices generally in the economy are arrived at by considerations other than those of short-run, market-driven profit maximization, CED projects will find it difficult to prosper without some degree of subsidization.

Subsidies for CED projects can take many forms, from someone picking up the bottom-line losses of a project to the provision of a wage or training subsidy, a protected market for products at a higher than market price, physical assets at less than cost, cheap capital, a protective tariff or tax on competitors' products, or help towards

[1] Drawn partly from "Economics for Community Economic Development Practitioners," with Laura Lamb, in Eric Shragge and Mike Toye (eds), *Community Economic Development: Building for Social Change*, University College, Cape Breton Press, 2006. Also published in John Loxley, Jim Silver, and Kathleen Sexsmith, (eds), *Doing Community Economic Development*, Fernwood Books, Halifax, 2007. Drawn partly from Chapter 5 of *Transforming or Reforming Capitalism: Towards a Theory of Community Economic Development*, Fernwood Publishers, Halifax, and CCPA-Manitoba, 2007.

meeting overhead costs. All of these can be found, in one way or the other, around the world.

In places where CED is very well established along convergence lines, with many enterprises and agencies providing a range of goods and services, some products may be subsidized by others. In this case, "cross-subsidization" is said to be taking place. Some examples of cross-subsidization in CED may include a community-owned credit union's provision of credit on favourable terms to other community-based projects, or a locally owned restaurant being supplied with locally produced food at prices not determined by the market. Another form of cross-subsidization occurs when locally produced products are being sold at prices higher than those seen elsewhere, in which case it is the consumers who are subsidizing CED activities. The extensive cross-subsidization of CED projects in a community through higher final sales prices than those in neighbouring communities is justified by the jobs the project creates and which would not otherwise exist (see *We're the Boss*, National Film Board, 1990, a film about the experiences of Evangeline in Prince Edward Island). In this respect, support for CED projects is not unlike support for fair trade products or for cooperatives generally; consumers may, quite simply, have to pay more to support broader social goals.

Usually one resorts to the principles of cost-benefit analysis to provide an economic rationale for subsidization. Projects that are not commercially viable may yet be socially viable if the market does not accurately capture the true costs and benefits to society of the project in question. Market prices do not, in fact, normally capture the true *opportunity cost* of employing resources, or in other words, the forgone opportunities which arise when resources are not put toward the use that optimizes social benefits. Thus, for a community experiencing widespread unemployment, the true social cost of employing labour is not the wage that would have to be paid to hire workers, but rather the loss of output to society of using funds to offer work to the unemployed instead of other, potentially more productive purposes. Often, that loss is zero or negligible, in which case a subsidy could be justified because it would put wages well below market levels, improving the apparent profitability of the project. The rationale for this subsidy is, therefore, one of job creation, wherein the state or some other entity would have to pay the project the difference between market and social wage costs. The correct way to proceed, in general, is to calculate true social costs and benefits, analyze effects on project accounting, and then limit subsidies to the amount that brings the project out of deficit spending.

In reality, however, these calculations are difficult to make, and government policy-makers may find them hard to follow. In such cases, another closely related approach may be pursued. This other approach to the determination of government subsidy consists of measuring a project's *fiscal impact*, and gearing the amount of the subsidy to improving the fiscal position of government(s). Such improvement may come from a number of sources. First, if the project increases employment it may reduce either Employment Insurance (EI) claims (expenditures made by the federal government) or social assistance payments (usually paid by provincial or municipal governments). Second, once employed, workers will contribute to government revenues through EI payments, as well as income, sales, and other taxes. Third, projects may reduce social problems either directly or indirectly—logically, when unemployment is reduced, government spending to address social problems should go down. In theory, it is possible to add up all these positive fiscal impacts and to use the result to justify government subsidization of CED projects.

Though there are similarities in the two approaches, they can, and normally will, give different results for the amount of subsidy considered to be justified. Politicians can usually relate more easily to the fiscal impact approach, finding it more accessible than justifications for subsidies based on cost-benefit analyses. One potential problem of this preferred method, however, is that net fiscal benefits are spread among the different levels of government, so that the level of government which gains the most may not be the one that has made the greatest amount of subsidy available. Despite this drawback, it is worthwhile to undertake fiscal impact studies to justify state support for CED undertakings.

Subsidies may be a feature of all alternative CED strategies (except, by definition, a pure subsistence strategy). However, export base strategies are not likely to work where production costs are too high to compete in the external market. Import substitution approaches may need some additional form of protection so that import substitutes can compete against cheaper goods and services produced outside the community. Finally, the basis of a convergent CED strategy can be formed where state and third-sector funding is available for activities such as housing, education and training, which take on a huge importance in this approach because they immediately address people's basic needs as well as provide sources of income, employment, and linkages.

Voluntary labour inputs from members of the community are another source of project "subsidization," which is often important but under-recognized. It is also often gendered, with women playing disproportionate roles. It needs to be recognized, therefore, that pursuing a convergence strategy might place new demands on community members, especially on women. Nonetheless, successful pursuit of the strategy might reduce other burdens on women by improving childcare facilities, creating job opportunities, improving incomes, and reducing the social problems that affect them.

FURTHER REFLECTIONS ON SUBSIDIZATION OF CED PROJECTS

Laura Lamb (2007) has made a convincing economic and fiscal case for the state to consider subsidizing CED activities. Her approach also puts upper limits on the amount of any subsidy. The case for subsidization she presents rests on the argument that CED projects are likely to be much smaller than the private sector projects they compete against. One could further the case for subsidization by arguing that in many CED projects, the labour pool from which workers are specifically drawn is a disadvantaged one, often lacking skills and work experience, and frequently coping with severe personal and social problems. More often than not, the attachment of this pool to the labour force proper is at best precarious but creating or strengthening that attachment may bring significant benefits to society at large as well as benefits to the individuals involved. Thus, increased employment opportunities would reduce social assistance payments and might help reduce such social problems as crime, residential turnover, school absenteeism among children, family violence, and addictions. The economic and fiscal implications of these potential benefits would justify the subsidization of projects employing this pool of potential workers. This would constitute a powerful additional argument to the one based on scale.

A labour force case for subsidizations raises important questions about *the form* of subsidies, questions that are equally valid, though less obvious, when scale is the justification.

FORMS OF CED SUBSIDY

There are essentially three forms of subsidies: labour subsidies and capital subsidies, which reduce costs, and price subsidies (Shaffer, 1989: 216–218). Labour subsidies take the form of covering training costs, reducing wage costs, or giving projects tax credits on their profits for the number of jobs they create. Government financial support is, therefore, tied to improving labour quality or increasing the number of jobs created. Capital subsidies effectively reduce the cost of the buildings, machinery, and cash needed to operate a business. They are usually more numerous and take more forms than labour or price subsidies. They may take the form of grants, soft loans which are loans on favourable terms (lower interest or longer than market repayment periods), or favourable tax treatment of capital assets. Thus, business entities might be allowed to write off capital assets against income for tax purposes more quickly than the assets wear out (depreciate). This reduces tax payable in the early years of a project when cash flow might be tight. This last form is available only to those CED projects making profits. Price supports may take the form of the public sector protecting the market for products of CED ventures, by giving them preference when making purchases, or paying higher than market prices for their products.

How should subsidization programs be best constituted to obtain the desired results for CED projects while, at the same time, preserving fiscal integrity and accountability to the electorate at large? Are these two outcomes necessarily consistent or might they be competing? CED observers tend to be silent on these points though public finance analysis does offer some insights. First of all, it is generally agreed in the economics literature that explicit subsidization is superior to other possible forms of support (e.g., tariff protection for local industry) because it is usually both explicit and transparent in the books of the government and subject to periodic review (see Grubel, 1981: 144). Secondly, if the object is to increase employment, then a subsidy tied explicitly to employment targets is preferable to one tied to capital usage, output, or sales, or simple bottom-line losses. For, though capital subsidies may themselves increase employment if they stimulate an increase in output, they are even then less likely to be the cheapest way to increase jobs if this is the main objective (Shaffer, 1989: 218–220). Where scale deficiencies are being compensated for, however, subsidization might also sensibly be tied to size of sales or output or to capital employed. In reality, both scale and labour force characteristics might be the rationale for subsidization and hence a hybrid approach to subsidization might be in order. In practice, however, CED projects rarely have the luxury of selecting the form of subsidization but rather have to struggle for any kind of support, and especially once a project is up and running. Front-end subsidization is often all that is available and, where this is the case, it favours capital usage or initial training or overhead costs; it does not provide ongoing support in line with the ongoing social and fiscal benefits that CED projects often provide.

Where ongoing subsidization is available, tying it explicitly to higher operating or labour costs, rather than simply covering bottom-line losses, is to be preferred both by the government because of its transparency and by the CED project because it highlights the economic and social rationale for the assistance perhaps offering better protection from political whims. Ongoing subsidization in the form of price support for products, through sheltered markets (e.g., giving preference to goods produced by minorities) or higher prices (e.g., allowing targeted groups to sell products at a higher price than that charged by private business) is obviously attractive to CED projects but there is some loss of transparency for governments.

SUBSIDIES IN GAP-FILLING VERSUS TRANSFORMATIVE CED

Given the deficiencies of capitalism that gap-filling CED is designed to rectify, some degree of subsidization is likely to be necessary and hence the policy rationale for it must be made clear. Sympathetic governments, funding agencies, or foundations must be presented with a clear economic and social case for departures from a break-even or positive bottom line for the CED projects they support. Where possible, a positive fiscal case should also be made when government funding is involved. Once CED is widespread, or transformative in nature, however, the idea of generalized subsidization makes less sense and instead, prices of inputs and products should be adjusted for their economic and social implications.

This issue appears not to have been addressed in CED analysis but it was confronted in earlier development theorizing. Thus, Samir Amin (1976) argued that rational pricing under socialism would involve minimizing the necessary social labour time (the quantity of labour in a given societal setting) required to create new production structures and to train workers. Precisely how this might be achieved in practice, if at all, was part of much earlier debates about the rationality of pricing under socialism between Lange and Taylor (1938) on the one hand, and Hayek (1935), Robbins (1934), and Mises (1935), on the other. Reflecting on the shortcomings of USSR experience, Alec Nove (1983) proposed an approach to pricing under socialism which combined labour values with use values and consumer demand, i.e., a blend of Marxist and market-oriented approaches. More recently, in discussing "parecon," Albert and Hahnel (1991a) and Albert (1997) have posed the idea of "flexible" prices based not on the market or the views or quantitative techniques of central planners, but on "social consultation and compromise" (Albert and Hahnel, 1991a: 60). That is, prices would be indicative, subject to change as best estimates change in the planning process, and would be explicitly formed on the basis of a social process of consultation informed by, but not driven by, quantitative information.

There is, thus, no single way of tackling the issue of prices in transforming an economy. The point is that CED literature has not engaged this issue but would need to if the CED movement were to achieve a significant presence in the economy. Albert and Hahnel's approach, which explicitly provides for community input into pricing decisions, seems to offer a promising starting point.

RETROSPECTIVE ON CHAPTERS 10 AND 11

Without undertaking a comprehensive survey of Aboriginal financing and the performance of financing agencies over the past 25 years, it is difficult to offer an update on Chapter 10. But there are a few salient themes that come to mind. The first is that there is a larger Aboriginal presence in funding agencies dealing with Aboriginal People and more Aboriginal agencies as well. Tribal Councils are now well established and have been very assertive in promoting both job creation and economic and business development. Aboriginal capital corporations are active and seem relatively stable. There are many more Aboriginal economic development officers than there used to be. Tribal Council Investments Group, Manitoba, is a highly successful joint venture between seven Tribal Councils that was established over 20 years ago (Wuttunee, 2004). It now has assets in the region of $30 million. And, as we have seen, community enterprises are flourishing in a number of First Nations communities.

The second theme I would now emphasize, having been persuaded of this by Fred Wien and the Harvard Group, is that I would stress the need for a limitation on direct political intervention in the day-to-day affairs of Aboriginal businesses. This separation would distance managers and possibly boards from misguided intervention in which financial performance is undermined for political reasons. General policy direction could still be influenced by politicians and I believe this is appropriate in small communities. I also believe a similar separation between Aboriginal "civil servants" and Chief and Council would be a desirable one. There should be more continuity among staff in Aboriginal organizations and the ability of staff to protect themselves against arbitrary treatment by being able to form trade unions. Furthermore, there is increasing agreement that band council elections every two years are an undesirable recipe for instability, and for myopic, short-term-oriented and inexperienced governance.

The third theme I would stress is that there should be no room for paternalism in assessing the performance of Aboriginal businesses. My good friend, the late Van Hall, who was much loved by the Aboriginal community for his commitment and dedication, was unequivocal on this point. In improving the performance of the Communities Economic Development Fund in the mid- to late 1970s, Van was adamant that loans had to be repaid, even if it meant taking coins out of Coke or Pepsi machines (most of which Van might have put in anyhow!). In return, he would spend endless hours with Aboriginal managers, helping them with their books, their financing, and their management problems. Excusing or overlooking poor business performance is a recipe for closure and failure. Pointing it out and helping address it is a much better approach.

The fourth theme is that there have been significant advances in Aboriginal procurement over the last decade. Governments at both the federal and provincial levels have made provision for Aboriginal preferences both in general purchasing and for specific large projects. Private companies have also found it expedient to enter into joint business projects and to offer incentives for procurement to Aboriginal businesses. These developments can be very important to fledgling Aboriginal businesses as they provide a guaranteed and stable market for their products. Federal procurement reached almost $0.5 billion in 2003 (Aboriginal Human Resource Council, 2009) and will have grown significantly since. The Manitoba government has a general procurement policy which provides for three levels of consideration to be given to Aboriginal businesses in provincial procurement: set-asides, reserved only for Aboriginal businesses, where goods being purchased relate directly to Aboriginal needs (e.g., cultural goods or purchased for specifically Aboriginal diabetics); mandatory consideration for partnerships where Aboriginal capacity is in doubt; and situations where it might be desirable to encourage Aboriginal participation (Manitoba Government, 2009). A key element of this policy is an Aboriginal Business Directory. To 2010, 345 companies (which must have at least 51% Aboriginal ownership and employ at least one-third Aboriginal employmees if six or more workers are employed) have registered voluntarily, 181 of them in Winnipeg and 11 in Thompson. The province and the Federal government also provided for an Aboriginal set-aside procurement arrangement for the expansion of the Winnipeg Floodway, and by 2009, $53 million in contracts had been awarded under this provision (Manitoba Floodway Authority, 2009). In the Canadian private sector, two very large oil companies, Syncrude and Encana, have each conducted more than $1 billion in business with Aboriginal companies (Aboriginal Human Resource Council, 2009). It would be interesting to analyze the long-term impact of these arrangements but over the short run, these appear to be significant initiatives which should help strengthen Aboriginal businesses.

The fifth and final theme is that we have very little hard analysis about Aboriginal business performance and the performance of financial institutions set up to support Aboriginal business. In 1996, my graduate student, Neil Loughran, produced a thesis of monumental proportions evaluating the performance of three federal financing programs that operated in Manitoba in the 1970s and 1980s. His findings were very insightful for both the characteristics of businesses that failed but, more importantly, of how the financing institutions involved functioned. He found that despite operating in a context in which regional development strategies were supported by the provincial government, "(t)here was little effort to allocate support resources according to any development strategy or impact maximizing strategy" (Loughran, 1996: 496). The staff of the financing institutions were generalists with poor specialist skills, such as marketing, economic analysis, or business planning; they were sympathetic but overworked and subjected to intense political pressures to move funds into projects. Applications were screened out at an early stage, largely on the basis of applicant persistence or lack thereof and out of 1,596 received over this period, only 419 resulted in businesses being financed (ibid.: 499). Gross capital costs of these projects were $90 million and they created 3,000 jobs, at $30,000 per job. By 1994, "only one-quarter of the financed businesses are known to have been operating" (ibid.: 501), a survival rate of only 6% of initial applications. The programs had insufficient monitoring or follow-up provisions to ascertain how businesses were doing and few resources to assist them after start-up.

Loughran also performed regression analysis on the project data and found that project survival was positively correlated with social enterprises, whether or not owned by governments. This was explainable perhaps, by their ability to cross-subsidize their businesses (ibid.: 506), but no evidence was presented in support of this hypothesis. Band-owned businesses had a relatively high rate of survival, because of guaranteed markets and local financial and political support (ibid.: 520). The survival rate of privately owned non-Aboriginal businesses was almost double that of private Aboriginal businesses (Ibid: 509). The survival rate of existing businesses that had previously had financial assistance was much higher than that of new businesses. Perhaps surprisingly, there was a negative association between business survival and educational levels (ibid.: 522). Businesses that produced primary products for export had a lower survival rate than other, more internal looking projects (ibid.: 524).

Ideally, this type of analysis should be carried out routinely on government programs, but it is not. Loughran chose not to publish his work, perhaps because he did not want his findings to reflect badly on the staff involved or on the intended goal of the programs, and it is rarely cited. Its relevance today is questionable given the institutional developments which have taken place both in government and in the Aboriginal economy, but it stands as a useful historical account of how well-intended financial schemes actually performed in practice.

CHAPTER 12

CHALLENGES AND OPPORTUNITIES

It is anticipated that the Aboriginal population in Canada will grow from 1.07 million in 2001 to between 1.39 and 1.43 million by 2017. The rate of growth of the Aboriginal population, at 1.8% per annum, is significantly higher than that for the population as a whole, which is 0.7%. Thus, the share of Aboriginal People in the total population will rise, from 3.4% to 4.1% by 2017. Bill C-31 transfers of identity from mothers would further increase the Aboriginal population, perhaps by as much as 0.4 million, bringing the total to as much as 1.47 million by 2017 (Statistics Canada, 2005).

As the population ages, the proportion of Aboriginal children may fall from 32.9% of the total to 28.6%, but this would still represent a net addition of around 70,000 children. More strikingly, the number of young adults entering the labour force will rise by almost 42%, from 170,300 in 2001 to 241,700 in 2017. The number of Aboriginal seniors will more than double to 92,500 by 2017. The proportion of Aboriginal People living on reserve is expected to rise from 33% to around 40%, while that of those living in urban areas will fall. However, given the population increase, both reserves and urban areas expected to have to accommodate an additional 130,000 people each.

In Manitoba, the Aboriginal population is expected to grow from around 159,000 in 2001 to 231,000 with Bill C-31 transfers, and those living on reserve from 58,000 to 91,000. The percentage of the population represented by children under 14 years of age will rise significantly from 24 in 2001 to 31% in 2017. The proportion of young Aboriginal adults (aged 20 to 29 years) will rise from 17% in 2001 to 23% by 2017 (Statistics Canada, 2005). Aboriginal youth would then, potentially, represent a significant proportion of the total labour force.

Busby (2010) has estimated the proportion of the labour force likely to be filled by Aboriginal People over the next 10 years using two assumptions about the level of immigration; first a continuation of trends over the past 10 years, together with a reduction of interprovincial out-migration, and second, a sharp increase in immigration and a sharp decline in interprovincial out-migration. In either case, Aboriginal People assume a potentially huge importance in the labour force, rising from 13.8% to between 17.2 and 16.1% by 2017. In the first case, they would provide almost all the net addition to the labour force, after baby-boomer retirements, of around 26,000. In the second, they would be called upon to provide one in three workers needed. Drawing on the works of Richards (2008, 2009), Mendelson (2006), Sharpe and Arsenault (2010), and others, Busby concludes that public policy should focus on reducing the secondary school dropout rates of Aboriginal youth and increasing their representation in post-secondary institutions. The former would be achieved by giving school divisions greater discretion over Aboriginal education, by achieving greater Aboriginal participation in school governance and by measuring and publishing Aboriginal student performance (Richards 2009). The latter would require more financial assistance and greater attention to solving non-financial challenges such as "high-school performance, parental education, relocation to urban centres, family responsibilities, age, on-campus racism, and peer influences" (Busby, 2010: 6).

Population trends in Canada and especially in provinces like Manitoba with a high proportion of Aboriginal People offer enormous opportunities for Aboriginal People of working age. But the obstacles mentioned above are not easily overcome and will require significant community empowerment and state intervention. Thus, high school performance is not unrelated to early childhood development where many experts believe problems of poverty and non-participation originate. Early childhood education is, in turn, closely affected by living conditions, diet, and the taking of children into care away from their homes and communities. Addressing secondary school dropout rates and improving access to post-secondary education will require, therefore, a frontal attack on these deeper social issues. There are, as Jim Silver (2000) would put it, "solutions that work" that are known; the issue is one of implementing them aggressively and on a sustained basis.

For instance, the outrageously high rate of Aboriginal children in care could be reduced by policies designed to assist parenting and the retention of children in the family or community (Wien, Blackstock, Loxley, and Trocme, 2007). Ways of improving the housing stock both on reserve and in urban areas are well known but require a firm commitment of resources. Enabling the Aboriginal community to take advantage of job opportunities over the next generation will require a shift in public policy priorities to address these serious social issues. Greater Aboriginal militancy will probably be required to bring this shift about.

There can be no doubt that it will be through education, training, and employment in the general economy that the economic and social well-being of Aboriginal People will be improved in the future, just as it has in the past. Opportunities for employment in Aboriginal organizations will continue to be important and as the first wave of Aboriginal employees retire, but the growth here is unlikely to be as high as it was over the past two decades as government services were devolved. But opportunities in other levels of government and in the private sector, including non-profits, will increase with baby-boomer retirement. Employment equity and human rights approaches will still be needed, especially for access to management positions; hence the need for post-secondary education.

Community economic development should, however, be of increasing importance given the strengthening institutional structure in Manitoba and the obvious successes of communities like the Nisichawayasikh Cree Nation. The Aboriginal co-ownership of new Hydro dams might be extended to other northern resource companies, with accompanying CED spin-offs, if sufficient political levers can be found. Aboriginal social enterprises are also likely to flourish in Winnipeg as the Neechi Commons takes off and as the Aboriginal Centre shifts its focus. The need to offer constructive alternatives to Aboriginal youth who have dropped out of the education system and perhaps even fallen afoul of the legal system, as

OPK and BUILD do, will be an ongoing one. And CED will, hopefully, be increasingly attractive to the non-Aboriginal population too, as a means of addressing poverty. But for both communities, CED will also offer a different approach to organizing society, gradually replacing private ownership with a variety of social enterprises characterized by greater democracy, more transparency, greater income and gender equality, and much more awareness of the need to balance resource use between generations.

APPENDIX I
INPUT-OUTPUT AND INCOME FLOW ANALYSIS

In order to explain how different strategies are likely to affect a community economy, it is necessary to examine how economists analyze the structure of income and production. Table 1 represents an input-output table of a community economy. Reading across each row one can see how the *output* of each sector is allocated between i) sales to other sectors in the community as intermediate inputs to enable their output to be produced, e.g., wheat output is sold as an input to flour producers; ii) final demands in the form of consumption, investment (including changes in inventory), government purchases for use in the community, or sales outside the community, i.e., exports. All output must be accounted for in these ways.

Reading down the columns one can see the *inputs* required to produce the output of a given sector. These inputs consist of the value of goods purchased from other sectors within the community, the value of goods bought from outside the community (imports), plus the total cost of wages, rents, interest and direct taxes paid plus any profits (or minus any losses) earned.

One can therefore analyze the total value of production of a commodity or, as in the table, of a sector producing similar commodities, from the point of view of its end uses (sales) or from the point of view of the composition of its inputs (costs). It is clear that when profits are regarded as an input, the value of all inputs must equal the value of production or sales.

This table helps shed light on how integrated a community economy is in the sense of the strength of interdependence between sectors. To the extent that a sector's output depends on inputs purchased from other sectors in the community economy then *backward linkages* are said to exist. For sector 1, in the table, agriculture, the strength of these would be measured by the sum of the entries in column 1 expressed as a percentage of the output of sector 1, i.e., backward linkages in agriculture =

$$\frac{x11 + x21 + x31 \ldots xn1}{X1} \%$$

It is apparent that the larger are imports into the community, i.e., purchases of inputs from outside the community, the smaller will be the backward linkage effects of projects, other things being equal.

To the extent that a sector's output is sold as inputs to other sectors of the community economy, then *forward linkages* are said to exist. For sector 1, agriculture, the strength of these would be measured by the sum of the entries in the intermediate demand section of Row 1 as a percentage of total output of sector 1, i.e., forward linkages from agriculture =

$$\frac{x11 + 12 + x13 \ldots + x1n}{X1} \%$$

TABLE 1—INPUT-OUTPUT TABLE

	Intermediate Demands						Final Demand				
PURCHASES BY: / SALES TO	Agriculture	Hunting, Fishing & Trapping	Forestry	Mining	Manufacturing	Transport Utilities Services	Household Consumption	Private Investment	Government Spending	Exports	TOTAL VALUE OF PRODUCTION
Agriculture	x_{11}	x_{12}	x_{13}	x_{14}	x_{15}	x_{16}	Y_c	Y_I	Y_G	Y_x	X_1
Hunting, Fishing, Trapping	x_{21}	x_{22}	x_{23}	x_{24}	x_{25}	x_{26}	Y_c	Y_I	Y_G	Y_x	X_2
Forestry	x_{31}	x_{32}	x_{33}	x_{34}	x_{35}	x_{36}	Y_c	Y_I	Y_G	Y_x	X_3
Mining	x_{41}	x_{42}	x_{43}	x_{44}	x_{45}	x_{46}	Y_c	Y_I	Y_G	Y_x	X_4
Manufacturing	x_{51}	x_{52}	x_{53}	x_{54}	x_{55}	x_{56}	Y_c	Y_I	Y_G	Y_x	X_5
Transport, Utilities, Services	x_{61}	x_{62}	x_{63}	x_{64}	x_{65}	x_{66}	Y_c	Y_I	Y_G	Y_x	X_6
IMPORTS	m_1	m_2	m_3	m_4	m_5	m_6	M_c	M_I	M_G	M_x	
VALUE ADDED											
Wages											
Profits											
Interest											
Rent											
Taxes											
Depreciation											
TOTAL VALUE ADDED	V_1	V_2	V_3	V_4	V_5	V_6					
TOTAL VALUE OF PRODUCTION	X_1	X_2	X_3	X_4	X_5	X_6					

Final demand linkages can be calculated in a similar way as the sum of consumption and investment demands of a particular product within a community. It is apparent that the greater the proportion of production sold outside the community as exports, the smaller will be forward and final demand linkages.

Both the backward and forward linkages measured above are direct ones only. It is possible to calculate the strength of indirect linkages thereby recognizing that the output of one sector can have a multiplier effect on the community by being used as an input to another sector, the output of which is an input to yet other sectors, and so on. Those interested in pursuing this should consult Kenny (1981); for our purposes it is sufficient that the principle of linkages be made clear.

Apart from clarifying the structure of production in a community economy, such a table also shows what happens to value added or to incomes created through economic activities within the community. Incomes generated in a community can take the form of wages, salaries, profits, rents, interest. Analysis of these can shed light on the social structure of the community on income distribution and on property relationships. It is, however, also possible to identify incomes generated in the community earned by people who are not resident in the community. These earnings will represent "leakages" from the local economy in much the same way that spending on imports represents a leakage.

Finally, some incomes received in a community are generated independently of production. These could be on account of income earned elsewhere through ownership of assets on which interest or dividends are paid or through work performed elsewhere. They could also be the result of transfer payments by the state for family allowance, UIC, welfare, or old age pensions. Since these items are independent of production within the community, the input-output table does not include them; they do not constitute value added within the community. They should, however, be included in any estimate of community income.

APPENDIX II

JOHN LOXLEY: PRACTICAL INVOLVEMENT IN ABORIGINAL, NORTHERN, AND COMMUNITY ECONOMIC DEVELOPMENT

Positions Held
1. Chair of the Board of Directors, Pollock's Hardware Co-op Ltd., Winnipeg, 2008 on.
2. Conducted an Organizational and Operational Review of the University College of the North, for the Governing Council of UCN, Manitoba, 2008–09.
3. Member, Expert Advisory Committee of Assembly of First Nations Make Poverty History Campaign, 2008 on.
4. Principal Investigator of a $1,000,000 SSHRC/CURA proposal (involving the Canadian Centre for Policy Alternatives, the University of Winnipeg, and several community groups) to examine community economic development in inner city and Aboriginal communities, August 2007.
5. Academic Representative on Winnipeg Partnership Agreement, Social Economy and Community Development Advisory Committee, 2005–8.
6. Consultant to the First Nations Child and Family Caring Society, Ottawa, on a new funding formula for First Nations child welfare agencies in Canada, October 2004–2008.
7. Member of Board of Directors, Ogijiita Pimatiswin Kinamatwin, Aboriginal Youth Housing Renovation Project, for ex-inmates. May 2004 to date.
8. Consultant to Sayisi Dene and Northlands Dene on economic development, June–September 2001.
9. Consultant to Assembly of Manitoba Chiefs on the Governance Initiative of Robert Nault, Minister for Indian Affairs, June 2001.

10. Principal Investigator of an $895,000 SSHRC/INE Research Alliance Grant (involving the Canadian Centre for Policy Alternatives, the University of Winnipeg, Brandon University, and several community groups) to examine community economic development and the new economy, November 2002–06.
11. Member of a research team funded by The National Crime Prevention Centre to evaluate the Ndaawin Program designed to prevent sexual exploitation of (mainly Aboriginal) children and youth through prostitution. Project leader Jane Ursel, Director, RESOLVE, Centre of Excellence in Research on Family Violence and Violence Against Women, University of Manitoba, 2001–2004.
12. Member of Joint Assembly of Manitoba Chiefs and Canadian Bankers' Association committee on Phasing the Transition to Financial Independence for First Nations, representing AMC, 1994–95.
13. Chairperson of SEED Winnipeg, a community-based micro-lending scheme, 1999 to 2003. Vice-Chair of SEED Winnipeg, 1993–1999.
14. Economic advisor to Royal Commission on Aboriginal Peoples, 1992–95.
15. Economic Advisor to Assembly of Manitoba Chiefs, January 1992–1997.
16. Consultant to Native Economic Development Program, DRIE, 1985 and 1986.
17. Member of the Board of Directors of Métis Economic Development Corporation, September 1984 to June 1986.
18. Instructor in Economic Development and Planning for training course for tribal council economic development officers organized by the All Chiefs' Budget Committee of Manitoba, October 1983 to June 1984.
19. Advisor to the Budget Committee of Manitoba Indian Chiefs, 1982 to 1985.
20. Chairman of a Committee appointed jointly by God's River Indian Band and the Department of Indian and Northern Affairs to investigate the planning process of God's River, May-August 1979.
21. Chairman, Communities Economic Development Fund (a Manitoba Government Crown Corporation), 1975–78.
22. Chairman and President, Channel Area Loggers (a Manitoba Government Crown Corporation), 1975–78.
23. Secretary (Deputy Minister), Resource and Economic Development Sub-Committee of Cabinet, Government of the Province of Manitoba, Canada, 1975–77.

Books, Papers, Reviews and Unpublished Reports Dealing with Aboriginal Issues and Community Economic Development

Loxley, John, Kathleen Sexsmith, and Jim Silver (eds.). 2007. *Doing Community Economic Development*. Halifax: Fernwood Press and CCPA-Manitoba.

Loxley, John (ed.). 2007. *Transforming or Reforming Capitalism: Towards a Theory of Community Economic Development*. Halifax: Fernwood Press and CCPA-Manitoba.

Loxley, John and Dan Simpson. *Government Policies Towards CED and the Social Economy in Quebec and Manitoba*. 2008. Victoria: Canadian CED Network and Saskatoon: the Centre for the Study of Co-operatives, University of Saskatchewan. At <www.usaskstudies.coop/socialeconomy/files/LLL_Final_Reports/Report_CL5_04_MB.pdf>.

Loxley, John. 2007. "The State of Community Economic Development in Winnipeg." In Loxley, John, Jim Silver, and Kathleen Sexsmith (eds.), *Doing Community Economic Development*. Halifax: Fernwood Press.

Loxley, John, Fred Wien, Cindy Blackstock, and Nico Trocme. 2007. "Keeping First Nations Children at Home: Few Federal Policy Changes Could Make a Big Difference." *First Peoples Child and Family Review* 3, 1.

Loxley, John and Laura Lamb. 2006. "Economics for Community Economic Development Practitioners." In Shragge, Eric and Mike Toye (eds.), *Community Economic Development: Building for Social Change*, University College: Cape Breton Press. Also published in Loxley, John, Jim Silver, and Kathleen Sexsmith, (eds.). 2007. *Doing Community Economic Development*. Halifax: Fernwood Press.

Loxley, John, Fred Wien, and Cindy Blackstock. 2004. *Bridging Econometrics with First Nations Child and Family Service Agency Practice*. First Nations Child and Family Service Agency Funding Formula Research Project, First Nations Child and Family Caring Society of Canada, Ottawa. <fncfcs.com>.

Loxley, John, Cindy Blackstock, Tara Prakash, and Fred Wien. 2005. *Wen:de: We are coming to the light of day. Stage Two*. First Nations Child and Family Service Agency Funding Formula Research Project, First Nations Child and Family Caring Society of Canada, Ottawa, also at <fncfcs.com>.

Loxley, John, Linda DeRiviere, Tara Prakash, Cindy Blackstock, Fred Wien, and Shelley Thomas Prokop. 2005. *Wen:de: —We are Coming to the Light of Day: Phase 3 Report*. Ottawa. First Nations Child and Family Service Agency Funding Formula Research Project, First Nations Child and Family Caring Society of Canada.

Loxley, John. 2003. "Financing Community Economic Development in Winnipeg." *Économie et Solidarité* 34, 1.

Loxley, John and Fred Wien. 2003. "Urban Aboriginal Economic Development." In Newhouse, David and Evelyn Peters (eds.), *Not Strangers in These Parts: Urban Aboriginal Peoples*, Ottawa: Policy Research Initiative.

Loxley, John. 2002 "Sustainable Urban Economic Development: An Aboriginal Perspective." *Journal of Aboriginal Economic Development* 3, 1.

Loxley, John, Wanda A. Wuttune, and Alison Dubois. 2002. "Gambling on Casinos." *Journal of Aboriginal Economic Development* 2, 2.

Loxley, John. 2001. "Book Review: Market Solutions for Native Poverty: Social Policy for the Third Solitude by Helmar Drost, Brian Lee Crowley and Richard Schwindt," *Journal of Aboriginal Economic Development*.

Loxley, John. 2000. "Aboriginal Economic Development in Winnipeg." In Jim Silver (ed.), *Solutions that Work: Fighting Poverty in Winnipeg*. Halifax: Fernwood Press and Manitoba: CCPA.

Loxley, John, Fred Wien, David Newhouse, and Steven Cornell. 2000. *Governance Issues in the Métis Settlements of Northern Alberta*. Edmonton: Métis Settlement General Council.

Loxley, John. 1993. "Democratising Economic Policy Formulation: The Manitoba Experience." In G. Albo et al. (eds.), *A Different Kind of State? Popular Power and Democratic Administration*. Toronto: Oxford University Press.

Loxley, John. 1996. "Aboriginal People in the Winnipeg Economy." Ottawa: Royal Commission on Aboriginal Peoples. Available on CD-ROM in RCAP Papers.

Loxley, John. 1993. "Child Care Arrangements and the Aboriginal Community in Winnipeg." Ottawa: A report prepared for the Royal Commission on Aboriginal Peoples.

Loxley, John. 1992. "Manitoba: Dynamics of North-South Relationships." In G. Lithman et. al. (eds.) *People and Land in Northern Manitoba*. Winnipeg: University of Manitoba.

Loxley, John. 1986. *The Economics of Community Development*. Report prepared for Native Economic Development Program, DRIE. January.

Loxley, John. 1981. "The Great Northern Plan." *Studies in Political Economy* 6.

PhD Theses Supervised

1. Tom Simms. 2010. *The Ideology of Community Economic Development.* Interdisciplinary Program, University of Manitoba.
2. Laura Lamb. 2007. *The Economic Theory of Community Economic Development and of the New Economy.* Department of Economics, University of Manitoba.
3. Laurie Dean. 2004. *Community Economic Development in Winnipeg's North End: Social, Cultural, Economic and Policy Aspects.* Interdisciplinary Program, University of Manitoba.
4. Bret Nickels. 2003. *A Field of Dreams: The Story of the Manitoba Indian Agricultural Program (MIAP).* Interdisciplinary Program, University of Manitoba.
5. Joan Larsen. 2002. *Econometric Modelling of Obstacles to Economic Development in Greenland.* Department of Economics, University of Manitoba.
6. Wanda Wuttunee. 2000. *Economic Development in Selected Aboriginal Communities: Lessons in Strength, Resilience and Celebration.* Interdisciplinary Program, University of Manitoba.
7. Neil Loughran. 1998. *A study of three federal government programs that financed economic and business development projects in communities of Northern Manitoba with substantial Aboriginal populations.* Interdisciplinary Program, University of Manitoba.

MA Theses Supervised

1. Lynne Fernandez. 2005. *Government Policy Towards Community Economic Development in Canada.* Department of Economics, University of Manitoba.
2. Gabriela Sparling. 1992. *An Analysis of the Socio-economic and Housing Conditions of Winnipeg's Native Single Parent Population.* Joint MA in Public Administration, University of Manitoba–University of Winnipeg.
3. Richard Kenny. 1981. *Economic Base and Input-Output Analysis: The Techniques and Their Application to a Mining Community's Economy.* Natural Resource Institute, University of Manitoba.
4. Michael Fisher. 1981. *An Assessment of Methods of Collecting and Evaluating Subsistence Fish and Marine Mammal Harvesting Data in the Northwest Territories.* Natural Resource Institute, University of Manitoba.

BIBLIOGRAPHY

Aboriginal Council Discussion Paper. 1992. "Self-Determination for Urban Aboriginal People." (Based upon Assorted Aborginal Experiences from the Urban Area of Winnipeg) Presentation to Royal Commission on Aboriginal Peoples. Edmonton, Alberta. June 21–23.

Aboriginal Human Resource Council. 2009. *Introduction to Successful Aboriginal Procurement Strategies for Corporate Canada.* <aboriginalhr.ca>

Albert, Michael. 1997. *Thinking Forward, Learning to Conceptualize Economic Vision.* Winnipeg: Arbeiter Ring Publishing.

Albert, Michael and Robin Hahnel. 1991a. *The Political Economy of Participatory Economics.* Princeton: Princeton University Press.

Alexie, S. 2004. "Love, hunger, money." At <protecting_knowledge-owner@egroups.com, Lheidli Tenneh Nation>. December 13.

All-Chief's Budget Committee, Midas Economic Development Institution. 1984. "A Manitoba Approach to Indian Economic Development Concept and Proposals." Assembly of Manitoba Chiefs. April.

Amin, Samir. 1976. *Unequal Development: An Essay on Social Formations and Peripheral Capitalism.* New York: Monthly Review Press.

Assembly of First Nations. 1984. Speaking Notes on Oral Presentation to the Standing Committee on Indian Affairs and Northern Development on Indian Economic Development. Ottawa. December 12.

Assembly of First Nations. 2006. *The Royal Commission on Aboriginal Peoples After 10 Years: A Report Card*, Ottawa. At <afn.ca/cmslib/general/afn_rcap.pdf>.

Assiniboine Credit Union. 2002. "Community Economic Development Initiatives." Winnipeg. Mimeo.

Balassa, Bela. 1982. *Development Strategies in Semi-Industrial Economies.* Baltimore: Johns Hopkins University Press.

Baran, P. 1957. *The Political Economy of Growth.* New York: Monthly Review Press.

Batten, T.R. 1974. "The Major Issues and Future Direction of Community Development." *Community Development Journal* 9, 2: 96–103.

Belanger, Yale. D. 2006. *Gambling with the Future: The Evolution of Aboriginal Gaming in Canada.* Saskatoon: Purich Publishing.

Bendavid, A. 1972. *Regional Economic Analysis for Practitioners.* New York: Praeger Publishers.

Berger, Thomas R. 1977. "Northern Frontier, Northern Homeland." *The Report of the Mackenzie Pipeline Inquiry.* Vol. 1. Ottawa: Minister of Supply and Service.

Black, E. 1996. "Gambling Mania: Lessons from the Manitoba Experience." *Canadian Public Administration* 39, 1.

Black, Errol and Jim Silver (eds.). 1991. *Hard Bargains: The Manitoba Labour Movement Confronts the 1990's.* Winnipeg: Manitoba Labour History Series.

Board of Pollock's Hardware Co-op Ltd. 2010. *Forming a Co-operative in Manitoba: The Pollock's Hardware Co-op Experience.* A Paper Prepared for the Co-operatives Promotion Board, Winnipeg, Manitoba, September.

Broadband Communications North Inc. (BCN). 2010. Communities Map. At <gobcn.ca>.

Brox, Ottar. 1968. "Newfoundland Fishermen in the Age of Industry—A Sociology of Economic Dualism." *Newfoundland Social and Economic Studies* 9. Memorial University of Newfoundland: Institute of Social and Economic Research.

BUILD, 2010, *Warm Up Winnipeg*, At BUILD website: <warmupwinnipeg.ca/programs.html>.

Burke, J. 1976. *Paper Tomahawks—From Red Tape to Red Power.* Winnipeg: Queenston House.

Busby, Colin. 2010. *Manitoba's Demographic Challenge: Why Improving Aboriginal Education Outcomes is Vital for Economic Prosperity.* C.D. Howe Institute. e-brief. <cdhowe.org>. May.

Callahan, M. 1997. "Feminist Community Organizing in Canada: Postcards from the Edge," in B. Wharf and M. Clague (eds.), *Community Organizing: Canadian Experience.* Toronto: Oxford University Press.

Campbell, J.A. 1918. "The Northern Manitoba Mineral Belt." In J.A. Campbell (ed.) *Manitoba's Northland including Hudson Bay Region and Rice Lake Gold Area.* The Pas: Manitoba. Department of Geology and Mineralogy, University of Manitoba.

... 1918b. "Some Resources of Northern Manitoba." In J.A. Campbell (ed.) *Manitoba's Northland including Hudson Bay Region and Rice Lake Gold Area*. The Pas: Manitoba. Department of Geology and Mineralogy, University of Manitoba.

Canadian Council on Rural Development (CCRD). 1976. A Development Strategy for the Mid-North of Canada. Ottawa.

Canadian Medical Association Journal News Desk. 2000.

Cardinal, Douglas. Undated. "Neeginan: A Vision of Hope and Healing." North Main Task Force. Winnipeg.

Cash, Martin. 2008. "Funding Plan to Fuel First Nations Growth," *Winnipeg Free Press*. September 24, B7.

Cates, Farley. 2003. "Community Based Housing Development in Winnipeg." Paper prepared for: Building on the Momentum—CD/CED Gathering. Winnipeg. November 26.

CED Network Manitoba (CCEDNET). 2009. "Creating a Robust Social Enterprise Sector in Winnipeg, Manitoba."

Chief of the First Nations Community. 2001. *Winnipeg Free Press*. March 10.

Chorney, Paul. 2003. "Neighbourhood Development Activity in Winnipeg." Paper prepared for: Building on the Momentum—CD/CED Gathering. Winnipeg. November 26.

Clapp, John M. 1977. "The Relationships among Regional Input-Output, Intersectoral Flows and Rows-Only Analysis." *International Regional Science Review* 2, 1 (Fall).

Clatworthy, Stewart J. 1981(a). *Patterns of Native Employment in the Winnipeg Labour Market*. Winnipeg: Institute of Urban Studies, University of Winnipeg.

... 1981(b). *Issues Concerning the Role of Native Women in the Winnipeg Labour*. Winnipeg: Institute of Urban Studies, University of Winnipeg.

... 1981(c). *The Effects of Education on Native Behaviour in the Urban Labour Market*. Winnipeg: Institute of Urban Studies, University of Winnipeg.

... 1983 (a). *Native Housing Conditions in Winnipeg*. Winnipeg: Institute of Urban Studies, University of Winnipeg.

... 1983 (b). *The Effects of Length of Urban Residency on Native Labour Market Behaviour*. Winnipeg: Institute of Urban Studies, University of Winnipeg.

... 1987. "Final Evaluation of the Winnipeg Core Area Agreement Employment and Affirmative Action Program." Winnipeg: Core Area Initiative. September.

Cleverley, Fred. 2001. "Racism not Issue in Casino Debate." *Winnipeg Free Press*, May 1: A10

Combs, H.C. 1990. *The Return of Scarcity: Strategies For An Economic Future*. New York, Melbourne, and Sydney: Cambridge University Press.

COMEF. 1963. *Manitoba 1962–1975*. Report of the Committee on Manitoba's Economic Future. Winnipeg: COMEF.

Community Inquiry Board. 1990. *Community Inquiry Into Inner City Revitalization: Final Report*. Winnipeg. June 25.

Community Ownership Solutions. 2002. Winnipeg. Pamphlet.

Community Resilience Team. 1999. *The Community Resilience Manual: A Resource for Rural Recovery & Renewal*. Centre for Community Enterprise, B.C.

Conn, Melanie. 1989. "Community Economic Development in Canada From a Women's Perspective." Saskatoon: *Newest Review* December.

Conn, Melanie. n.d. "Women, Co-ops and CED." *Making Waves*, 12, 1.

Conyers, Diana. 1982. *An Introduction to Social Planning in the Third World*. New York: John Wiley & Sons.

Cook, Malcolm, Tim Johnston, and Maxine Larway. 2004. *Impact of Information Technology on Community Economic Development Processes in Northern Manitoba Communities*. Report by the Northern e-BIZ Centre for the Manitoba Research Alliance into CED and the New Economy, Winnipeg. At <manitobaresearchallianceced.ca/Documents/40-MarchITFinal-revised3.pdf>.

Cornell, Stephen and Joseph P. Kalt. 2003. "Sovereignty and Nation-Building: The Development Challenge in Indian Country Today." Joint Occasional Papers on Native Affairs, No. 2003-03.

Damas and Smith Limited. 1975. *Neeginan: A Report on the Feasibility Study*. Prepared for Neeginan (Manitoba) Incorporated. April.

Daugherty, Wayne. 1982. *A Guide to Native Political Associations in Canada*. Ottawa: Treaties and Historical Research Centre.

Dene Advisory Committee. 1982. *Economic Development Program Planning for Dene Communities*. Toronto: Prepared for DIAND.

Department of Finance. 2002. *Canada's Credit Unions and Caisses Populaires*. Ottawa. At <fin.gc.ca/toce/2002/ccu_e.html>.

Department of Indian and Northern Affairs, Canada. 1976. *The Manitoba Region Housing Survey*. Ottawa: Department of Indian and Northern Affairs.

Department of Regional Economic Expansion, Canada. 1974. *Manitoba's Changing Northland*. Ottawa: Department of Regional Economic Expansion.

DesBrisay, David. 1994. *The Gaming Industry in Aboriginal Communities*. Ottawa: Royal Commission on Aboriginal Peoples, Public Policy and Aboriginal Peoples Section.

Development Education Centre. 1983. *Strategies for Self-Reliance: Canadian Native and Third World Community-Based Development*. Toronto: Prepared for DIAND.

DIAND. 1980. "Indian Conditions and Employment Development." Discussion Paper.

Dimitrakopoulou, Hari. 1993. *Women and Sustainable Economic Development in Northern Manitoba*. Thompson, Manitoba: Northern Manitoba Economic Development Commission.

G.Dixon, C.Johnson, S.Leigh, and N. Turnbull. 1982. "Feminist Perspectives and Practice." In Craig, Derricourt and Loney (eds.), *Community Work and the State*. London: Routledge and Kegan Paul.

Driscoll, David T. 1996. *The Role of Financial Institutions in Community and Economic Development*. Ottawa: Caledon Institute of Social Policy.

D.P.A. Consulting Ltd. 1982. *Local Economic Development Assistance Program: Interim Evaluation*. Ottawa: For Employment and Immigration Canada.

Duboff, Carly. 2004. *A Scan of Community Economic Development Organizations, Rural Communities and First Nations in Manitoba and their Participation in the New Economy* MA Thesis. Winnipeg. Manitoba Research Alliance into CED and the New Economy. At <manitobaresearchallianceced.ca/Documents/16-CEDProjectScan.pdf>.

Elias, P.D. 1975. "Certain Employment Patterns in the Northern Manitoba Industrial Sectors of Hydro Construction, Forestry, Mining and Provincial Government Administration." Winnipeg: Planning Secretariat of Cabinet, Manitoba. Mimeo.

... 1975b. "Metropolis and Hinterland in Northern Manitoba." Winnipeg: The Manitoba Museum of Man and Nature.

... 1976. "Employment patterns and the Health Working Group Report." Northern Strategy Exercise. Mimeo.

Epstein Associates Inc. 1987. *Final Evaluation of the Winnipeg Core Area Agreement Economic Stimulus Programs (Sector 2 Programs)*. Submitted to Stewart J. Clatworthy, Evaluation Manager, Winnipeg Core Area Initiative. November.

Evans, J. 1976. Conference on Northern Development organized by the Communities Economic Development Fund, Manitoba. March 10–12.

Fairbairn, Brett, June Bold, Murray Fulton, Lou Hammond Ketilson, and Daniel Ish. 1995. *Co-operatives and Community Development: Economics in Social Perspective*. Saskatoon: Centre for the Study of Co-operatives, University of Saskatchewan.

Falconer, Patrick. 1985. "Appendices for the Report on: Urban Native Community Economic Development and NEDP's Element 11: Problems, Prospects and Policies." Submitted for consideration August 30.

Falconer, Patrick. 1990. "The Overlooked of the Neglected: Native Single Mothers in Major Cities on the Prairies." In Silver, Jim and Jeremy Hull (eds.), *The Political Economy of Manitoba*. Regina: Canadian Plains Research Centre, University of Regina.

Faux, Geoffrey. 1971. *CDC's: New Hope for the Inner City*. New York: The Twentieth Century Fund.

Feit, Harvey A. 1987. "Waswanipi Cree Management of Land and Wildlife: Cree Ethno-ecology Revisited." In Bruce Alden Cox (ed.), *Native People, Native Lands: Canadian Indians, Inuit and Métis*. Ottawa: Carleton University Press.

Filkin, Elizabeth and Michael Naish. 1982. "Whose Side Are We On? The Damage Done by Neutralism." In Craig, Derricourt and Loney (eds.), *Community Work and the State*. London: Routledge and Kegan Paul.

Findlay, Isobel M. and Wanda Wuttunee. 2007. "Aboriginal Women's Community Economic Development: Measuring and Promoting Success." IRPP *Choices*, 13, 4.

Flanagan, Tom, Christopher Alcantra, and André Le Dressay. 2010. *Beyond the Indian Act: Restoring Aboriginal Property Rights*. Montreal and Kingston: McGill-Queen's University Press.

Fontaine, Grand Chief Phil. 1999. "Statement by Grand Chief of the Assembly of First Nations." *The Journal of Aboriginal Economic Development*, 1, 1.

Franz, Klaus. 1999. *Indian Reservations in the United States*. Chicago: University of Chicago Press.

Freylejer, Leandro. 2009. "The Social and Economic [Under] Development of Northern Manitoba Communities Over the Past Two and a Half Decades. "Paper Submitted to the Manitoba Research Alliance for Transforming Inner-Cities and Aboriginal Communities, Canadian Centre For Policy Alternatives-Manitoba. Mimeo. June 4.

Fulham, Richard Scott. 1987. "Economic Strategy for Urban Indians." Urban Indian Association of Manitoba. October.

Fulham, Stanley A. 1981. *In Search of a Future*. Winnipeg: KINEW.

"Gaming World International/White Earth Contract Breached." At <yvwiiusdinvnohii.net/upnews/ojibgame.htm>.

Garrity, Paul. 1972. "Community Economic Development and Low Income Housing Development." In Weistart, John C. (ed.), *Community Economic Development*. New York: Oceana Publications.

Gilmore, Donald R. 1960. *Developing the "Little" Economies*. New York: Committee for Economic Development.

Griffiths, Hywel. 1974. "The Aims & Objectives of Community Development." *Community Development Journal* 9, 2.

Grubel, Herbert G. 1981. *International Economics*, Revised Edition. Hoewood, Illinois: Richard D. Irwin Inc.

Gunn, Christopher and Hazel Dayton Gunn. 1991. *Reclaiming Capital: Democratic Initiatives and Community Economic Development*. Ithica, New York: Cornell University Press.

Hallet, Bruce. 2006. *Aboriginal People in Manitoba*. Ottawa: Service Canada.

Hansen, W.L. and C.M.Tiebout. 1963. "An Intersectoral Flows Analysis of the California Economy." *The Review of Economics and Statistics*, 45.

Hayek, F.A. (ed). 1935. *Collectivist Economic Planning*. London: Routledge and Kegan Paul.

Heller, Agnes. 1974. *The Theory of Need in Marx*. London: Allison and Busby.

Hendry, M.C. 1918. "Water Power Resources of Manitoba." In J.A. Campbell (ed.) *Manitoba's Northland including Hudson Bay Region and Rice Lake Gold Area*. The Pas: Manitoba. Department of Geology and Mineralogy, University of Manitoba.

Henin, Calvin. 2006. *Dances with Dependency: Indigenous Success Through Self-Reliance*. Vancouver, BC: Orca Spirit.

Hetherington, J.A.C. 1972. "Community Participation: A Critical View." In Weistart, John C. (ed.), *Community Economic Development*. New York: Oceana Publications.

Hickling-Johnston. 1975. *Manitoba Northern Transportation Study*. Report prepared for the Province of Manitoba.

Hill, R. 2001. Presentation at Oklahoma Tribal Governance Symposium. Norman, Oklahoma: University of Oklahoma Press. March 12.

House of Commons. 1983. *Indian Self Government in Canada*. Ottawa: Report of the Special Committee.

House of Representatives. 1997. *Tax Policy: A profile of the Indian Gaming Industry*. Ottawa: Ways and Means Committee. At <taxboard.com/ GAOReport/gao97-91.html>.

Hull, Jeremy. 1984. *Native Women and Work: Summary Report of a Winnipeg Survey*. Winnipeg: Institute of Urban Studies, University of Winnipeg.

Hull, Jeremy. 1991. "Aboriginal People and the Labour Movement." In Black, Errol and Jim Silver (eds.). 1991. *Hard Bargains: The Manitoba Labour Movement Confronts the 1990s*. Winnipeg: Manitoba Labour History Series.

Hultin, D. 2004. *New Partnerships in Hydro Development*. Winnipeg: Manitoba Research Alliance on CED in the New Economy. At <manitobaresearchalliance-tiac.ca>.

Human Resources Canada. 1998. *Report on First Nations, Métis, Inuit and Non-Status Peoples in Winnipeg's Urban Community*. Information Generated from the Place Louis Riel Round Table held November 9 and 10. Ottawa. Human Resources Canada.

Hunter, Heather. 2000. "In the Face of Poverty, What a Community School Can Do." In Jim Silver (ed.), *Solutions that Work: Fighting Poverty in Winnipeg*. Halifax: Fernwood Publishing and Manitoba: CCPA.

Hutchinson, Brian. 1999. "Losing Bet: Gambling Hasn't Fixed Windsor's Economy. It's Just Addicted It." *Report on Business Magazine*. November.

INAC. 2010. *Urban Reserves in Canada*. At <ainc-inac.gc.ca/ai/scr/mb/fnmb/ urs/index-eng.asp>.

Indian Chiefs of Alberta. 1970. *The Red Paper*. Presentation to Right Honourable P.E. Trudeau, Prime Minister and the Government of Canada.

Indian Tribes of Manitoba. 1971. *Wahbung: Our Tomorrows*. Winnipeg: Manitoba Indian Brotherhood.

Jackson, E.T. 1984. *Community Economic Self-Help and Small Scale Fisheries*. Ottawa: Department of Fisheries and Oceans.

Jackson, Edward T. and Jonathon C. Pierce. 1993. "Mobilizing Capital for Regional Development." In D. McNair and M. Lewis (eds.), *Regional Development From the Bottom Up: Selected Papers of the Local Development Series*. Vancouver: Centre for Community Enterprise/Westcoast Development Group.

Jordan, J. 1983. "Future Directions of Cooperatives." In Campfens (ed.), *Rethinking Community Development in a Changing Society.* Guelph: Ontario Community Development Society.

Kalt, J. & S. Cornell. 1993. *What Can Tribes Do? Strategies and Institutions in American Indian Economic Development.*" Los Angeles: University of California.

Kenny, Richards L. 1981. *Economic Base and Input-Output Analysis: The Techniques and Their Application to a Mining Community's Economy.* MNRM Practicum. Winnipeg: Natural Resources Institute, University of Manitoba.

Kierans, E. 1973. *Report on Natural Resource Policy in Manitoba.* Winnipeg: Government of Manitoba.

Kirk, R. 2001. Personal Communication with Wanda Wuttunee. Winnipeg, Manitoba. April 11.

Kotlar, Milton. 1972. "The Politics of Community Economic Development." In Weistart (ed.), *Community Economic Development.* New York: Oceana Publications.

Krech, Shepard III. 1999. *The Ecological Indian: Myth and History.* New York: W.W. Norton & Company.

Krotz, Larry. 1980. *Urban Indians: The Strangers in Canada's Cities.* Edmonton: Hurtig Publishers.

Kulchyski, Peter. 2004a. "È-nakàskakowaàhk (A Step Back): Nisichawayasihk Cree Nation and The Wuskwatim Project." *Canadian Centre for Policy Alternatives Review,* May.

Kulchyski, Peter. 2005. "Peter Kulchyski Responds. " *Canadian Dimension,* January-February.

Kusch, Larry. 2010. "Urban Reserve Leaps Ahead: City Agrees to Long Plain Project on Parcel in Polo Park Area." *Winnipeg Free Press,* July 23: A3.

Lagasse, Jean H. 1959. "A Study of the Population of Indian Ancestry Living in Manitoba." In *The People of Indian Ancestry in Greater Winnipeg. Appendix.* Winnipeg: The Social and Economic Research Office, Dept. of Agriculture and Immigration.

Lamb, Laura. 2007. "Towards an Economic Theory of Community Economic Development." In John Loxley (ed.), *Transforming or Reforming Capitalism: Towards a Theory of Community Economic Development.* Halifax: Fernwood Publishing.

Lane, T. 1966. "The Urban Base Multiplier: An Evaluation of the State of the Art." *Land Economics* 42, 3.

Lange, O. and F. Taylor. 1938. *On the Economic Theory of Socialism.* Minneapolis: University of Minnesota Press.

LaRusic, J.E. 1978. *The Income Security Program for Cree Hunters and Trappers.* DINA: May.

T.H. Lee, D.P. Lewis, and J.R. Moore. 1971. "Multi-region Intersectoral Flows Analysis." *Journal of Regional Science* 11, 1.

Lett, Dan. 2000. "Hasty Approach Muddying Issue of Native Casinos." *Winnipeg Free Press*, May 1: A4.

Lett, Dan & Tracy Tjaden. 2000. "Casino Losers Demand Answers." *Winnipeg Free Press*, June 4: A1.

Lewis, Mike and R.A. Lockhart. 1999. *CED in the High Arctic: Progress and Prospects—A Documentary Review.* Centre for Community Enterprise, B.C.

Lezubski, Darren, Jim Silver, and Errol Black. 2000. "High and Rising: The Growth of Poverty in Winnipeg." In Jim Silver (ed.), *Solutions That Work: Fighting Poverty in Winnipeg.* Halifax: Fernwood Publishing. Winnipeg: CCPA, Manitoba.

Loewen, Garry. 2003a. "Employment Development Activity in Winnipeg." Paper prepared for: Building on the Momentum—CD/CED Gathering. Winnipeg. November 26.

Loewen, Garry. 2003b. "Social Enterprise Development in Winnipeg." Paper prepared for: Building on the Momentum—CD/CED Gathering. Winnipeg. November 26.

Loney, Martin. 1982. "Policies for Community Care in the Context of Mass Unemployment." In Craig, Derricourt, and Loney (eds.), *Community Work and the State.* London: Routledge and Keagan Paul.

Loney, Shaun. 2010. "BUILD: A Community-Based Solution to Energy Poverty and Unemployment in Low-Income Neighbourhoods." *CEDWorks.* May. At <cedworks.com/files/pdf/free/i42010JUL30_BUILD.pdf>.

Lotz, Jim. 1977. *Understanding Canada: Regional & Community Development in a New Nation.* Toronto: NC Press Ltd.

Loughran, N.E. 1996. *A Study of Three Federal Government Programs that Financed Economic and Business Development Projects in Communities of Northern Manitoba with Substantial Aboriginal Populations.* PhD Thesis in Interdisciplinary Studies, University of Manitoba.

Loughran, N. E. 1985 "Community Development Corporations and Cooperatives: A Study of the Effectiveness of Two Vehicles for Broad Based Community Economic Development." Term paper for Professor John Loxley, University of Manitoba. Mimeo.

Loxley, J. 1980. "Fiscal Sociology and the Fiscal Crisis of the State." Paper read to the Conference on The State and the Economy. University of Manitoba.

Loxley, J. 1981. "The Great Northern Plan." *Studies in Political Economy*, 6 Autumn.

Loxley, John. 1986. *The Economics of Community Development, A Report Prepared for the Native Economic Development Program*. Winnipeg: H.K.L. and Associates.

Loxley, John. 1993. *Child Care Arrangements and the Aboriginal Community in Winnipeg*. Winnipeg: A Report Prepared for the Royal Commission on Aboriginal People. November.

Loxley, John. 1996. *Aboriginal People in the Winnipeg Economy*. Winnipeg. A Report Prepared for the Royal Commission on Aboriginal Peoples. February 1994; revised September 1996.

Loxley, John. 2000, "Aboriginal Economic Development in Winnipeg." In Jim Silver (ed.), *Solutions That Work: Fighting Poverty in Winnipeg*. Winnipeg: Canadian Centre for Policy Alternatives-Manitoba, Halifax: Fernwood Publishing.

Loxley, John. 2002. "Sustainable Urban Economic Development: An Aboriginal Perspective." *Journal of Aboriginal Economic Development* 3, 1.

Loxley, John. 2003. "Financing Community Economic Development in Winnipeg." *Économie et Solidarité* 34, 1.

Loxley, John. 2007. "Some Remaining Theoretical Challenge" in J. Loxley (ed.) *Transforming or Reforming Capitalism: Towards a Theory of Community Economic Development*. Halifax: Fernwood Publishing.

Loxley, John and Fred Wien. 2003. "Urban Aboriginal Economic Development." In David Newhouse and Evelyn Peters (eds.), *Not Strangers in These Parts: Urban Aboriginal Peoples*. Ottawa: Policy Research Initiative.

Loxley, John and Laura Lamb. 2006. "Economics for Community Economic Development Practitioners." In Eric Shragge and Mike Toye (eds.), *Community Economic Development: Building for Social Change*. University College, Cape Breton Press.

Loxley, John and Russ Rothney. 1983. "Some Thoughts on Participation in Planning." All Chiefs' Budget Committee of Manitoba, Budget and Financial Analyst Training Program. Mimeo.

Loxley, John, Jim Silver and Kathleen Sexsmith, (eds.). 2007. *Doing Community Economic Development*. Halifax: Fernwood Publishing.

Mahmood, S.T. and A.K. Ghosh, (eds.). *Handbook on Community Economic Development*. Washington, DC: Government Printing Office.

Manitoba First Nations Casino Project Selection Committee. 2000. Manitoba First Nations Casino Project: Request For Proposals. Winnipeg: January 19.

Manitoba Floodway Authority. 2009, *Aboriginal Set-Aside Initiative* <floodwayauthority.mb.ca/aboriginal_setaside.html>.

Manitoba Government. 1971. Northern Manitoba-Northern Working Group: Internal Working Papers. Winnipeg, Manitoba: Planning & Priorities Committee of Cabinet.

Manitoba Government. 1973. "Guidelines for the Seventies," 1, 2 and 3.

Manitoba Government. 2006. "Community Economic Development" in The 2006 Manitoba Budget and Budget Papers, Budget Paper F. Winnipeg: Department of Finance.

Manitoba Government. 2009. "Aboriginal Procurement Initiative: Overview." *Procurement Bulletin*, 96. Procurement Services Branch. <gov.mb.ca/mit/psb/api/Bulletin%2096.pdf>.

Manitoba Government. 2010. *Aboriginal Business Directory*. Procurement Services Branch. <manitoba.ca/mit/psb/api/abr.pdf>.

Manitoba Hydro. 2010. *Building a Powerful Future: 59th Annual Report for the Year ended March 31, 2010*. Winnipeg.

Manitoba Indian Brotherhood. 1971. *Wahbung: Our Tomorrows*. Winnipeg: Manitoba Indian Brotherhood.

Manitoba Indian Women's Association. 1973. *Summary Report of Meeting and Organization Chart*. Manitoba Indian Women's Association Annual Meeting at the Balmoral Hotel, Winnipeg. November 20–22.

Manitoba Planning Secretariat of Cabinet. 1975. *Macro-Data Working Group Report*. Mimeo. July.

Mason, W.D. 2000. *Indian Gaming: Tribal Sovereignty and American Politics*. Norman, Oklahoma: University of Oklahoma Press.

Macleod, G.H. 1979. "Community Development Corporations: Theory and Practice." *Critere* 25.

McArthur, Doug. 1989. "Aboriginal Economies and Underdevelopment, " Society for Socialist Studies, Laval University. June. Mimeo.

McCallum, John. 1999."Aboriginal Economic Development: Overview," *The Journal of Aboriginal Economic Development*. 1, 1.

McCracken, Molly, with Kate Dykman, Francine Parent and Ivy Lopez. 2007. "Young Women Work: Community Economic Development to Reduce Young Women's Poverty," in John Loxley, Jim Silver and Kathleen Sexsmith (eds.). 2007. *Doing Community Economic Development*. Halifax: Fernwood Publishers and CCPA-Manitoba

McMurtry Tara. 1993. "The Loan Circle Programme as a Model of Alternative Community Economics." In Eric Shragge (ed.), *Community Economic Development: In Search of Empowerment*. Montreal: Black Rose Books.

McRobie, George. 1981. *Small is Possible*. New York: Harper and Row.

MEDTP Inc. 1986. *Currents of Change: Métis Economic Development*. Winnipeg: Pemmican Publications.

Mendell, Marguerite and Lance Evoy. 1993. "Democratizing Capital: Alternative Investment Strategies." In Eric Shragge (ed.), *Community Economic Development: In Search of Empowerment*. Montreal: Black Rose Books.

Mendelson, Michael. 2006. "Aboriginal Peoples and Postsecondary Education in Canada." Ottawa: Caledon Institute of Social Policy.

Métis National Council. 1984. *Métis Self-Determination*. Brochure #1.

Métis National Council. 1984. *Who Are The Métis?* Brochure #2.

Métis National Council. 1984. *What Rights Do Métis Seek?* Brochure #3.

Métis National Council. 1984. *Why A Métis Register?* Brochure #5.

Métis National Council. 1984. *Métis Lands*. Brochure #6.

Métis National Council. 1984. *Métis Local Government*. Brochure #7.

Métis National Council. 1984. *Political Autonomy*. Brochure #8.

Métis National Council. 1984. *Hunting, Fishing, Trapping & Gathering*. Brochure #10.

Métis National Council. 1984. *Métis—A Federal or Provincial Responsibility*. Brochure #11.

Mises, L. 1935. "Economic Calculation in the Socialist Commonwealth," in Hayek, F.A. (ed). 1935. *Collectivist Economic Planning*. London: Routledge and Kegan Paul.

Morduch, Jonathon. 1999. "The Microfinance Promise. "*Journal of Economic Literature* XXXVII (December).

National Council of Welfare. 1998. *Banking and Poor People: Talk is Cheap*. Ottawa: Minister of Public Works and Government Services.

National Film Board of Canada. 1990. *We're the Boss*. Directed by Brian Pollard. Ottawa: NFB.

National Indian Brotherhood. 1973. *Statement on Economic Development of Indian Communities*. Prepared for the Western-Federal Provincial Conference.

National Indian Brotherhood/Department of Indian Affairs. 1976. *A Strategy for the Socio-Economic Development of Indian People*. Report of the Socio-Economic Development Strategy Task Force. Vancouver.

National Indian Socio-Economic Development Committee. 1979. "To Have What is One's Own." *Beaver Report*. Ottawa. October.

Neff, Gina. 1996. "Microcredit, Microresults." *Left Business Observer* 74 (October) At <leftbusinessobserver.com/Micro.html>.

Nelson House Development Corporation. 2010. *Newsletter,* August. At <ncncree.com/ncn/documents/DevCorpNewsletter.pdf>.

Newhouse, David. 2000. "Modern Aboriginal Economies: Capitalism with a Red Face," *The Journal of Aboriginal Economic Development*, 1, 2: 55–61.

Nicholls, W.M. and W.A. Dyson, 1983. *The Informal Economy*. Ottawa: Vanier Institute of the Family.

Ninacs, William A. 2000. "Overview of Current Community Economic Development Activity in Quebec". Victoriaville, Quebec: The Canadian CED Network. Mimeo.

Ninacs, William A. and Louis Favreau. 1993. *CED in Quebec: Features in the Early 1990s*. Centre for Community Enterprise, B.C.

Nisichawayasihk Cree Nation. 2010a. *ATEC*. At <ncncree.com/ncn/atecinfo.html>.

Nisichawayasihk Cree Nation. 2010b. *Urban Reserve*. At <ncncree.com/ncn/urbanreserve.html>.

Nisichawayasihk Cree Nation. 2010c. *Nisichawayasihk Cree Nation Trust Office*. At <trustoffice.ca/>.

North, D.C. 1975. "Location Theory and Regional Economic Growth." In *Regional Policy Readings in Theory and Applications*. J.F. Friedman and W. Alonso (eds.). Cambridge, Massachusetts: M.J.T. Press.

Northern Manitoba Economic Development Commission. 1992. *Northern Manitoba: A Benchmark Report*. Thompson, Manitoba.

Nourse, H.O. 1968. *Regional Economies*. New York: McGraw-Hill Book Company.

Nove, Alec. 1983. *The Economics of Feasible Socialism*. London: George Allen and Unwin.

O'Connell, Dorothy. 1983. "Low Income Women & Community Development Projects: Self-Help and the Experts." In Campfens (ed) *Rethinking Community Development in a Changing Society*. Guelph: Ontario Community Development Society.

Olshewski, Doug, CAW Winnipeg 2001. On CBC Information Radio, March 12.

Owen, Bruce. 2008. "Betting on Hotel as Tourist Draw," *Winnipeg Free Press*. August 30: B9.

Owen, Bruce. 2010. "Spirit Sands Casino Moves Ahead," *Winnipeg Free Press*. August 26: A7.

Pasquaretta, P. 1994. "On the 'Indianness' of Bingo: Gambling and the Native American Community." *Critical Inquiry* 20 (Summer).

Perry, Stewart. 2001. *The North End Community Renewal Corporation: A Case Study of a Successful CEDO Take-Off*. Centre for Community Enterprise. October 26.

Primrose, Jerry and W. Elvis Thomas. 2005. "Debating the Wuskwatim Hydroelectric Deal." *Canadian Dimension*, January-February.

Pruitt, William O. 1989. "The Northern Environmental Imperative." Paper read to conference on The Role of Circumpolar Universities in Northern Development. Thunder Bay: Lakehead University.

Rahman, Aminur. 1998, "Microcredit Initiatives for Equitable and Sustainable Development: Who Pays?" *World Development* 26, 12.

Report of the Royal Commission on Aboriginal Peoples. 1996. Ottawa: Communications Group. <collectionscanada.gc.ca/webarchives/20071115053257/http://www.ainc-inac.gc.ca/ch/rcap/sg/sgmm_e.html>.

Richard, Pierre. 2004. *Transformed by Community Economic Development: Southwest Montreal Now Has a Future as Well as a Past*. Centre for Community Enterprise.

Richards, John. 2008. "Closing the Aboriginal/Non-Aboriginal Education Gaps." C.D. Howe Institute. Backgrounder 116. Toronto: C.D. Howe Institute. October.

… 2009. "Dropouts: The Achilles' Heel of Canada's High-School System." C.D. Howe Institute. Commentary no. 296. Toronto: C.D. Howe Institute. October.

Robson-Haddow, Jennifer. 2002. "Asset Building and IDAs: What We Don't Know (But Should)." *Making Waves* 13, 1.

Ross, David P. and Peter J. Usher. 1986. *From the Roots Up. Economic Development as if Community Mattered*. Toronto: Lorimer Press.

Rothney, R. 1992. "Neechi Foods Co-op Ltd.: Lessons in Community Development." Winnipeg: Family Economic Development Inc. July.

Rothney, R. and S. Watson. 1975. *A Brief Economic History of Northern Manitoba*. Winnipeg: Manitoba Department of Northern Affairs.

Royal Society of Canada, Panel on Aboriginal Casinos. 2007. "Aboriginal Casinos: Who's Cashing In?" Ottawa: RSC.

Sanders, Carol. 2000. "Band Elders Support Headingly Casino Foes." *Winnipeg Free Press*, December 6: A7.

Sanders, Douglas Esmond. 1973. *Native People in Areas of Internal National Expansion: Indians and Inuit in Canada*. Copenhagen: International Work Group for Indigenous Affairs.

Saskatchewan Liquor and Gaming Authority News Release. 2000. "Strong, Immediate Action by SLGA on SIGA Audit." At <gov.sk.ca/newsrel/2000/11/15-737-attachment.html> November 15.

Saskatchewan, Provincial Auditor. 2000. "Audit Finds Improper Use of Gaming Money." At <auditor.sk.ca/provwebnew.nsf/html/2000flvol2sknews>.

Sawchuk, Joe. 1978. *The Métis of Manitoba: Reformulation of an Ethnic Identity*. Toronto: Peter Martin Associates.

Schumacher, E.F. 1974. *Small is Beautiful—A Study of Economics as if People Mattered*. London: Abacus.

SEED Winnipeg. Various years. Winnipeg: Annual Report.

SEED Winnipeg. 2002b. "Winnipeg Individual Development Account Pilot Project." In Annual Report. September 2001 to August 2002. September.

SEED Winnipeg. 2010. *Annual Report*. 2009–2010. Winnipeg. At <seedwinnipeg.ca/documents/SEED2010ANNUALREPORTREVISED.pdf>.

Shaffer, Ron. 1989. *Community Economics: Economic Structure and Change in Smaller Communities*. Ames: Iowa State University Press.

Sharpe, Andrew and Jean-François Arsenault. 2010. "Investing in Aboriginal Education: An Economic Perspective." CSLS Research Report 2010–3. Ottawa: Centre for the Study of Living Standards. March.

Simms, Tom. 2010. *The Ideology of Community Economic Development*. Interdisciplinary PhD Thesis. University of Manitoba, Winnipeg.

Smith, Dean Howard. 2000. *Modern Tribal Development: Paths to Self-Sufficiency and Cultural Integrity in Indian Country*. Walnut Creek, CA: Altmira Press.

Social Planning Council of Winnipeg. 1982. *A Review of Changes in the Demographic, Educational, Economic and Social Conditions of the Registered Indian Population of Manitoba—1971 to 1981*. Winnipeg: Social Planning Council. May.

Social Planning Council of Winnipeg. 1989. *Winnipeg Census Data Insights & Trends: An Information Kit.* Winnipeg: Social Planning Council of Winnipeg.

Social Planning Council of Winnipeg. 1992. "Toward a Solution to End Child Poverty in Manitoba" in *Child Poverty in Manitoba: An Approach Towards its Elimination.* Winnipeg: Social Planning Council.

Stanford, Jim. 1999. *Paper Boom: Why Real Prosperity Requires a New Approach to Canada's Economy.* Ottawa: Canadian Centre for Policy Alternatives and Toronto: James Lorimer and Co. Ltd.

Statistics Canada. 1993. "Schooling, Work and Related Activities, Income, Expenses and Mobility." In 1991 *Aboriginal Peoples Survey.* Ottawa: Statistics Canada.

Statistics Canada. 2005. *Projections of the Aboriginal Populations, Canada, Provinces and Territories 2001 to 2017.* Ottawa. <statcan.gc.ca/pub/91-547-x/2005001/4155166-eng.htm>.

Statutes of Manitoba. 1991. The Community Development Bonds Act, Chapter C160. Assented to July 26.

Stein, Barry A. 1974. *Size, Efficiency and Community Enterprise.* Cambridge, Massachusetts: Centre for Community Economic Development.

Stevens, Harvey. 1982. *A Review of Changes in the Living Conditions of the Registered Indian Population of Manitoba During the 1970's.* Winnipeg: Social Planning Council of Winnipeg.

Strang, William A. 1972. "Minority Economic Development: The Problem of Business Failures." In Weistart (ed.), *Community Economic Development.* New York: Oceana Publications.

Streeton, P. 1979. "A Basic Needs Approach to Economic Development." In K.P. Jameston and C.K. Wilber (eds.), *Directions in Economic Development.* Indiana: University of Notre Dame Press.

Sturdivant, Frederic D. 1972. "Community Development Corporations: The Problem of Mixed Objectives." In Weistart (ed.), *Community Economic Development.* New York: Oceana Publications.

Thalassa Research Associates. 1983. *The Economic Foundations of Self-Government.* A Report Prepared for the House of Commons Special Committee on Indian Self-Government. Victoria, B.C.

Thomas, C.Y. 1974. *Dependence and Transformation: The Economics of the Transition to Socialism.* New York: Monthly Review Press.

Thunderbird Consulting. *An Economic Strategy for The Manitoba Métis Federation*. Presented to The MMF Economic Development Technical Group. Winnipeg.

Tiebout, C.M. 1962. *The Community Economic Base Study. Supplementary Paper No. 16*. New York: Committee for Economic Development.

Tudiver, Neil. 1973. *Why Aid Doesn't Help: Organizing for Community Economic Development in Central Appalachia*. PhD Thesis in Business Administration. University of Michigan.

Tyrell, J.B. 1917. "Northern Manitoba as a Mining Country." In J.A. Campbell (ed.) *Northern Manitoba: Mining, Timber and Pulpwood, Water Powers, Fish and Furs, Agriculture, the Hudson Bay Route*. The Pas: Manitoba. Department of Geology and Mineralogy, University of Manitoba.

United Nations Development Programme. 2002. "Proceedings of International Workshop of the Anti-Poverty Partnership Initiatives Trust Fund (APPI Trust Fund): Fighting Urban Poverty." York University Centre for Research on Latin America and the Caribbean. May.

Usher, Peter. 1987. "Indigenous Management Systems and the Conservation of Wildlife in the Canadian North." *Alternatives*, 3.

Usher, Peter J. 1978. "Staple Production and Ideology in Northern Canada." Mimeo.

Usiskin, Len. 1996. "Pension Funds: Their Potential for Gaining Democratic Control Over Investment, Reducing Capital Mobility and Financing Community-Based Economic Development Initiatives." MA Comprehensive Exam Research paper. Department of Economics, University of Manitoba. August.

Usiskin, Len, Laverne Szejvolt, and Mike Keeling. 2001. *Quint: CED and Affordable Housing in Saskatoon*. Ottawa: Caledon Institute of Public Policy. March.

Waldram, James B. 1988. *As Long as the Rivers Run: Hydroelectric Development and Native Communities in Western Canada*. Winnipeg: University of Manitoba Press.

Wallace, J.R. 1918. "The Resources of Manitoba and Their Development. " In "The Significance of Manitoba's Northland." In J.A. Campbell (ed.) *Manitoba's Northland including Hudson Bay Region and Rice Lake Gold Area*. The Pas: Manitoba. Department of Geology and Mineralogy, University of Manitoba.

Wallace, R.C. and J.S. DeLury. 1916. "Geographical Features of Rice Lake District." In J.A. Campbell (ed.) *Manitoba's Northland including Hudson Bay Region and Rice Lake Gold Area.* The Pas: Manitoba. Department of Geology and Mineralogy, University of Manitoba.

Watkins, M.H. 1963. "A Staple Theory of Economic Growth," *The Canadian Journal of Economies and Political Science* xxix, 2 (May).

Watkins, M.H. (ed.). 1977. *Dene Nation—The Colony Within.* Toronto: University of Toronto Press.

Watkins, M.H. 1977. "The Staple Theory Revisited." *Journal of Canadian Studies* xii, 5.

Weaver, Sally M. 1984. "A Commentary on the Penner Report." *Canadian Public Policy* x: 2.

Weistart, John C. (ed.). 1972. *Community Economic Development.* New York: Oceana Publications.

Welfare Council of Greater Winnipeg. 1954. Annual Report. Winnipeg.

West Broadway Development Corporation. 2002. Annual Report. Winnipeg.

Wien, Fred. 1986. *Rebuilding the Economic Base of Indian Communities: The Micmac in Nova Scotia.* Montreal: The Institute for Research on Public Policy.

Wien, Fred. 1999. "The Royal Commission Report: Nine Steps to Rebuild Aboriginal Economies," *The Journal of Aboriginal Economic Development*, 1, 1.

Wien, Fred, Cindy Blackstock, John Loxley, and Nico Trocme. 2007. "Keeping First Nations Children at Home: Few Federal Policy Changes Could Make a Big Difference." *First Peoples Child and Family Review* 3, 1.

Williams, Joan and Catherine Scott. 1981. *Community Economic Development in Rural Canada. Handbook for Practitioners.* Ottawa: Supply & Services.

Winnipeg Core Area Initiative. 1986. *Canada-Manitoba-Winnipeg Tripartite Agreement 1986–1991.* Public Information Program of the Winnipeg Core Initiative.

Winnipeg Core Area Initiative. 1987. *Final Status Report. Program Activities To September 30, 1987 Under the 1981–1986 Core Area Agreement.* Public Information Program of the Winnipeg Core Initiative.

Winnipeg Core Area Initiative. 1989. *Status Report. Programs and Projects to September 30 Under the 1986–1991 Core Area Agreement.* Public Information Program of the Winnipeg Core Area Initiative.

Winnipeg Core Area Initiative. 1992. *Canada-Manitoba-Winnipeg Tripartite Agreement for Development of the Winnipeg Core Area. Selected Indicators of Program Objectives Achievement.* Evaluation Program. August.

Winnipeg Core Area Initiative. 1992. *Partnerships for Renewal—Canada-Manitoba-Winnipeg Tripartite Agreement 1981–1992.* Public Information Program of the Winnipeg Core Area Initiative.

Winnipeg Native Family Economic Development Inc. 1993. *It's Up to All of Us: A Guide to Community Economic Development in Winnipeg's Inner City.* February.

Winnipeg Partnership Agreement. 2005. Annual Report. 2005. <winnipegpartnership.mb.ca/pdf/annual_rpt_2005.pdf>.

Wismer, Susan and David Pell. 1981. *Community Profit: Community Based Economic Development in Canada.* Toronto: Is Five Press.

Wismer, Susan and David Pell. 1983. "Community-Based Economic Development and Community Self-Reliance." In Campfens, H. (ed.), *Rethinking Community Development in a Changing Society.* Guelph: Ontario Community Development Society.

Working Margins Consulting. 1991. *Evaluation of the Winnipeg Core Area Employment and Affirmative Action Initiative: Detailed Findings Report.* Winnipeg. September.

Wuttunee, Wanda. 2004. *Living Rhythms: Lessons in Aboriginal Economic Resilience and Vision.* Montreal and Kingston: McGill-Queen's University Press.

INDEX

A
Abitibi, 104, 117
Aboriginal Business Development Centre, 167
Aboriginal Business Directory, 255
Aboriginal businesses, 12, 69, 235–40. *See also* co-ops; private enterprise
   casinos, 11, 73–79, 87–88
   limiting political intervention, 253
   overlooking poor business performance, 254
   promotion of, 173
   small business failure, 235–40, 254, 256
   survival rate, 256
Aboriginal capital corporations, 187, 231–32, 253
Aboriginal Centre of Winnipeg, 166–69, 179–80, 194, 232, 259
Aboriginal children, 257–59. *See also* Aboriginal youth; child welfare services; childcare
   educational accomplishments, 152, 186
   infant mortality, 95
Aboriginal Council of Winnipeg (ACW), 153, 160, 162–64, 167, 172, 175
Aboriginal development
   need for new Native-owned and controlled institutions, 58, 65
   requirements for success, 241–43
Aboriginal development bank (proposed), 89
Aboriginal development corporations, 65
Aboriginal economic development in Winnipeg, 151–88
   political divisions, 175
Aboriginal elites, 82. *See also* Aboriginal leadership
Aboriginal employment, 89–90, 94, 118
   casinos, 73–74, 88
   female, 157–58
   in hydro development, 145
   in public sector, 82, 84
   racial discrimination and, 101, 103–4, 157
   Winnipeg, 152, 156–60, 170–71, 174, 183–84
Aboriginal gang activity, 168
Aboriginal incomes, 157–58, 176. *See also* wages
Aboriginal institutional development, 65
Aboriginal institutional framework in Winnipeg, 231
Aboriginal joint-ownership of hydro projects, 145–47
Aboriginal Justice Inquiry, 143, 231
Aboriginal labour force participation. *See* Aboriginal employment

Aboriginal leadership, 69–70, 109, 127
  ambiguous position, 23, 108
  band council elections, 254
  class interests among, 124
  commitment to the community, 241
  importance of good leadership, 85–86
  individual wealth, 30, 70, 109, 241
  in inner city Winnipeg, 180
  petty bourgeois aspirations among, 124
  state financing, 108–9
  and white working class, 127
Aboriginal People. *See also* Métis
  collectivist orientation of, 65, 82, 85
  community development focus, 60
  demographics, 12, 154–56, 225, 257
  dependence on state transfer payments, 37, 82, 84, 102, 130 (*See also* social assistance; welfare)
  economic development literature by, 57–71
  education of (*See* education)
  growing political awareness, 105, 142
  history ignored, 98, 133
  importance in the labour force, 12, 257–58
  integration, 135
  kinship or tribal relationships, 36, 67
  land claims, 57, 61, 63–64, 89
  negative effects of industrialization, 103
  Non-Status Indians, 106, 154, 161, 185
  permanent jobs (*See* Aboriginal employment)
  petty commodity producers, 102, 107 (*See also* traditional staples of furs, fish, wild rice)
  self-determination, 45, 162
  self-government, 57–60, 63, 70–71, 89, 184, 187–88
  Status Indians, 60, 62, 106, 152–54, 161–62, 185
  suicide and homicide rates, 95, 143
  traditional culture (*See* traditional Aboriginal values and culture)
  urban, 64, 84, 162, 172
Aboriginal Peoples Survey (APS) (1991), 156
Aboriginal poverty. *See* poverty
Aboriginal procurement, 254
Aboriginal way of life. *See* traditional Aboriginal way of life
Aboriginal Women's Unity Coalition, 163
Aboriginal youth, 12, 179
  secondary school drop out rates, 258–59
  social assistance for returning to school, 188
accountability, 82, 85, 249
  to the community, 241
  in First Nations casinos, 78–79
  management, 227
affirmative action, 165, 176, 180, 182, 187
  confusion with business development goals, 240
agriculture, 101, 132, 134
Alternative Financial Services Coalition (AFSC), 201–2, 218
Andrew Street Family Centre, 200
Assembly of First Nations, 69, 90–91
Assembly of Manitoba Chiefs (AMC), 153, 161–62, 174–75, 186
  All-Chiefs Budget Committee, 171
asset-building programs for low-income earners, 193, 210, 233. *See also* Individual Development Accounts (IDAs)
  learn$ave program, 201–2

Assiniboine Credit Union, 189, 199, 205, 209, 213–14, 218, 231–33
   Community Loan Centre, 196, 202
   importance to CED initiative in Winnipeg, 183, 196–98, 234
   technical advice and assistance to other credit unions, 200
Assiniboine Indians, 99
Atoskiwin Training and Employment Centre of Excellence (ATEC), 147

B
basic goods, 46–48, 110
basic needs, 27, 248
Beaver Report, 59–61
Black, Salway, 86
blame the victim strategy, 97, 104. *See also* racism
Brandon, 88
Broadband Communications North Inc. (BCN), 149
Brokenhead, 77–78, 88
Bruntland Commission, 131, 138
Build-a-Business Program, 197, 202
Building Urban Industries for Local Development (BUILD), 233, 260

C
Calmeadow Foundation, 192, 198
Campbell, J.A., 131, 134
Canada Mortgage and Housing Corporation (CMHC), 215
Canada/Manitoba Economic Partnership Agreement, 199
Canadian Aboriginal Economic Development Strategy (CAEDS), 231
Canadian Auto Workers union (CAW), 74
Canadian Centre for Policy Alternatives – Manitoba, 218, 220

Canadian Community Economic Development Network (CCEDNET), 209, 217, 234
Canadian Council on Rural Development, 48, 55
Canadian Human Rights Commission, 174
Canadian society at large, 138
capital
   equity, 213–15, 223, 234
   foreign, 11
   labour-sponsored venture capital, 193
   local pool of, 242
   shortage in Native communities, 30, 70
capital subsidies, 250
capitalism, crisis of, 121
Capitalism with a Red Face, 85–86
capitalist values and private enterprise, 16
   compatibility with traditional Aboriginal culture, 85–86
Cardinal, Douglas, 169
Cardinal, Harold, 169
Casino Regina, 76
casinos, 11, 73–79, 87–88
   Aboriginal employment, 73–74, 88
   accountability in First Nations casinos, 78–79
   as economic development strategy, 73–79
   profitability, 76–79, 88
   spin-off businesses, 79
   success and failure of First Nations casinos, 77–78
   unionization, 74
Centre for Aboriginal Human Resource Development (CAHRD), 232

charitable foundations, 208, 219.
  See also names of individual
  foundations
  complement to state funding, 209
  money into CED initiatives, 193
child welfare services
  Aboriginal children in care,
    258–59
  Aboriginal People's involvement, 143
  devolution, 231
childcare, 90, 155, 157, 159, 171–72, 187
Cho!ces, 196
Christmas Lite campaign, 182, 200
Churchill, 122, 132, 136
City of Winnipeg Act, 212
class consciousness, 128
class interests among Aboriginal
  leadership, 124
class relationships in fur trading
  companies, 99, 101
class structure in Northern
  Manitoba, 106–9, 120, 122, 142
Clatworthy, Stewart, 154, 157–58, 187
collective land tenure system, 16
collective ownership. *See also*
  community ownership and control
  community input in, 32–33
  democracy in, 32–33
colonialism, 29–30, 84, 99–100, 106,
  109, 114, 125
  "decolonization," 172
COMEF report, 134–36
communal ownership. *See* collective
  ownership; community ownership
Communities Economic
  Development Fund, 254
Community and Worker Ownership
  Program, 199
community development (CD), 22–23,
  29, 35, 65
  definition, 19

economic strategy, 21–22, 25
  local business objections to, 24
  mobilizing role, 27
  not politically neutral, 25
  ownership and control, 29–34, 69
  private enterprise in, 29–30, 69, 165
  redistribution of power, 23–24, 56
  stimuli for, 20
  technical support and advice from
    national organizations, 34
  used to discourage legitimate
    demands, 24
Community Development Business
  Association (CDBA), 174
community development
  corporations (CDCs), 33, 192
community economic development
  (CED), 9, 12, 20, 169, 217–29, 233
  Aboriginalization, 172
  alternative vision of society, 229
  boards of directors, 227–28
  cultural foundation, 221
  financing, 189–216, 219, 222, 234
  gap-filling *vs* transformative,
    250–51
  goals, 228–29
  housing, 44, 218
  increasing importance of, 259
  incubator approach, 194–95
  infrastructure for, 189
  institutional base, 218
  management of, 226–27
  Neechi approach, 171–73, 194–95
  need, issue of, 25–28
  Nisichawayasihk Cree Nation, 147
  poverty alleviation, 228–29, 260
  riskiness of, 191, 193
  subsidies in, 245–51, 256
  supportive academic environment
    for, 220

training programs, 186, 222
Winnipeg as focal point, 211, 217
Community Education Development (CEDA), 181, 185, 199, 208, 218
community gardens, 148
Community Inquiry into Inner City Revitalization, 179–81, 190
community- or worker-owned larger-scale business projects, 210–11. *See also* co-ops
community ownership and control, 46, 82, 173
    ideological rejection of, 31, 34
community ownership solutions (COS), 203–5, 210, 218, 223
community participation, 19, 46, 50, 116, 122–23, 172, 241
Community Profit (Wismer), 53
community self-reliance. *See* self-reliance
comparative advantage, 39
compensation, 64–65
    for loss of land, 62, 129
    for loss of livelihoods, 144, 147–48
comprehensive land claims, 61–64, 129
Conawapa dam, 137
Conawapa station, 146
Conn, Melanie, 81
consensus, 16, 85
construction industry, 94, 112, 117
consumption, 16, 138
convergence or self-reliance strategies, 34–35, 44–52, 54, 68–69, 117–18, 121, 241–42
    community development literature on, 48–49
    C.Y. Thomas's, 10, 110, 112, 127–28
    importance of state funding, 49
    Neechi Foods approach, 169, 172, 194

new demands on community members (especially women), 248
    ownership of land and, 129
    political requirements, 49
    relevance to the Micmac, 141
    retention of income leakages, 47
    retention of spending power, 49
convergence theory, 231
cooperation between communities, 52
cooperative ownership, 194
cooperatively owned financial institutions, 191–92
co-ops, 224, 233–34
    client or worker owned, 33, 195, 217
    as social enterprise, 224
    suitable form for social enterprise in Winnipeg, 225
cottage industries, 101
Country Food Program, 148
credit circles, 192–93, 198–99
credit union or caisse populaire, 191, 224
Crocus Investment Fund, 185, 199, 203, 205, 209–10
    collapse of, 223
Cross Lake, 144
cross-subsidization in CED, 246, 256
Crown corporations, 33–34, 50, 52
Crown land, 114

D

"decolonization," 172
democracy, 46, 93, 112, 260
democracy / efficiency trade-off, 31
democratic, participatory management styles, 226
democratic decision-taking, 194, 228
Dene Nation of the Northwest Territories, 45, 128
    comprehensive land claim, 61–63, 129

focus on community ownership, 70
hope to confirm rather than extinguish title, 63
Department of Aboriginal Relations, 89
Department of Human Resources, Canada, 193
Department of Indian Affairs, 58–60, 84
Department of Indian Affairs and Northern Development, 89
Department of Intergovernmental Affairs (provincial), 203
Department of Northern Affairs (DNA), 116
Department of Regional Economic Expansion (DREE), 115, 121
dependency theory, 98
dependent economies, 46, 110
development banks, 192
diet, 47, 96, 103, 112, 118
Dimitrakopoulou, Hari, 141
direct production, 159–60
diversifying the funding base of CED activities, 208–9, 212–13, 222
Diversity Foods, 234
dual economy strategy, 35, 42, 45, 129
dualism, 97–98, 135–36. *See also* racism
"The Dynamics of North-South Relations," 148

E

early childhood education, 91, 258
early childhood interventions, 225
economic base technique, 39
economic development. *See also* community economic development (CED)
  preserving and reinforcing tradition and culture, 66, 86, 188

Economic Development Boards (proposed), 59
economic development literature by Aboriginal People, 57–71
economic development opportunities for Aboriginal People, 145–46
Economic Development Training Program, 172
economic differentiation, 69–70
An Economic Strategy for The Manitoba Métis Federation, 166
economies of scale, 51, 111
education, 47, 84, 91, 96, 112, 143, 153, 156. *See also* training
  Aboriginalization, 172
  early childhood education, 91, 258
  need for national Aboriginal education strategy, 83
  post-secondary education, 258
  reform, 225
  secondary school, 258–59
education, training and employment services, 218, 232
educational performance of Aboriginal children, 152, 186
efficiency, 50. *See also* scale
efficiency / democracy trade-off, 31
Elias, P.D., 94–95, 98–100, 103–4, 107
employment, 233. *See also* Aboriginal employment
  long-term, 146, 170
  make-work, 105
  short-term, 38, 107
  skilled jobs held by outsiders, 44, 46
employment and training agencies, 218, 232
employment creation, 12, 118, 137
employment equity, 12, 174, 182, 187
Employment Insurance (EI), 157–58, 247

employment subsidies, 248–50
Encana, 255
export, 11, 101, 133, 137
export promotion strategies, 35, 39, 43, 45
   input-output analysis, 40
   volatility of prices, 41
export-import economy, 87
extinguishment of Aboriginal title, 42, 62–63, 102

F

federal procurement, 254
felt needs, 25–26, 28
Filmon government, 161
Financial Foundations Resource Centre, 201
Financial Management Training curriculum, 201
First Nations Economic Development Advisory Council (proposed), 161–62
First Nations Fiscal and Statistical Management Act (2004), 83
First Nations Land Management Act (1999), 83
First Peoples Economic Growth Fund, 88
fiscal impact approach to justify subsidies, 247
Fontaine, Phil, 90
forestry, 94, 101, 133. *See also* modern staples of mineral, forestry, hydro, oil and gas
Fox Lake Cree Nation, 145
front-end subsidization, 250
Fulham, Stan, 64, 164–65, 173, 194
   acceptance of market values, 174
   in favour of expanding private enterprise, 69

G

gaming. *See* casinos
Gaming World International, 76
gender equity, 228
government funding. *See* state funding
government procurement policies, 219
government purchasing, 52–53, 165, 254
government services strategy, 35, 38, 44, 47
government transfers. *See* state transfers
Grameen Bank, 192–93
grassroots community activism, 173, 195
"The Great Northern Plan," 10, 93–130, 142, 231
Greening of the Assiniboine, 196, 205
grow bond approach, 212

H

Hall, Van, 254
Harvard Project on American Indian Economic Development, 82, 87, 253
health and health care, 38, 95, 103, 105, 137, 143
public health, 47, 112, 170
Helin, Calvin, 82–84
housing, 38, 47, 91, 96, 112, 117, 153
   housing deprivation, 143
   housing problems, 153, 168, 178, 180, 186
   importance to CED, 44, 218
   improving housing stock, 190, 214–15, 225, 259
housing co-ops, 224
Hudson Bay Mining and Smelting, 137
Hudson's Bay Company, 99–100, 105
Human Resources Development Canada, 202

hybrid approach to subsidization, 250
hydro development, 94, 120, 133, 136.
    See also Manitoba Hydro
    partnerships with local First
    Nations communities, 145–46, 223
Hydro Northern Training Initiative
    (HNTI), 145

I

import substitution strategies, 35, 43,
    46, 84, 87
    efficiency issues, 45
    local incomes "leaked" out of the
        region, 44
    outside management and skilled
        labour, 44
    subsidies and, 247
income distribution, 39, 43, 228
income inequalities, 46, 95
    equalization, 112
income leakages, 44, 49, 170. *See also*
    surplus drain
income-security for hunters and
    trappers, 63, 148
incubator approach to CED, 167, 169,
    174, 194
Independent Living Resource
    Centre (ILRC), 202
Indian Act, 58, 61, 68, 83, 105
Indian and Métis Friendship
    Centre, 165
Indian and Métis Friendship
    Societies, 84
Indian Chiefs of Alberta, 59
Indian Chiefs of Manitoba, 59–60, 69
Indian Métis Friendship Centre, 153
Indigenous Women's Collective, 163
Individual Development Accounts
    (IDAS), 193, 200–201, 211
individualism, 16, 31, 67, 195
infant mortality, 95

informal economy, 36, 160
inner city problems, 168–69, 180.
    See also housing; Winnipeg Core
    Area Initiative (WCAI)
    income leakage, 170
Inner City Renovations (ICR), 203,
    218, 233
integration for Aboriginal People, 135
international development theory,
    10–11
Internet access in the North, 148–49
Investors Group, 201
It's Up To All Of Us guide, 169

J

Jacobs, Jane, 49, 87
James Bay Agreement, 64, 90, 146
    bias against community and
        convergence-type projects, 63
    extinguishment of title, 62–63
    no Aboriginal rights to minerals, 62
    and traditional Aboriginal way of
        life, 63
James Bay Native Development
    Corporation, 62
job creation, 12, 118, 137. *See also*
    employment
Jubilee Fund, 202–3, 205, 218, 232–33
Just Housing, 181, 214

K

Kahn-Tineta-Horn, 165
Keeyask generating station, 145–46
Krech, Shepard, 81

L

labour force case for subsidization,
    248–50
labour-sponsored venture capital, 193
Lamb, Laura, 248
land, 10, 60, 89

Aboriginal title, 42, 62–63, 102
  claims (*See* land claims)
  collective land tenure system, 16
  Crown land, 114
  Indian reserves, 116
  and modern staples, 42, 102
  Native attachment to, 67, 108
  ownership and control of, 15, 50
  respected as giver of life, 15
  stewardship, 16
  and traditional staples, 42
  urban reserves, 165, 232–33
land claims, 57, 61, 89, 129
  bargaining ability and, 63–64
  Métis, 62
leadership. *See* Aboriginal leadership
learn$ave program, 201–2
Limestone Project, 145
LITE, 209, 213, 218
  funding, 200, 205
Loan Loss Reserve (LLR), 231–32
Long Plain First Nation, 232
Lotz, Jim, 24, 48, 55
Loughran, Neil, 255–56
Louis Riel Capital Corporation, 161, 231

M

Ma Mawi Wi Chi Itata Centre, 168, 172
  New Directions Project, 179
management. *See also* Aboriginal leadership
  accountability, 227
  autocratic management behaviour, 226–28
  of community economic development (CED), 32, 226–27
  democratic, participatory management styles, 226
  failure of small businesses from inadequate management, 235–36
Manitoba Association for Native Languages, 179
Manitoba Conservative government, 121
Manitoba Federation of Labour, 126
Manitoba First Nations casinos, 88
  income distribution from, 76
  potential spinoffs and employment, 79
Manitoba Forest Industries paper plant (Manfor), 104, 117
Manitoba Hydro, 142, 144, 146. *See also* Northern Flood Agreement
  fibre optic lines, 148
  financial compensation (*See* compensation)
  flooding of northern communities, 103
  joint venture with Nisichawayasihk Cree Nation, 145
  profits, 104
Manitoba Indian and Métis Annual Conferences, 151
Manitoba Indian Brotherhood (MIB), 108, 116–17, 174
  focus on reserve-based members, 153
  Northern Strategy exercise and, 124, 127
Manitoba Indian Development Association, 174
Manitoba Indian Women's Association (MIWA), 153
Manitoba Keewatinook Ininew Okimowin, 145
Manitoba Lotteries Commission, 77–78, 88
Manitoba Métis Community Investments Inc., 161

Manitoba Métis Federation (MMF), 60, 108, 116–17, 153, 160, 166, 171, 175, 185
  business agreement with Manitoba Hydro, 145
  institutional capacity for planning and development, 161
  land claim, 62, 65
  Northern Strategy exercise and, 124, 127
  training programs, 186
Manitoba NDP government, 61, 93, 114–15, 120–21, 231
  Aboriginal MLAS, 144
  commitment to CED, 219, 234
  distanced itself from labour, 125
  election of, 199
Manitoba Research Alliance, 220
market forces, 27–28, 50–51
Marx, Karl, 106–7, 109
Marxist dependency theory, 141
Marxist framework, 98
Matheson Island, 97
McArthur, Doug, 142
Medicine Wheel, 85–86
Memberton First Nation, 83
Mennonite Central Committee (MCC), 181, 199
Mennonite Economic Development Associates (MEDA), 182
merchant capitalism, 99
Métis, 64, 106, 161. *See also* Manitoba Métis Federation (MMF)
Métis Construction Company, 161
Métis National Council, 59
  emphasis on land and resource base, 60–61
Micmac economy in Nova Scotia, 141
micro-business development, 199, 210
  SEED funding for, 234

micro-lending programs, 192–93
middle class, 30, 108, 241
migration, 104, 108, 135, 137
  policies encouraging, 38
migration to the city, 11, 66, 104, 113, 154
  different motivation for men and women, 154–55
  reconnecting skilled migrants to home communities, 84
mineral development, 133. *See also* modern staples of mineral, forestry, hydro, oil and gas
mineral rights, 62
mining, 94, 101, 104
Minister for Aboriginal Relations, 89
modern staples of mineral, forestry, hydro, oil and gas, 41, 45, 133
  capital and skill intensive production, 42
  "divergent" economy, 102
  effect on traditional staples, 103
  few job prospects for local residents, 42
  need for clear title to land, 42, 102
  regulation, 45, 129
Moffat family, 209
Mondragon restaurant worker co-op, 224
Montreal Community Loan Association, 192

N

National Indian Brotherhood, 60, 69
Native Development Corporation (NDC), 164
Native Economic Development and Employment Council (NEDECO), 164
Native Economic Development Program, 10

Native economic way of life. *See*
    traditional Aboriginal way of life
Native Industrial Centre, 164
Native leaders. *See* Aboriginal
    leadership
Native People. *See* Aboriginal
    People
Native Women's Transition Centre,
    179, 200
Nee Gawn Ah Kai Day Care, 172
Neechi approach, 171, 188
    grassroots community activism, 173
    against market ideology, 195
    prospects for long-term self-
        reliance, 195
Neechi Commons, 232, 259
Neechi Foods Co-op Ltd., 81, 170,
    179, 186, 190, 200, 220, 224
    community-based economic
        development approach, 194
    It's Up To All Of Us guide, 169
Neechi Principles, 174, 194, 206, 210,
    215, 217, 219, 221, 231
need, 25–28, 110
Neeginan or Thunderbird House, 194
Neeginan proposal, 165–66, 168–69,
    175, 181
neighbourhood corporations, 213
Neighbourhoods Alive! Program, 219
Nelson House, 143–44
neo-colonialism, 109
New Democratic Party. *See*
    Manitoba NDP government
Newhouse, David, 85–86
Nishga in British Columbia, 128
    ownership and control of land, 129
Nisichawayasihk Cree Nation, 259
    community-based economic
        development, 147
    Hydro compensation, 144, 148
    joint ownership in Wuskwatim
        project, 145
    NCN Development Corporation, 147
    partnering with BCN to provide
        Internet, 148
non-monetary values, recognition
    of, 28, 242
Non-Status Indians, 106, 154, 161, 185
North End Community Renewal
    Corporation, 182, 204, 208, 220
North End Community Renovation
    Enterprise, 215
North End Development, 218
North End Housing Project, 215, 218
North West Company, 100
Northeastern Alberta Aboriginal
    Association, 83
North-End Housing Aboriginal
    Youth Training Project, 200
North-End Housing Project, 210
Northern Flood Agreement, 144
Northern Manitoba
    Aboriginal People ignored in
        early visions, 133 (*See also*
        underdevelopment)
    changing perceptions of, 131–39
    cutbacks in social services, 121
    economy, 11, 106, 132–34, 143
    education, 96
    employment, 94
    income levels, 95–96
    industrial capitalist expansion, 106
    mineral potential, 132
    natural resources, 131–32
    population, 94
    seen as key to industrial develop-
        ment of province as a whole, 132
"Northern Manitoba Development
    Strategy," 93

Northern Manitoba Economic
  Development Commission on
  women and sustainability, 141
Northern Star Workers'
  Cooperative, 200
Northern Strategy exercise, 10–11,
  97, 115, 137, 141–42, 171. *See also*
  "The Great Northern Plan"; The
  Thomas strategy
  Aboriginal opposition to, 119, 124–25
  conflict over "community
    participation," 122–23
  failure (reasons for), 120–30
  left existing private appropriation
    of surplus intact, 121
  Marxist framework of analysis, 98
  Native interest (after the fact),
    126–27
  no attempt to implement, 119, 121
  participation by Native People, 116
  possibility of an alternative
    strategy, 126
  utopian, 126
Northern Working-Group Report
  (1971), 136
Northlands agreement, 115, 121
Norway House, 143–44
nutrition, 47, 96, 103, 112, 118

O

O'Connell, Dorothy, 56
Ogijiita Pimatiswin Kinamatwin, 218
Opaskwayak Cree First Nation, 77,
  143, 232
organized labour. *See* unions
Original Women's Network, 163
Osayoos Indian Band, 83
"Our Place." *See* Neeginan proposal
ownership and control
  in community development (CD),
    29–34

land and resources, 21, 45, 50, 57,
  60–61, 89, 129

P

"parecon," 251
The Pas, 77, 88, 131, 136, 143
Pasquia project, 134
paternalism, 239, 254
patriarchy, 56
Payuk Inter-Tribal Co-op, 171, 195
Peace of the Brave Treaty, 146–47
Pell, David, 24–25, 48, 53, 55
Penner Report, 59–60
pension plan investing in CED
  activities, 193, 212, 214
Polar Gas Pipelines, 122
*The Political Economy of
  Underdevelopment* (Szentes), 10
Pollock's Hardware Co-op Ltd.,
  233
Portage La Prairie Jail for women,
  151
post-secondary education, 258–59
Potowatamin Band in Wisconsin
  support for Manitoba First
  Nations, 144
poverty, 70, 156–57, 159–60, 201, 210, 215
  Aboriginal culture and, 86
  alleviation or eradication, 12, 81,
    203, 228–29, 260
  complexity of poverty in
    Winnipeg, 11, 225–26
  education as path out of, 83, 258
  Northern, 9–10, 95–97, 106, 109,
    142–43
  and poverty-line wages, 27, 157, 245
  Royal Commission on Aboriginal
    People on, 91
  of single-parent families, 187
prejudice and stereotyping. *See* racism
price subsidies, 249–50

Primrose, Jerry, 147
private enterprise, 50
　in community development, 29–30, 165
　government support for, 195
　Helin's fixation with, 84
　ideological preference for, 31
　Red Paper support for, 69
private ownership, 69
profit, goal of, 31–34, 42
profits
　exported, 41, 101, 104, 118, 133
　ploughing back in, 242
profits and rents, control of, 41, 129. *See also* dual economy strategy
proletariat, 100–101, 106, 109, 113, 115, 125–26
property tax credits, 212
protected markets. *See* sheltered markets
Provincial Council of Women, 151
public health, 47, 112, 170
public sector funding. *See* state funding
purchasing power of government, 52–53, 165, 254

Q
Quebec, 191–92

R
racism, 97, 101, 103–4, 109, 136, 157, 239
　among white workers, 126
railroad, 105, 132–33
recreational facilities, 38, 47, 112
"red capitalism," 85–86
Red Paper, 58, 67
　assumptions on compatibility and coexistence, 67–68
　community development focus, 60
　on private enterprise, 69
Red River College, 222
Red River Rebellions, 101
Red River Settlement, 100
regional planning, 52, 59
renewable resources, 35, 42, 45, 129. *See also* traditional staples of furs, fish, wild rice
Repap project, 137
Report of the Committee for Manitoba's Economic Future. *See* COMEF
Report of the Royal Commission on Aboriginal Peoples, 88–91
Report on Northern Transportation (1974), 136
reserve army of the unemployed, 100–101, 106–7, 126
Resource and Economic Development (RED) Secretariat, 115–16, 119
resource base insufficient for community development (myth), 136
resource development, 11, 137
　Aboriginal opposition to until land claims are settled, 138
　emphasized at expense of community development, 138
　regulation, 45, 129
retirement funds. *See* pension plan investing in CED activities
Roseau River Anishinabe First Nation, 232
Round Table on Aboriginal People in Winnipeg's Urban Community, 175
Royal Bank, 183
Royal Commission on Aboriginal Peoples, 11, 88–91

S

Salway Black, Sherry, 86
Saskatchewan First Nations casinos, 76, 88
  Aboriginal employment, 74
  income distribution from, 75–76
  unionization, 74–75
Saskatchewan Indian Gaming Authority (SIGA), 78
  resistance to unionization, 74–75
Saskatchewan Liquor and Gaming Authority (SLGA), 78
Sault Ste. Marie Tribe of Chippewa Indians in Michigan, 79
Saving Circle Individual Development Account Pilot Project, 201
scale, 21, 110, 134, 139
  critical minimum level, 51–52
  large-scale production, 11, 133–34
Schreyer, Ed, 9, 135
Scott, Catherine, 31, 53, 55
secondary school
  Aboriginal drop out rates, 258–59
SEED Winnipeg, 181, 183, 189, 201, 208–9, 218–20
  asset-building programs, 233
  and the Assiniboine Credit Union, 197–200
  Build-a-Business Program, 197, 202
  core funding, 199, 205
  Credit Circle pilot project, 198
  funding for micro-businesses and social enterprises, 234
  mentor dimension, 182
self-determination, 45, 130, 162
self-employment, 159–60
self-government, 57–58, 63, 184, 187–88
  Aboriginal self-government in urban areas, 60
  and economic development link, 59
  requirement for state funding and resources, 70–71, 89
self-reliance, 36, 57, 170, 172, 195. *See also* convergence or self-reliance strategies
self-respect, 15, 66, 170, 194
self-sufficiency, 60, 118
set-asides, 166, 254–55
sexism, 68
"Shaman economics," 82
sheltered markets, 52–53, 245
Shore, Fred, 81
Silver, Jim, 259
single mothers on social assistance, 157, 198
single parent families, 154, 187
small business failure, 235, 240
  inadequate internal controls, 235–37
  from lack of capital, 236
  management weakness, 236
  state funding agencies' contributions to, 237–40
small enterprise (in CED activities), 195
small manufacturing, 43
small-scale production, 194
  efficiency, 50
Smith, Dean Howard, 86–87
social and economic differentiation in Aboriginal communities, 10–11, 25, 57, 69, 82, 142, 160
Social and Enterprise Development Innovations (SEDI), 202
social assistance, 91, 152–54, 157–58. *See also* state transfers
  for Aboriginal youth returning to school, 188
  RCAP recommendations on, 90
  single mothers on, 157, 198
  subsidization of traditional pursuits (hunting and trapping), 90

Social Capital Partners, 204
social enterprise sector, 218, 223–25, 232, 234, 256, 259
  SEED funding for, 234
social inclusion, 228
social problems reduction
  to justify subsidies, 247
social relations of production, 101
Social Research and Demonstration Corporation (SRDC), 202
socialism, 110, 112
  pricing under, 251
Solidarity Fund of the Quebec Federation of Labour, 193
Southeast Resource Development Council, Inc., 163
specific land claims, 61–62, 64
Spirit Sands casino, 88
Split Lake, 143–44
stabilization of Aboriginal neighbourhoods in Winnipeg, 156, 170, 186, 218, 225
staple economy, 143
  modern staples of mineral, forestry, hydro, oil and gas, 41–42, 45, 102–3, 133
  traditional staples of furs, fish, wild rice, 41, 107
staple theory, 39, 41
  economic diversification and, 40
state control of natural resources, 114
state funding, 29–30, 33, 70–71, 255–56. *See also* state transfers
  change of government and, 234
  dispensed as political largesse, 241
  importance in Winnipeg CED, 205–6
  needs to be planned and coordinated, 70
  reliability and predictability, 58, 206–8, 234, 238

state funding agencies
  expectation of Native business failure, 239
  lacking business expertise, 238
  need for Aboriginal staff, 239
  need for integrated and comprehensive approach to planning, 240
  racism and paternalism, 239
state role in the North, 104, 114, 133. *See also* Manitoba Hydro
  promoting large investments, 135, 137
  sacrificing interests of Aboriginal People, 122
  smaller communities and, 137
  subsidizing merchant and industrial capital activities, 105
  supporting accumulation of capital by non-residents, 120
state transfers, 82, 95, 106–7, 154, 158, 176. *See also* state funding
Status Indians, 60, 62, 152, 161
  ambiguous position off the reserve, 162
  tied to reserve system, 106
  in Winnipeg, 153–54, 185
status quo, 23, 26–27, 48, 91, 123
Studies in Political Economy, 9
subsidies for hunters and trappers, 63, 148
subsidies in CED, 245–51
subsidization, 28–29, 33, 37, 44, 51, 53
  accountability to electorate at large, 249
  cost-benefit analysis to justify, 246–47
  front-end, 250
  voluntary labour as form of, 248
subsistence strategies, 10, 35, 45, 47, 54, 107
  in pre-capitalist economies, 36

subtraction approach, 97–98.
  See also racism
Supreme Court of Canada, 74
surplus drain, 41, 101, 104, 118, 133
Swan Lake First Nation, 88, 232
Syncrude, 255
Szentes, Tamas, 10, 98
  The Political Economy of Underdevelopment, 10

T

Taking Charge project, 198
tariff protection, 44, 245
Tataskweyak Cree Nation, 145
tax credits, 205, 209, 211–12, 214, 219, 233
tax increment financing, 219
technocratic skills, 67
technology, 21, 32, 54, 111–12
  geared to local skill and employment levels, 50, 54
  new technologies helpful to the North, 148
  that emphasize small-scale production, 139
Thomas, C.Y., 10, 109–12, 231
Thomas, Elvis, 147
Thomas Sill Foundation, 199, 201, 208, 219
The Thomas strategy, 109–15
  assumes society is in transition to socialism, 110, 112
  mobilization aim, 114
Thomas-type strategy, 130
Thompson, 122
throwaway mentality, 138
Thunderbird Consulting, 166
Thunderbird House, 169, 194
tourism, 132–33
traditional Aboriginal values and culture, 10, 15, 85, 90
  adaptation to capitalism, 85–86
  collegial decision-taking and, 67–69
  economic development consistent with (or supporting), 58, 66
  egalitarianism and sharing, 16, 85
  elders in, 16, 67, 85
  enoughness, 16, 81
  possibilities for preservation or revival, 66–68
  stewardship, 81
traditional Aboriginal way of life, 67, 101, 108, 135, 139, 148
  collectivist orientation, 85
  erosion, 17
  James Bay Agreement and, 63
  learning from, 17
  resource management, 15–16
  sustainability, 16
  in synchronization with nature, 16
traditional staples of furs, fish, wild rice, 67, 107
  labour intensive and small scale, 41
  subsistence element, 41
training, 12, 145–47, 153, 176–77, 182, 192, 233. *See also* education
  CD/CED Training Intermediary, 222
  lack of, 156
  in skills appropriate to community development, 170
training and apprenticeship initiatives, 225
training and retention of staff in CED, 242
training programs, 37, 48, 105, 197, 218
  Credit Circle pilot project, 198
training programs (under WCAI), 176–77
transportation, 38, 101, 111. *See also* railroad
Treaty Land Entitlement process, 232–33

Tribal Council Investments Group, Manitoba, 253
Tribal Councils, 65, 127, 143, 149, 161–63, 174–75, 185, 253
  promoting job creation and economic development, 253
Tribal Wi-Chi-Way-Win Capital Corporation (TWCC), 231
Tyrell, J.B., 132

U

underdevelopment, 9, 93, 96, 113, 122, 130
  explanation and causes, 97
  Marxist theory on, 98
  symptoms, 94–96
unemployment, 94, 156, 176–77, 184, 210
  Aboriginal people in Winnipeg, 154
  class of permanently unemployed persons, 99–102, 106–7, 126
Unemployment Insurance, 157–58, 247
unionization rights, 68, 227, 254
unions, 122
  hostility towards, 75–76
  potential for unity with Aboriginal People, 126, 128
  progressive leadership, 126
United Way, 193, 198–99, 201, 205, 208–9, 214, 219, 233
urban Aboriginal People, 64, 84
  links to reserves and rural Métis, 83–84, 172
  no land base, 162
urban centres in Northern Manitoba, 94, 121
Urban Entrepreneurs with Disabilities Program, 202, 205, 218
Urban Indian Association, 153, 161, 167
urban reserves, 165, 232
U.S. development banks, 192
U.S. environmental lobbies, 144

V

Vancouver City Credit Union (VanCity), 191
Vanier Institute of the Family, 36
voluntary labour as form of subsidization, 248

W

wage labour, 36–37, 45, 100, 107–8, 142
wage or training subsidies, 245
wages, 42, 74, 100, 107, 195, 237, 246, 264
  decent, 42, 160, 224, 245
  poverty line, 27, 157, 245
  to those who stay home and care for children, 187
Wahbung-Our Tomorrows, 59–60
War Lake First Nation, 145
Waswanipi, 15
Watkins, Mel, 45, 102, 106, 129
welfare, 58, 95, 105, 137, 170. *See also* social assistance; state transfers
welfare and/or migration strategies, 35, 37–38
welfare communities, 37
welfare trap, 82, 84
West Broadway Development Corporation, 206, 218, 220
Western Economic Diversification (WED), 199, 203, 219
White Bear Reserve casino, 76
White Earth Band of Chippewa, Michigan, 76
White Paper (1969), 58
white proletariat / Native People, 125
  common experience of exploitation, 126
white working class, 127
Wien, Fred, 141, 253
Williams, Joan, 31, 53, 55
Winnipeg, 11, 62, 77

Aboriginal demographics (1990s), 154–56
Aboriginal economic development, 151–88
Aboriginal population, 151–52, 154, 225
  complexity of poverty in, 225–26
  employment and training agencies, 218
  focal point for community economic development, 217, 221
  inner city, 168–70, 180 (*See also* housing)
  Métis population, 151–52, 154
  Non-Status Indians, 154, 185
  social enterprise sector, 218
  social purchasing portal, 218
  social service agencies, 218
  stabilization of Aboriginal neighbourhoods, 156, 170, 186, 218, 225
Winnipeg Chamber of Commerce, 182
Winnipeg Coalition of Native Child Welfare, 172
Winnipeg Core Area Initiative (WCAI), 176–81. *See also* inner city problems
  Employment and Affirmative Action component, 176–77
  employment creation, 177–78
  funding for CED, 189
  funds for housing and community infrastructure, 178
  Neighbourhood and Community Development, 179
Winnipeg Council of Treaty and Status Indians, 153, 160
Winnipeg Development Agreement (WDA), 181, 190
Winnipeg Floodway extension, 223, 255
Winnipeg Foundation, 199, 209, 220, 233
Winnipeg IDA Project, 200–201
Winnipeg Indian Council, 153
Winnipeg Individual Savings Account Pilot Project, 201
Winnipeg Métis Development Corporation, 161
Winnipeg Native Family Economic Development (WNFED), 171, 173
Winnipeg Partnership Agreement, 219, 224, 234
Winnipeg Tribal Council, 175
Wismer, Susan, 24–25, 48, 55
  Community Profit, 53
women, 160, 163, 184, 192–93, 195, 201, 248
  exclusion from decision-taking roles, 55
  informal economy and, 36
  involvement in CED, 81
  need for representation in self-government, 187
  participation in economic activities, 21, 54–56
  participation in the northern economy, 141
  proportion of employed Aboriginal people, 157–58
  single mothers, 154, 157, 187, 198
  on staff and board of SEED, 234
  and traditional Aboriginal values and culture, 68
Women's World Finance Manitoba Association, 198
worker or cooperative ownership of large-scale operations, 195
workers' cooperatives, 200, 217, 224. *See also* co-ops
Wuskwatim and Keeyask Training Consortium (WKTC), 145

Wuskwatim project, 145, 147
Wuttunee, Wanda, 81, 86

Y
Yellowquill College, 232
York Factory First Nation, 145
York Landing, 144